Red Lights

Red Lights

THE LIVES OF SEX WORKERS
IN POSTSOCIALIST CHINA

Tiantian Zheng

University of Minnesota Press

Minneapolis

London

Frontispiece: Dalian Victoria Plaza, called "Nightless City" by the residents of Dalian. One of the author's field sites is located in this district. Photograph by Tiantian Zheng.

Part of chapter 3 was previously published as "Claim for Equal Social Status: An Ethnography of China's Sex Industry," in *Working in China: Ethnographies of Labor and Workplace Transformation,* ed. Ching Kwan Lee (New York: Routledge, 2007), 124–44, reprinted courtesy of Routledge; and as "Complexity of Life and Resistance: Informal Networks of Rural Migrant Karaoke Bar Hostesses in Urban Chinese Sex Industry," *China: An International Journal* 6, no. 1 (March 2008): 69–95. Part of chapter 4 previously appeared as "Cool Masculinity: Male Clients' Sex Consumption and Business Alliance in Urban China's Sex Industry," *Journal of Contemporary China* 15, no. 46 (2006): 161–82. Part of chapter 6 was published as "Consumption, Body Image, and Rural–Urban Apartheid in Contemporary China," *City and Society* 15, no. 2 (2003): 143–63; and as "From Peasant Women to Bar Hostesses: Gender and Modernity in Post-Mao Dalian," in *On the Move: Women in Rural–Urban Migration in Contemporary China,* ed. Arianne Gaetano and Tamara Jacka (New York: Columbia University Press, 2004), reprinted courtesy of Columbia University. Part of chapter 7 was published as "Commodifying Romance and Searching for Love: Rural Migrant Bar Hostesses' Moral Vision in Post-Mao Dalian," *Modern China* 34, no. 3 (2008).

Published by the University of Minnesota Press
111 Third Avenue South, Suite 290
Minneapolis, MN 55401-2520
http://www.upress.umn.edu

Library of Congress Cataloging-in-Publication Data

Zheng, Tiantian.
Red lights : the lives of sex workers in postsocialist China / Tiantian Zheng.
p. cm.
Includes bibliographical references and index.
ISBN 978-0-8166-5902-9 (hc : alk. paper) — ISBN 978-0-8166-5903-6 (pb : alk. paper)
1. Prostitution—China—History. 2. Sex-oriented businesses—China.
3. China—Social conditions. I. Title.
HQ250.A5Z44 2009
306.740951'09049—dc22
2008047510

Printed in the United States of America on acid-free paper

The University of Minnesota is an equal-opportunity educator and employer.

15 14 13 12 11 10 09   10 9 8 7 6 5 4 3 2 1

I dedicate this book to

SUSAN BROWNELL and JACK WORTMAN

Contents

MASCULINITY, POWER, AND THE CHINESE STATE

IT WAS AROUND 9 P.M. ON A FRIDAY NIGHT. I was sitting with hostesses in the opening hallway to the entrance of a karaoke bar in the red light district of Dalian, a leading city in Northeast China. As we were joking, laughing, and talking to each other, waiter Wang burst through the bar door and yelled, "Everyone upstairs! Fast! The police are coming this way any moment! They are raiding the karaoke bar next door now!" Hearing these words, twenty-five hostesses panicked and raced to the small dormitory room upstairs that served as their hideout whenever news about police raids spread along the street from one bar to another. I ran with them. We frantically filed into the room and hid under the bunk beds. Waiter Wang followed us to the room and said, "Be careful not to make any sounds!" With these words, he closed the door and we heard the lock click outside the door. His steps faded away into the stairway. We were locked in the dark room. Hostess Dee was next to me and held my hand fast; both of our hands were soaked with sweat. All of us were holding our breath, waiting for the approaching steps of the police. No one spoke or coughed for fear that any sound would reveal our hideout.

I found myself panicking and could hear my rapid heartbeat. Visions of being caught by the police flashed through my mind. I would be identified and arrested as a prostitute and a spy from America intending to disclose dark secrets of China to the outside world and blemish the reputation of the Party. My mind whirled, trying to think of words and ways to respond to the police interrogation, or worse—police abuse. I did not realize how many minutes had passed before I heard the heavy steps of several policemen coming upstairs, getting closer and closer. Finally they stopped at the door of our room. A low voice asked, "What's in this room?" Waiter Wang answered calmly, "This room is only for storage, Sir." There was a long silence. After about five minutes, the heavy steps finally retreated downstairs. The room seemed safe for the time being, but still none of us made a sound. I realized that we should be expecting more police, or the return of the previous police, at any moment. After more than forty minutes, the waiters shouted from below, "Okay, okay, they're gone. You can come out now!" Immediately hostesses yelled to each other: "I almost died from holding my breath too long!" "Me too!" "That was too intense! Thank goodness I didn't cough!" "Yeah! We escaped from the police!"

I was at that time a Ph.D. student in anthropology at Yale University and in the midst of two years of ethnographic fieldwork that I carried out in karaoke bars between 1999 and 2002. How had I, a privileged urban Chinese, come to identify so closely with these hostesses that I was willing to risk my own well-being?

Sex, the State, and the Postcolonial Legacy in Dalian

I am a Chinese woman who came of age during the turbulent social changes in China from the 1980s to the 1990s, which revived the sex industry and created new inequities for women. I am also a native of the port city of Dalian, in Liaoning Province, a city with a unique colonial history. Dalian was occupied and settled by the Japanese from 1905 to 1945. No other regions in mainland China were under Japanese colonial rule for so long. This book describes how the postcolonial legacy of the Japanese occupation is being played out.

In 1984, following the promising results of more liberal economic policies in Shenzhen, Zhuhai, Shantou, and Xiamen, the State Council granted Dalian the status of "special economic zone" (SEZ). By the late 1990s, municipal propaganda boasted that Dalian had developed into the "Hong Kong of the North," the "International Transportation Hinge," an "advanced industrial base," a "modern environmental city," and the "Center of Finance, Trade, and Tourism in Northeast Asia." It had grown rapidly from a fishing village in the nineteenth century to a metropolis with a population of 6.5 million.

Unlike other Chinese cities, Dalian has had to manage a complex and unusual system of prostitution that included the system of comfort women during the Japanese occupation as well as diverse ethnicities since prostitutes came from Manchuria, Korea, and Japan. The experiences of DalianChinese men under Japanese colonialism established an enduring model of masculinity based on bodily resistance, which I will explore in chapter 2. Dalian men have felt ambivalence toward the Japanese, the Maoist state, and even the post-Mao state, unlike the almost universal hatred felt against the Japanese in other parts of China.

Within the fifty-odd years of Communist rule, China's sex industry has gone from bust to boom. During the Maoist era, all kinds of commodity consumption, including commercial sex, were strictly regulated and highly politicized. The Communist Party attempted to level previous class distinctions and promote its egalitarian ideology by eliminating all forms of conspicuous consumption and "reactionary" leisure activities.[1] The time, form, and content of leisure activities fell under the scrutiny and supervision of the state (here and below I mean the state apparatus), and leisure itself was conceptualized as a form of collective action. In political study classes, unsanctioned leisure activities were denounced as capitalist behavior, and state propaganda advocated the ethos of "hard work and simple living."[2]

Since 1978, the state's pro-consumption stance has opened the way for the reemergence of nightclubs and other leisure sites. Such consumption outlets had been condemned and eradicated from the communist landscape. The Maoist state classified nightclubs, dance halls, and bars as emblems of a nonproletarian and decadent bourgeois lifestyle. To avoid any residual negative connotations from the previous era, nightclubs in the current post-Mao period were referred to as karaoke bars, karaoke plazas, or *liange ting* (literally, "singing practice halls"). These new consumption sites were prominent in the more economically prosperous SEZs.[3] Patrons were mainly middle-aged businessmen, government officials, policemen, and foreign investors. Clients could partake of the services offered by hostesses and at the same time engage in "social interactions" *(yingchou)* that helped cement "relationships" *(guanxi)* with their business partners or their patrons in the government.[4] Hostesses played an indispensable role in the rituals of these male-centered worlds of business and politics.

The hostesses or escorts who worked at karaoke bars were referred to by the Chinese government as *sanpei xiaojie,* literally, "young women who accompanied men in three ways." These ways were generally understood to include varying combinations of alcohol consumption, dancing and singing, and sexual services. These women, mainly seventeen to twenty-three years of age, formed a steadily growing contingent of illegal sex workers. Their services typically included drinking, singing, dancing, playing games, flirting, and caressing. Beyond the standard package, some hostesses offered sexual services upon the request of the clients for an additional fee.

Hostesses first emerged in modest numbers at the end of the 1980s. Their numbers expanded rapidly in the mid-1990s as karaoke bars became favored sites not just for male recreation but also for transactions between male businessmen and political elites. Paradoxically, the state agents who were responsible for policing the activities of hostesses in these bars comprised one of the main segments of their customer base.

During the 1990s, the imported karaoke bar from Japan enticed Chinese men into a sense of liberation while serving the purposes of Japanese businessmen. The karaoke bar was part of the Japanese strategy to gain entry into the Chinese market and in turn was appropriated by Dalian men to help them recover from the profound sense of emasculation created during the Maoist era. Karaoke bars can be found almost every few steps throughout the city. Jian Ping, a reporter for the *New Weekly* magazine, calls the whole city "a gigantic sauna salon or KTV bar."[5] According to the city's police chief in 2001, Dalian was at that time home to four thousand nightclubs, saunas, and KTV (karaoke TV) bars.

Dalian's rapid growth has made it a magnet for labor migrants. By the year 1998, the most conservative estimate placed the floating population in Dalian at around three hundred thousand. Institutional (that is, by way of the household registration policy) and social discrimination have forced the vast majority of these migrants onto the lowest rung of the labor market. Migrants commonly work as construction workers, garbage collectors, restaurant waitresses, domestic maids, factory workers, and bar hostesses. A substantial number of female migrants find employment in Dalian's booming sex industry. In 2001, the city police chief estimated that 80 percent of the total population of migrant women worked as hostesses in the nightclub industry. He might have been exaggerating, but this figure suggests that a high percentage of migrant women work as bar hostesses.

Of the two hundred hostesses with whom I worked, only four were from cities. They were extremely averse to exposing their rural origins. At the beginning of my field research, hostesses always told me that they were from large, metropolitan cities such as Dalian, Shanghai, and Anshan. It was only after becoming close friends that they confided to me that they were actually from rural areas on the outskirts of these cities. I accompanied two of my hostess friends when they visited their rural hometowns. In chapter 6, I describe how they operated as "brokers of modernity" in the countryside. As migrants and sex workers, hostesses encounter virulent institutional and social discrimination in the city. Acutely aware of their status as second-class citizens, hostesses attempt to claim an urban identity through their consumption practices and through exploiting the superior social, cultural, and economic resources possessed by their clients. They rebel against the state's portrayal of them as country bumpkins incapable of becoming full-fledged urbanites. Chapter 7 details how they refashion their bodies through conspicuous consumption of "modern" commodities such as foreign fashions and claim full urban membership by projecting their refashioned bodies.

MASCULINITY, POWER, AND THE CHINESE STATE

This is the first book-length treatment of the critical period in Chinese history characterized by the hand-in-glove rise of the postsocialist state and the sex industry. This intermingling of state and private spheres (which have never been clearly separated) was an important development in the shaping of new state-society relationships. My account of the mutual constitution of hostesses, clients, and the state challenges the assumption that dichotomizes the state and its subjects. My aim is to deepen the trend of anthropological inquiry into the state-subject relationship through an ethnographic approach. In this book, I show the relationship between the hostesses and the state as a dynamic interaction rather than two polarized entities. As I will demonstrate in the following chapters, hostesses appropriate the dominant cultural symbols to maintain a sense of autonomy and dignity, yet at the same time paradoxically reproducing state hegemony. In this sense, hostesses are not just victims or agents: they are both agents and victims acted upon, as they struggle to find ways to feel empowered while in an objective position of disempowerment.

Indeed, the way in which prostitution is intertwined with rural-urban migration, the entertainment industry, and state power is unique to China. As I will demonstrate in the following chapters, state production and management of the entertainment industry characterized prostitution until the Mao era. For thousands of years, the dynasties and states produced, regulated, sometimes threatened to abolish, yet at the same time profited from prostitution in economic and political terms. The subjugation of women has always been the basis of male identity in China. For example, before the May Fourth Movement in 1919, the courtesan house was a site that produced an elite masculinity of self-control and cool demeanor. Elite masculinities had to be validated by the courtesans, the arbiters of their maleness, as worldly, urbane, knowledgeable, sophisticated, and refined.[6] These values were so important that there were guidebooks instructing men in appropriate conduct. A customer had to learn the aesthetics and etiquette of frequenting courtesans in order to obtain respect from other men, avoid ridicule from courtesans, and demonstrate his sophistication. If he failed in these manners, he lowered his own status and risked exposure in front of his fellow customers as a "country bumpkin."[7]

Unlike Europe, China did not have a hereditary, landed aristocracy or clerical hierarchy but was ruled by the Confucian scholar-officials who gained their elite status through the examination system.[8] The literati, or gentry class, served as the intermediaries between the imperial state and the people, and controlled material, social, and symbolic resources.[9] The merchants leading the commercial expansion joined the gentry by buying land and cultivating literati lifestyles rather than remaining a distinct class.[10] In so doing, they added commercial wealth to the resources available to elites and confirmed their elite status.[11]

It is important to note that concerns about masculine identity at this secure time of "culturalism"[12] have to do with social class and have no reference point outside of China. With Western intrusion into China, Chinese male insecurity was linked to the perceived decline of China and contributed to the growth of Chinese nationalism. Elite masculinity was attacked because it was identified with the elite cultural tradition.[13]

At the turn of the century, nationalism began to produce a new model of masculinity. The powerless and impotent son had been replaced by a rebellious and sexually powerful male. This new masculinity demanded a new model companion: an educated and progressive modern woman on which men's individual development and national progress were predicated. For the first time in Chinese history, the sexual prowess of Chinese men was not measured internally as a means to establish social class but came to be measured against the outside predators whose military prowess identified them as more sexually potent. The conflict between the need for social order and the desire to maintain prostitution for economic reasons and to serve masculinity grew more intense during the nationalist period.

Starting in the 1930s, masculinity was complicated by war and the Japanese occupation. It was here in Dalian that Japanese imperialism based on Bushido (a feudal-military Japanese code of chivalry valuing honor above life) confronted Chinese masculinity first and for the longest period. Dalian men's adoption and transformation of soccer provided the primary basis for this new masculinity. While the Japanese colonialists intended to use calisthenics to cultivate Dalian schoolboys' subordination to a single, strong imperialist leader, Dalian men instead established a model of masculine identity based on bodily resistance. Dalian men's soccer playing was a form of overt resistance that constituted a conscious, collective, and structural form of independence and a powerful form of self-expression. By choosing soccer, Dalian men sought to demystify the naturalization of imposed inequality between the nations of Japan and China, based on men's strong or weak bodies. Soccer allowed Dalian-Chinese men to assert hypermasculinity, creativity, and aggressiveness to debunk the fabricated myth of the "Sick Man of East Asia" and the supposed degradation of Chinese men's bodies through calisthenics.[14]

After the Communist Party came to power in 1949, a new bureaucratic structure emerged that eviscerated the power base of the former elites and turned rural communities into "component cells."[15] Land reform destroyed the economic foundation of local society—lineage, markets, and religious organizations—and as a result, unlike the previous local elites who acted as brokers between imperial subjects and the central state, the new generation of political cadres simply acted as state agents.[16]

Although peasants were the mainstay of the revolution, they now found themselves its victims, subordinated to a caste of privileged urban aristocrats produced by Maoist policies. Before the Maoist state, imperial cities and towns were highly integrated into the countryside with a constant flow of people and goods between them.[17] The blurry boundary between town and country was eliminated by the Maoist state. Following Stalin's model of emphasizing heavy industry over light and industrial development over agriculture, the Maoist state invested in the cities. As a result, urban life was highly subsidized, with full access to a host of benefits.[18] As a result of peasants flooding into the cities, the Maoist state initiated the household registration system in 1958, which outlawed rural migration through the management of resource distribution, thereby establishing a two-tier urban-rural caste system in the society.[19] Rural residents found themselves on the losing end of a heavily lopsided distribution of social wealth.[20] Ironically, although the power of the Chinese Communist Party (CCP) originated in the countryside and then spread to the cities, in the end the CCP exploited the countryside much more intensely than ever before in Chinese history.

After the state initiated market reform and opening policy in 1978, the shift led to a change of social stratifications. With the legalization of private enterprises in 1988, a new class of private entrepreneurs emerged as the "new business elite."[21] These professional and technocratic managers of advanced sectors of the reformed economy, including joint venture, private, and state-owned enterprises, enjoyed a higher income and a better standard of living. Victor Nee suggests that the market economy led to the erosion of the redistributive state, and market institutions replaced politics as entrepreneurs overtook local bureaucrats in receiving economic rewards.[22] Others have disputed this claim and suggest that local bureaucrats' positional power still persisted as they took advantage of their privileged access and converted their political power to economic resources.[23] The result was a dual system of social stratification where bureaucrats and business elites coexisted and shared the benefits through clientele-based ties.[24] Hence the business elite could not transform their economic position into political power because the socialist-corporatist strategy of the state—state clientelism—was designed to prevent it.[25] State clientelism was most important in the private sector, since entrepreneurs, reliant on the discretionary favoritism of local officials for protection and resources, had to maneuver their way vis-à-vis the state bureaucracy.[26] As a result, entrepreneurs had to cultivate solidarity with officials through personal networks and bonding activities, including visits made to (and exploitation of) hostesses in karaoke bars.[27]

THE RISE OF ENTREPRENEURIAL MASCULINITY IN THE POST-MAO PERIOD

The Maoist state, with its emphasis on gender equality, had attempted to control men's sexuality through the suppression of female sexuality. The postsocialist state witnessed a revival of the state's conflicted relationship with prostitution. As I will discuss in chapter 3, bar owners, bar managers, bar bouncers, madams, and state officials manipulate state policy for their own ends by controlling and abusing the hostesses. An exploitative and violent environment was established in the sex industry through the interplay among state administrative and cultural power, the agendas of local officials, and the maneuverings of bar owners. The karaoke bar was the target of state law and police raids such as the one described above, in which state agents usurped and manipulated state policy for their own interest and profit. The state's antivice campaign not only failed to achieve the goals proclaimed in state propaganda but further eroded hostesses' working conditions.

Anthropologist Mayfair Yang observes that although post-Mao China is evolving into the fastest-growing capitalist economy in the world, those who study gender must pay heed to the state as well as to the market economy, because the state still plays the most crucial role in Chinese economic development. Yang quotes Manuel Castells in asserting that the post-Mao state still regards "economic development . . . not [as] a goal but a means" to state power.[28] Thus an inquiry into women's issues must examine the multiple relations that women have with the state.[29]

In China studies, entrepreneurial masculinity has been analyzed as inextricably linked to economic and state power.[30] However, we still do not know how this entrepreneurial masculinity is played out, contested, and reconfigured in lived experiences. This book will fill this lacuna through an ethnographic analysis of how entrepreneurial masculinity is constituted, performed, and refashioned in the new cultural context of karaoke bars. In the post-Mao era, hostesses provided a foil against which men could redefine themselves as "real men" and claim sexual consumption as a weapon against socialist morality and the socialist state. I argue that the transition from banquet to karaoke bars in the Chinese entrepreneurs' emulation of their economic superiors and competitors—Japanese businessmen—marked their rebellion and challenge against the monopoly of state power as represented by the banquet (which was the main form of state-sponsored consumption throughout the 1980s). Entrepreneurs regarded sex consumption as a form of resistance against the artificial shackles placed on human sexuality by an unnatural socialist system. Patronizing luxurious karaoke bars became a lifestyle, a modern and prestigious symbol, often only afforded by such wealthy clients as officials and local nouveaux riches.

In the 1990s, masculinity and marital stability came to be seen as dependent on women's enjoyment of sex. This radical notion that women should enjoy sex was not out of a concern for the happiness of women but, rather, reflected the new competitive, capitalist economic model where men proved themselves through entrepreneurial activity; men were judged not by birth status or education, but by their competitive abilities. The impact of this change on the relationship between men and women was profound. Women became a testing ground for male entrepreneurial ability. In this competitive world, it was the skill of men in charming women and keeping them under control that came to define their success. Because of the risks and social trust needed in the alliance between entrepreneurs and officials, the consumption of sex served as an institution for the preselection test and bonding activities, which ensured social trust. The most powerful men were identified as those who could emotionally and physically control the hostesses, exploit them freely, and then abandon them. The less powerful men engaged in sex-for-money transactions with a large number of hostesses. The weakest men were those who became emotionally involved with the hostesses. Hence, in the new, fluid urban entrepreneurial environment, men resurrected their lost masculinity by emulating the economically successful Japanese and Taiwanese businessmen in the consumption of women. Their subjugation of women represented the recovery of their manhood in post-Mao China.

My ethnography of the karaoke bars, where this process took place, not only displays the kind of entrepreneurial masculinity sought there but also demonstrates the responding femininity performed there. I argue that the hostesses take advantage of the clients' use of them. They perform an obedient and promiscuous role to satisfy the clients. In return, they redis-tribute the clients' social and economic resources and claim for themselves a cosmopolitan image.

This study aims to build on recent anthropological inquiries into body symbolism by linking it to individual agency, the burgeoning market economy, and state power in China. In chapter 4, I analyze a particular example of body symbolism: the clients' metaphoric use of *liang* (grain) in their reference to having sex with their wives as *jiao gong liang* (turning in the grain tax). This section draws on Susan Brownell's insights into the relationship between body symbolism and the workings of state power.[31] Brownell notes that the classic Chinese symbolic view of the body was grounded in a social world where connections among people and the envi-ronment were more important than individuals. Stripped of individual autonomy, people have little control over a social life where their bodies are subject to the demands and pressures of the family and state.[32] Hence, the social tensions to fulfill their economic (for men) and reproductive (for women) duties are expressed in bodily symbolism where people can exercise more control over their bodily fluids. The athletes in Brownell's study expressed social stress in their concerns about reproductive and diges-tive physiology: menstrual blood, semen, and food.

Unlike the athletes in Brownell's study, my research subjects rebelled against state power and claimed freedom from state control. A significant question I ask is, Why the metaphor of *liang* (grain)? I detail how the his-tory of the hierarchical system of food rationing in colonial and Maoist Dalian placed the Japanese and Maoist states at the top of the food chain and men at the bottom. Meanwhile, men perceived their masculinity as lost in the alliance of the Maoist state and Chinese women to liberate women. Thus semen and food are the pivotal points for symbolizing state power and social relationships. In the post-Mao era, men's attempts to recover their lost sexual identity with free-ranging promiscuity in the kar-aoke bars were further curtailed by the continued presence of socialist moralities and state laws. Thus the clients made an analogy of turning in their *jing* (semen) to their wives just as the peasants turned in the grain tax to the state. The clients/peasants perceived themselves at the bottom of the hierarchy vis-à-vis their wives/the state. I argue that the greater strain the state applied to the clients' sexual function, the more clients operated on an economy of scarcity where the semen was perceived as finite. They assumed more control over their "limited" amount of semen and exercised what I call "misappropriation," that is, they allocated their semen between their wives and hostesses. Such a misappropriation of their *jing* was a mode of resistance, just as *liang* was misappropriated by peasants who rebelled by cheating the government of their taxes. The clients' subversive misappropriation was intended to maintain their bodies' independence as "impermeable, inviolable entities."[33]

Their wives responded by attempting to assume more control over their husbands' "scarce" semen. I discovered that many of the wives of clients did not work and those who did were unable to independently support themselves or maintain their current level of consumption. Caught in the web of dependency on their husbands and stress over their husbands' infidelities, the wives focused on their husbands' semen and claimed ownership, or at least a fair share of it, by making continuous sexual demands on their husbands.

Hostesses, on the other hand, defied the claim of both the state and client on their reproductive and sexual organs by taking an economic view of their bodies. Unlike the female athletes in Brownell's study, who expressed strong concerns about their reproductive organs in order to fulfill their duties to the state,[34] many hostesses had six to seven (sometimes even more) abortions, even though they were fully aware that multiple abortions would jeopardize their future ability to bear children. Disregarding their reproductive duties to the family and the state, hostesses assumed an absolute entrepreneurial ownership of their own bodies and marketed them for their own independent, autonomous, and instrumental uses. They viewed their bodies as an assemblage of fragmented parts, attached a price tag to different body parts, and demanded financial rewards from the clients according to the parts that they touched. They also refused the clients' free use of their bodies on the pretext of romance and love, and demanded its quantified monetary gains. In so doing, they subverted the gender and social hierarchy and reclaimed the commodification of their bodies as an empowering practice.

The grand historical trends in masculinity are the primary driving forces behind the emergence and proliferation of karaoke bars. In response to male power, women are forced into niches that they themselves have little control in shaping. This book is an ethnographic study of rural migrant women seeking to survive through sex work, urban men seeking their services for reasons related to their own position in the emerging post-Mao social structure, and the evolving Chinese patriarchal state. By examining the role of sex workers and the evolution of masculinity throughout China's past and present, I seek to explore how masculinity, power, and sex work intersect in the post-Mao era. I will demonstrate that hostesses are exploited by the state to shoulder the responsibilities of rural families and the rural economy, while the state's legal, economic, and social structures aggravate the hostesses' working conditions and facilitate a violent and exploitative entrepreneurial masculinity to be sought at karaoke bars.

DIFFERENT SOCIAL CLASS, SHARED CULTURE

Although the following chapters will tell the story of young Chinese girls, immigrants from the Chinese countryside to the seaport city of Dalian forced to make their way within the harsh world of the karaoke bars, it is also my story or, rather, the story of my unfolding understanding of the world since I was born. Long before my birth, the events that would give a unique twist to my life were already in motion. In 1946, as Mao's armies swept onto the Liaoning Peninsula, my fate was changing before any hint of my existence.

Both my mother's family and my father's family were wealthy landowners. One of my father's earliest memories was of himself as a seven-year-old boy crouching in terror with his older brother and sister, as red spattered the snow against the background of screams as his parents were beaten to death in a Maoist struggle session. As I now know, they were only two of more than three million landlords who died violently in the name of social justice. The question was never whether they were personally just; the only question was one of class. For this there was only one answer, a fatal one.

Although I was born into a world where ancestors and family past were crucial in defining one's self, my past had disappeared before my birth. Not even pictures of my grandparents remain, only the scarred memories of a seven-year-old boy now grown old and muted by the terror he experienced that day. Throughout my life every attempt to understand our family's past has been met with anguished tears. I was born in the middle of the "lost years" of Mao's Cultural Revolution. I grew up a remnant of a despised class, but accepting the voice of the Communist Party and revering the legacy of Mao. I struggled to gain the respect of my parents and to find my place in the rapidly changing and dangerous world I inhabited. In 1997 after receiving my M.A. from Dalian University of Foreign Languages, I secured a scholarship in women's studies at the University of Northern Iowa. A year later I entered the Ph.D. program in anthropology at Yale University.

My interest in China's rural poor was also due to my ambivalent status in the United States as a poor Chinese student who relied on financial aid and the maintenance of high grades to keep my legal status. My own experience helped me to identify with the victims I was studying in China and intensified my interest in my subject. Although not in as desperate a situation as the subjects I was studying, like them I was forced to face a new environment with limited resources to help with my adaptation. I came to feel a strong identity with them. As I came to know the history of women in China, I came to better understand my own history and who I am. It became apparent that although hostesses and I had very different vocations and lives, we resembled one another in one important way: we all lived lives of contradiction. On one level our contradiction was the same: we were part of a culture that taught the exploitation of daughters, but at the same time were filial daughters. On another level, studying in the United States taught me about my native country and myself as a Chinese woman.

In Chinese, we call the state "state family" *(guojia)*, and we call the Communist Party "our party" *(wodang)*. The loyalty and bond with parents, the state, and the Communist Party are deeply embedded in me. My sense of identity is hard to separate from my membership in these groups. In China, the smallest unit is not the individual, but some group of which an individual is a member. In the United States, I experienced loneliness that I had never felt while embedded in family, state, and party. This loneliness was the genesis of a deeper exploration of myself and my culture that gave me a perspective, a place to stand and look at my own culture in a way that I hadn't before. Demystifying what I had learned about the state and the Chinese Communist Party became for me a painful experience in the United States. I remember watching the film *The Gate of Heavenly*

Peace, which was the first time I had ever seen my country and my party criticized; the criticism was devastating. I could not help crying as I saw the mask ripped from the face of the party. I was horrified; the shattered image of the party was like the death of a parent. For my entire life the party had been a kind of parent, and now it was dead to me.

As I would find out, the film was only the beginning of my education in the States. When I first came to the United States, I proudly told everyone in class that women in China enjoyed equal rights, and communism made women equal to men. One day we were discussing the issue of single mothers in the United States. I was very frustrated with my classmates' discussion, insisting that the state should help these women with more welfare. I spoke from sincerely held cultural beliefs: "These women shouldn't have had sex before marriage. If they had adhered to this principle, they wouldn't now be suffering from the consequences." Unbeknownst to me, I had crossed the line of political correctness. Immediately everyone stopped talking and glared angrily at me. The class was silent for about two minutes before the professor dismissed the class. While my words had ended the class, it was not the end of the story. My classmates were waiting for me and began an intense diatribe. They accused me of not being a feminist. In frustration, I tried to talk to the professor, but to no avail. That event was the true beginning of my feminist education. As a young girl, it was drummed into me that a decent girl must be a virgin until her wedding night. Once again I was forced to examine the past and ideas that were so much part of my being that I never contemplated questioning them. Had I so absorbed patriarchal ideas that I had come to think of them as my own? Would it be possible for me to question values that were so fundamental to my own sense of identity? Was I simply the victim of patriarchal indoctrination as so many of my classmates believed?

I grew up in the post-Mao misogynist environment of the 1980s. My uncle made his daughter quit school and work to support her brother through school. I grew up listening to my uncle explain how girls' biology determined that their talents were inferior to boys. Although my grades were very high in junior high, he said girls who studied well in junior high would drop severely once they got into senior high. Their biology has determined their fate to be dominated by men in both talent and perseverance, he insisted. When I entered senior high, my grades were still the highest in the class, but I always heard boys in my class raise their voice and declare that the girls who now were receiving high grades would still end up in the kitchen at the stove, caring for the family. My mother also commented how she appreciated my father because he never complained about having two daughters. I sensed her disappointment in not having produced a boy and started living for the purpose of giving her honor as though she had a son. If my grades were not satisfactory, I would starve myself because I felt I did not deserve the food or even to live if I could not give my mother honor. I wanted to prove to my mother, my uncles, and my classmates that I could do better than boys.

Although I tried very hard to compete with the boys, I could not escape the fate of being a girl. During all the years of my youth it was a regular routine to be reprimanded because of the way I smiled, sat, stood, or spoke, and the only place to escape this was the bathroom, where I could hide and cry. My mother also trained me as a good Chinese girl not to be particular about food and eat everything presented to me, including large pieces of fat. She said, "If you don't, in the future your in-laws will think you were not properly raised." In China, girls are raised to please others.

My mother also told me that protecting my hymen was the most important duty for a woman before marriage. She said men would treat women horribly if they did not shed blood on the wedding night. The hymen determined whether you were going to be a happy or a miserable woman. She also said that the hymen could not be broken except through sexual intercourse, and that books and doctors who said otherwise were simply trying to save marriages and maintain the social order; otherwise, husbands would divorce their wives. Because of her indoctrination, I spent my life in fear and dread. I feared that I would never have a happy life and that no one would ever love me.

After I went to college, my mother continued to be a prominent part of my life. Once I returned home wearing a sleeveless shirt, and she immediately told me to take it off, saying that I shamed her by walking in the neighborhood dressed like this. I had contaminated her honor. Even as an adult in graduate school, the same type of situation occurred. Once coming back from a late dinner, I found that the gates were already locked so I had to climb over the wall to get back into campus. This led to vicious gossip and rumors about me. When I told my mother of this incident, she got on the train and came to my university. I stood outside of the train station to meet her. As soon as her eyes met mine she began scolding me: "You are not my daughter. I don't have a daughter like you. I have lived my whole life as a decent teacher without any shameful background; our whole family is respectable and honorable. Your sister is my daughter because she would never do anything like this to shame our family. You are nothing like your sister. You brought shame to us, and now my colleagues will laugh at us because of you." My heart felt like it was being torn open with a sharp knife. I cried and knelt before her on the steps of the train station. "I am sorry," I said through my tears. "I am not good enough to be your daughter. I am leaving right now and will no longer be your daughter to shame you anymore." I turned around and left heartbroken. This is an incident that I will never forget, and every time I recall it, my heart breaks because my mother disowned me when I desperately needed her help and support. Nothing was more hurtful and devastating than this.

As the years went by in the midst of reprimands and tears, I became the Chinese ideal of a soft-spoken, subservient woman living for my parents. I had internalized my mother's criticisms so much that I firmly believed certain things about women, including the virtue of chastity before marriage. As an anthropologist, I have come to understand that values such as chastity are particular to cultures, and not necessarily treated the same way in all cultures. I also now understand that women in the United States having children out of wedlock are often the unwitting victims of social conditions beyond their control. Nevertheless, my indoctrinated beliefs are still part of my identity, and I cannot fully eliminate them. When I studied Michel Foucault as a graduate student, I came to understand that I had so internalized patriarchal values that they had become powerful constraints and fetters on me.[35]

The indoctrination never stopped, even as I grew older and pursued my Ph.D. at Yale. When I returned to China to do my research with the hostesses in 2000, in order to fit in with the women I was studying and gain some sense of their personal aesthetics, I dressed as they dressed, iconoclastically but modestly. Even though I was twenty-eight years old, my parents summoned me into their room one day with serious faces. I was perplexed at the tense atmosphere and did not know what I had done wrong. They sat me in front of them and took turns lecturing me: "We have noticed your changes lately, and we are very concerned. We are concerned with your dress and your behavior. You are no longer a respectable woman. Keep in mind that you are a scholar, not a prostitute. You are going to make a living with your knowledge, not with your FACE and BODY. Look at the clothing you bought. Who wears that kind of clothes? Only prostitutes! You cannot let yourself be a prostitute. That's not you. . . ." I was deeply upset. Their reprimand left me speechless. I despaired that I would never escape the control of my parents. No matter how successful I became in my work, to them my work would never define me. To them, and even to me, I was still a Chinese woman—that was my identity.

My femininity and my sexuality needed to be controlled and policed at all times. My parents even believed that films, DVDs, and television were evil forces that corrupted women. Ever since I was twelve, they had forbidden me to watch TV dramas that involved love stories that could corrupt girls. Even as a mature woman, it was impossible for me to watch a DVD at home. It did not matter how old I was; all that mattered was that I was a woman.

When I was sixteen years old in my third year of senior high school, a male student came to my house to discuss a question with me. When he left, my mother towered over me in a rage, calling me "debased," "shameless," and "vile" *(xia jian)*. Confused, I asked in a timid voice why she was angry. She shouted at me that I was sitting too close to him and that was why I was dirty and low. I endured in silence. When she finished, I shut myself in my small room and started inflicting pain on my body. I pinched my arm black and blue. While feeling the pain, I cursed myself as dirty and debased. Later I had to endure additional attacks from her. Once, trusting her, I complained about some bodily discomfort I was experiencing. Her response was again rage. So I decided never to talk to her again about such topics.

The culture I lived in was patriarchal, even though the medium through which I experienced its rules and enforcements the most was, ironically, a female figure: my mother. My mother acted as an agent of the state to humiliate and mold me into a proper, respectable, subservient woman. I believed that she did it for my own good because I was going to step into a patriarchal society and would not flourish if I had not been properly shaped. In other words, she was preparing me to fit in and survive.

Even today, whenever I am doing research in the field, it is extremely common to hear misogynist and essentialist views about women. For instance, my male interviewees often comment that women live to be conquered and controlled. They say that men's biology determines their desire for sex and their desire to conquer women. For Chinese men, biology is the ultimate explanation and justification for all violence against women.

Biological determinism has dominated the discourse on sex and gender in China since the May Fourth Movement in 1919.[36] The onslaught of Western imperialism during the Republican era persuaded Chinese intellectuals to reevaluate Confucian culture and attribute national backwardness to weak bodies and a poor knowledge of sex. They replaced the cosmological yin-yang discourse with biological determinism and modern Western science as scientific proof of gender hierarchy. "Biological distinctions between male and female, which rarely assumed a primary function in imperial China, became essential," as Frank Dikotter puts it.[37] The alleged authority of modern science was claimed to legitimize the belief that gender and sexual behaviors were firmly determined by biological differences, and gender hierarchy was "natural and progressive."[38] This biological determinist strand continued until the Maoist and post-Mao eras.[39]

Chinese male intellectuals are not exempt from these beliefs. In 1999, when I attended a conference in Hong Kong, a famous male anthropology professor from Beijing University commented after learning that I studied under Helen Siu at Yale: "How could you have had the opportunity to study under her? I have never even had a chance to meet her. Did you have a boyfriend or a lover who had a special relationship with Helen Siu before you entered the program?" I was not surprised by this comment, although he had apparently forgotten that Helen Siu, the person he admired, was a woman. I am familiar with the biological determinist idea that women do not have the talents necessary for success. When women do succeed, it is almost always attributed to some sort of surreptitious transaction. This Chinese anthropologist also made the following comments about women in China: "All divorced women and unmarried older women in China have mental problems. They are abnormal," he insisted. "That's why I married a girl ten years younger than I."

At the beginning of my fieldwork, when I was introduced to hostesses by bar owners, the hostesses all appeared quite perplexed: "Why do you study us little people *[xiao renwu]*? What is so worthwhile about writing about us? Why don't you study professional urban women?" These three questions revealed a great deal about the hostesses' self-image. Describing themselves as "small fries" as opposed to "urban professional women," the hostesses convinced me that they carried heavy cultural and historical baggage with them when they migrated to the urban areas.

FILIALITY, PATRIARCHY, AND THE STATE

In writing this book, I learned a great deal about the nature of patriarchy in China, and it became my intent to explain the dilemmas of those girls trapped in prostitution. I do not see myself as any different from them. Even though I did not sell my body, I, too, have pawned my identity in deference to the patriarchal ideal of a Chinese woman. We all live and work for our parents, who are part of a culture that exploits and cages their children.

The nature of the state has changed tremendously in Chinese history, but the hand-in-hand collaboration of the state and the patriarchal family to subordinate women has not. Throughout China's history, women had been defined by the virtues of filiality and self-sacrifice, which mandated that women (most often rural women) were willingly or unwillingly sold, pawned, or abducted into prostitution for the survival of their parents or husbands. The Chinese state has always served the interest of masculine power and profited from prostitution in economic and political terms, except during the abolition period under Mao. In post-Mao China, various levels of the government, from national to local, are dependent on the sex industry. The state profits not only from the sex industry's stimulation of the local economy and its attraction of foreign investment, but also from the hostesses' financial support to their rural families and villages. In the absence of a state-sponsored welfare system, hostesses' remittances to their rural families alleviate the state's burden by taking care of the elderly and helping develop the rural economy.

To illustrate the enduring nature of the concept of filiality, I will take the readers with the hostesses back to their hometowns and examine carefully the relationship and interactions between these women and the communities they have left behind. As I will show in chapter 5, home to them is a temporary refuge from their dangerous lives in the city. The seeming contradiction between their desire for cosmopolitanism on the one hand and their continuing practice of filiality on the other only illustrates the depth of conviction in the Confucian value of filiality in spite of the New Culture movement,[40] Republicanism, Maoism, and post-Mao consumerism. I will demonstrate the continuing power of filiality by showing the intense loyalty demonstrated by these young women who, in spite of having violated rural codes of conduct, have not violated their duties to their parents. I will also show that by using filiality to assert their virtues, hostesses reproduce the structure that victimizes them.

During the post-Mao era, women were once again required to make sacrifices for the state. This usually took the form of laying off or encouraging women workers to return home, because after all, a woman's duty to the state was first defined as her commitment to her husband and children. As early as the 1980s, public discourse once again indicated that an ideal woman should be obedient and put her husband's interests first.[41] In 1988, the state-run journal *Chinese Women* opened a debate on whether women should return home or not. Many respondents agreed that female workers should return home where they belonged and allow men to have more job opportunities and enjoy higher wages. A large number of women either volunteered or were forced to retire. Since the late 1980s, women have been the first laid off when state-owned factories have reduced operations. Because men have held women in low esteem, they believe that they are incapable of competing in the market economy. Even today it is difficult for women to secure employment because many enterprises and government offices refuse to hire them.

Some observers even justified prostitution for women as part of a more general process by which female sexual attractiveness was commodified and sold in China.[42] After the Maoist androgynous ideal, recognition of biological differences between men and women resurfaced. The 1990s witnessed a proliferation of images of dramatically feminine beauties, slender and sexy, designed to appeal to male audiences.[43] Sexuality provided one of the few openings for women into the regular economy as sexual attractiveness came to be a vehicle for selling goods. Many jobs now require female applicants to meet a certain standard of sexual attractiveness. In other words, beauty has become a job requirement for women. As a result, in 2003 a large number of female college graduates attached their half-naked, colorful portraits to their résumés and emphasized that they could sing and dance, and that they were beautiful, decorous, gentle, and good at socializing and drinking alcohol.[44] In 1993 at a Shanghai trade fair, one enterprise hired fifty beautifully made-up young women to dance with guests after a banquet.[45] Some accounts suggested that sexual intercourse was a job requirement for women in occupations other than sex work and claimed that female employees were told they would lose their jobs if they refused to sleep with customers.[46]

It seems that in the patriarchal state where resources are in the hands of males, what is left for females is to find a sexual niche—that is, to decorate an essentially male world. For instance, when I worked in a bank in China, during a time of severe reduction of personnel, a poor migrant woman faced being laid off. She saved her position by agreeing to be the mistress of the bank manager. For a woman, clearly the line between what defines a sex worker and what is necessary to maintain employment is not substantial. In this patriarchal environment, it is not surprising that women have to use their looks and sexuality—the only accepted talents of women—to get ahead.

Although the patriarchal state instigated the proliferation of different forms of prostitution, the state blamed women themselves for their evil nature. Throughout history, women have been the focus of blame whenever there is a social disorder. In post-Mao China, female "third parties" *(disanzhe)*, mostly defined as migrant mistresses in public discourse, were severely condemned and punished as immoral women who built their happiness on others' bitterness and caused divorce and social disorder. The state's fear of marital instability—both real and perceived—has engendered great anxiety and even outright hostility toward these women. These sentiments coalesced to push the All-China Women's Federation *(fulian)*, other women's groups, and individual irate women to incorporate legal penalties against *third parties* (the formal term for mistresses) into revisions of the marriage law (2002). Although legislators ultimately rejected the proposed provisions, the Chinese government, through the judicial branch, has made clear its disapproval of migrant women's illicit relations with urban men. In a series of cases, Chinese courts have supported claims by adulterers and their wives (sometimes even in conjunction) that have stripped second wives of property rights to presents and cash gifts given by male patrons before the dissolution of the extramarital affair. The majority of these decisions are based on flimsy legal reasoning that only serves to highlight the extralegal considerations that inform case outcomes. Indeed, in one such instance the judge, unable to find a legal basis for his ruling, was forced to rely on the very vague and seldom invoked principle of "public order and good customs" *(gongxu liangsu)* to justify depriving a second wife of her ownership of property bestowed on her by her deceased lover. (The ruling also blatantly infringes on the deceased's right to dispose of his property postmortem.)

Migrant women, especially hostesses, are condemned as "unstable elements" destabilizing the social order and wrecking urban families, causing a crisis in national morality. The perception is that the transgressive sexuality of hostesses puts the party and state at risk. One newspaper alleges that more than 60 percent of government corruption is attributable to the sexual entanglements of officials with hostesses.[47] Hostesses' ability to seduce men is described as an almost magical power to enthrall and delude. This is called "the power of female charm" *(zise de liliang)* and "the weapon of beauty" *(meinv de wuqi)*.[48] According to these accounts, powerful men are the most likely to be targeted for seduction. The hostess uses her body to secure favors ranging from cash gifts to government jobs. This form of "sexual bribery" *(xing huilu)* is seen as even more dangerous than bribes of money. As the *China Youth Daily* reports, "Some leaders and cadre faced with the temptation of money have no problem refusing, but when faced with a woman's charm *[nuse]* start stumbling over themselves."[49] The article's author urgently calls for lawmakers to stamp out this harmful phenomenon by formally recognizing "power-sex transactions" *(quanse jiaohuan)* as a form of bribery punishable under criminal law.

Reports from newspapers, party periodicals, and other publications have been compiled into "internal documents" that serve as study materials for weekly political classes organized by government units.[50] Officials are urged to remain vigilant against the seductive powers of hostesses and to hold steadfast to party principles of public service and dedication. As reports dramatically illustrate, failure to abide by these guidelines comes at the penalty of ruined careers, broken families, and prison sentences. This reputation has earned hostesses the unflattering title of "beautiful disaster makers" *(hongyan huoshui)*, a concept similar to the sirens of classical Greek literature who led good men down the path to destruction.[51]

Popular media sites also reinforce this negative image of these women. The TV drama *Red Spider* portrays hostesses as sexually attractive but dangerous and evil.[52] They appear in sexy, tight dresses and are charming and seductive. They are also criminals who blackmail and murder male clients. The show highlights the control of these women in the arrest and handcuffing scenes. The arrested hostesses are disheveled as tears of regret stream down their faces. Seven or eight policemen forcibly press them onto a bed, pull their hair, and handcuff their wrists. This scene is not only intended to frighten real hostesses about the consequences of their behavior but also accommodates the male audience's fantasy of raping and controlling them. This TV series relates the stories of the short lives of ten female criminals. Rural migrant women are compared to red spiders, dangerous and poisonous. Their sexuality is under constant surveillance by the policemen and the state. Produced in a fake documentary form, the drama records the preexecution monologue of hostesses that is intended to instruct other women to control their sexual and moral conduct. In one series, a hostess poisons all of her clients and steals their possessions. When she is finally arrested, her mother tells the story of her daughter's migration to the city, "just as many women do." The fact that "she is not bad by nature" but "a product of circumstances" serves to warn other migrant women that they might end up like her unless they curb their sexuality.

If hostesses are portrayed as evil and dangerous "foxes"[53] in the state and popular media, how do the newly emerged Chinese feminists and social scientists represent them? Social scientists in China have accepted the party goal of ridding the country of Western pollution and restoring traditional Communist values in their research.[54] In doing so, they have subordinated their science to the goal of the state. Sociologist Chu Zhaorui and sexologist Liu Dalin follow state discourse and claim that the root of prostitution is found in the "flies" of Western capitalist erotic culture and the pollution of Western privatization, which harm Chinese marriages and families.[55] The intellectual youth writer Liang Xiaosheng compares hostesses in post-Mao China with prostitutes in the Republican era and concludes that hostesses have voluntarily chosen a life of vice and moral downfall.[56] His view is endorsed by both Chu Zhaorui and Liu Dalin, who describe hostesses as lazy women from poor backgrounds who have indulged in precocious sexual experiences and have enjoyed casual sexual conduct.[57] Liu Dalin thus admonishes these women to control their sexuality with reason, because reason represents "a holy, ideal, and happy human being."[58]

Sociologists Wang Jinling and Xu Sisun further insist on women's voluntary choice with a biological and pathological model. Wang and Xu conducted a detailed survey of 389 sex workers to investigate their biology, personality, intelligence, and psychology. They argue that sex workers share an early sexual maturation; distorted sexual psychology; deficient intelligence; high masculine vigor; and aberrant, abnormal personalities.[59] These characteristics are said to induce their liberal ideas regarding chastity and their voluntary choice of prostitution.[60]

State, popular, and intellectual representations condemn hostesses' voluntary engagement in the sex business as influenced by Western spiritual pollution and the abnormal psychology and biology of the women. Scholars provide social and scientific authority to regulate the transgressive behavior of hostesses. These scholars in recently rehabilitated disciplines like sociology, women's studies, and sexology label prostitution a vice and a crime, following the lead of the party-state, rather than a form of labor. Hershatter points out that for these scholars labeling this a "crime" is especially favored because, on the one hand, they hope to revive the long-restricted discussion of social problems and, on the other, labor is an old and obsolete topic that was exhausted during the Maoist period.[61] Almost all of them stand with the state on the issue of prostitution and busy themselves with proposing solutions. Further, Hershatter observes that formerly discredited scholars, through establishing prostitution as a legitimate object for study, are able to reestablish themselves as legitimate social commentators and redeem social science as a discipline.[62] This aligns them with masculine state power against the sex workers.

I would add that their work is clearly based on a preconceived outcome for their studies. Their methodology makes arbitrary assumptions that no competent social scientists would dare to make. For instance, they assert that these women, as they describe them, are more masculine than other women. The evidence for this is alleged hypersexuality. To assume that hypersexuality indicates masculinity is to assume as a premise what they are trying to prove.

MIGRATION AND SEX WORK

Migrants and employees of state-owned enterprises were losers in the reforms.[63] Despite their contributions to local and overall economic growth, unskilled and low-income migrants worked at the lowest rung of society and encountered severe institutional and social discrimination. They were blamed for the disturbing escalation in urban crime and disorder, and were denied civil, political, and residential rights.[64]

Most studies on migration and sex work outside of China have concentrated on macrolevel issues such as trafficking, human rights,[65] and economic and cultural changes that have weakened bonds to familiar institutions and loosened social mechanisms for control.[66] Sex work has been largely left out of Chinese anthropological work about migration and gender politics, and there is an outright lack of attention to the personal experiences of migrant sex workers. This study is unique in that it aims to expand the anthropological inquiry into the silenced voices and coping mechanisms of female migrants in relation to their clients and the state. Through this ethnography of migrant sex workers, I aim to fill the empirical and conceptual lacunae and contribute to a rich urban anthropology of China.

Recent approaches to migration have paid special heed to gender issues, debating whether migration can liberate rural migrant women or not.[67] These two different views come from the existing literature that focuses on factory workers and domestic maids.[68] This study departs from the previous model and examines how an unexplored population of migrant women—karaoke bar hostesses—experience gender exploitation and class domination in the flourishing Chinese sex industry. It complicates the thesis that economic capital can be directly translated into increased social power by demonstrating how the patriarchal state and new entrepreneurial masculinity constrain and shape rural migrant hostesses' identities.

However, while hostesses find it very difficult to become members of the mainstream urban community, it is clear that their lives in the city are preferable to the lives they leave behind in the countryside. As I will demonstrate in chapter 5, even when hostesses have had enough of risky life in the city where they have to evade the police and always worry about violent clients and thugs, they do not feel that they belong to their rural home anymore.

LIVING WITH AND WORKING AS A *XIAOJIE* (HOSTESS)

In 1999, I set out with a general interest in China's migrant population and social inequality with a focus on migrant women factory workers. Research in an embroidery factory allowed me to witness female workers' confinement within the factory walls, long hours, and strict working rules. During this time, I visited different departments of the municipal government and set up dinner appointments with twelve officials. Two of them worked at the top level of the local government, and the rest were high-level officials who worked in the subdivisions of the Bureau of Culture, Bureau of Resource Investment, Municipal Communist Party Committee, and Bureau of Social Management. To obtain their support for my research, I sought to establish friendships with them before proceeding with interviews. In the course of several rounds of gift giving and dinner conversations, they became friends. In the months to follow, each of them gradually introduced me to a web of their friends who were police officers, entrepreneurs, nouveaux riches, and other official colleagues. It is these people who form the major clientele base discussed in this book.

One evening I was invited by an official to a karaoke bar, where I encountered bar hostesses for the first time. The official told me that most of the hostesses came from rural areas. I was fascinated by these women's glamorous appearance and their full exposure to the high-consumption arenas in the city as compared with the poverty-stricken lives of women factory workers. Watching them socialize in their workplaces with important figures in the city, I was eager to learn about their opportunities for climbing the social ladder. With these questions in mind, I decided to switch the focus of my research to these bar hostesses.

When I told my official contacts about this research plan, I was suspected of being a spy sent by the United States. I was warned not to pursue the topic because of its political sensitivity. I was told that the study of "prostitution as a capitalist vice" discloses a "dark secret" of socialist China. As a result, China's reputation in the world could be ruined. I was also warned that government officials' corruption and decadent lives are an essential component of the phenomenon of "prostitution." Thus, they argued, a study of "prostitution" could jeopardize the image of the Chinese Communist Party in the world. The study could disrupt the "superior socialist morality" that China has endeavored to construct in the world, I was told. Whether I conducted this research would decide whether I was a patriot or a traitor, it was implied. Apart from the political issues, other friends also warned me of the physical risk and psychological travail involved in such research.

Fully informed of the risks and possible impediments, I embarked on my research on the hostesses. As expected, my initial research encountered a series of obstacles. My requests to conduct research in karaoke bars were repeatedly turned down by every bar owner I talked to. Officials were reluctant to "reveal any secret information" to me, contending that their own political positions would be jeopardized. I was fully aware of their suspicions of me throughout our interactions. Once, as I was singing songs with a couple of political officials and entrepreneurs in a karaoke bar, one of the officials suddenly grabbed my purse and started searching inside. I was too shocked at the moment to ask what he was looking for. In the end, he did not find anything except my keys and a mirror and returned the purse to me. He appeared much more relaxed after investigating my purse. Later, I realized that he was checking my purse to see if I had hidden a tape or video recorder there. The nature of my research raised everyone's suspicions of my "real identity" and created barriers in my relationships with them.

As time went by, my persistence in conducting the research and my sincerity in interacting with political officials bore fruit. I could see the suspicions subsiding and tensions thawing. Openly acknowledging their suspicion marked a big step out of their previous silence. One political official asked me to be his daughter's English tutor, and I agreed. In exchange, he introduced me to some karaoke bars to conduct my fieldwork. He himself was a regular customer of these establishments and therefore familiar with their proprietors. My identity and my research were fully explained to the bar owners. I assured them that I would not publicize the bar names to the outside world. Ultimately, I was intensively involved in three karaoke bars categorized respectively as high, middle, and low class. The ethnographic materials in this book were mainly drawn from these three bars, which were frequented by nouveaux riches, entrepreneurs, and local officials. I also visited other karaoke bars and altogether interacted with approximately two hundred bar hostesses from ten bars.[69]

The bar owners attempted to use the situation to their advantage. They seized the chance to ask for favors from the official, who as a senior government official controlled municipal resources. One bar owner, for example, hinted that he was interested in renting a plot of land in the city center. Because of the ideal position of this land in the heart of Dalian's largest commercial district, bidding for the land user rights would be intense. In the end, the bar owner himself called off the deal, saying that he was sick of constantly having to bribe and kowtow to political officials. Likewise, bosses saw me as a potential resource for their business and other plans. I was frequently grilled for information on business conditions in the United States, the best ways to go abroad, strategies for their children's education, and other matters.

Bar owners introduced me to hostesses as a university student from the United States who had come to do social research. As they explained, I had come to get a "real taste" *(tihui)* of hostesses' lives in order to write a book on the subject. My presence was greeted lukewarmly. The hostesses found it difficult to understand why anyone would want to study them. One hostess warned me that a female college student like me had been raped and murdered by a psychopathic customer while conducting her research. I do not know if this story is true, but it did shake me up a bit.

In the karaoke bars, my initial attempts to interact with hostesses were not very successful for a number of reasons. Their attention was squarely focused on business, and they would not talk to me. They did not even have time to listen to me, because their eyes were fixated on each entering client, and they concentrated on the selection process (*shitai,* try the stage). My cultural style also marked me as an outsider. They referred to me as "glasses" and "a college student." They ridiculed my student attire and my inability to understand or participate in their sex talk and jokes, and they distanced me from their circle. They did not believe I would be able to understand their lives, especially their inner turmoil, simply because I was not "in their shoes." They insisted that differences in experience and background would prevent me from knowing their pain. They were extremely wary of their own security from the assaults by the police, hooligans, and so on in their dangerous environment. They were also cautious in dealing with each other because any hostess might have some network with VIPs in the city that might harm them. So each hostess used a fake name, a fake hometown, and a fake personal story.

To overcome these barriers, I decided to increase the amount and intimacy of my interactions with them. I paid the rooming fees to the bar owner and lived with the hostesses in the karaoke bars. Thereafter, I became intensely involved in every aspect of their lives. On a typical day, we got up around noon and ordered a light meal from a nearby restaurant. The remainder of the afternoon was free for shopping or visiting the beauty parlor. We ordered dinner at around 6 P.M. Around that time the first customers of the evening would begin to trickle into the bar. While waiting to be selected, we sat in the bar lobby watching video compact discs or TV and chatting. Around midnight we ordered breakfast and went to bed between 2 and 3 A.M.

It was not my initial intention to research hostess-client dynamics by directly servicing clients as a hostess. However, objective circumstances mandated that I wait on clients. First, my personal profile fits within the range of hostesses' typical characteristics. I am Chinese and female. My fieldwork was conducted during my twenty-eighth and twenty-ninth years of life, which put me in the "autumn" of a hostess's career lifespan. This meant that a customer who saw me sitting in the KTV lounge would naturally assume that I was a hostess. Second, I was obliged to minimize the disruption of my research on the bar's normal business operations. According to KTV bar convention, a hostess can legitimately refuse to perform genital or oral sex acts with her customer. Although refusal can, and often does, spark conflicts between hostesses and clients, these incidents are considered to be a normal part of business. For a hostess to refuse to wait on a customer, however, is simply unheard of. This meant that if a customer chose me to wait on him, it would be very difficult for me to refuse.

To avoid clashes with customers, I took certain precautionary steps. First, I did not actively present myself to clients. When clients came into the lobby, I tried my best to be inconspicuous or, if circumstances mandated, slipped into a back room. Second, within the limits of hostesses' dress code, I did my best to appear conservative. Part of the requirement not to disturb bar business was that I adhere to the basic tenets of hostesses' dress code. Thus, I had to wear a skirt without stockings. Without violating these rules, I chose clothing that I felt would be the least appealing to customers, for example, longer skirts and solemn colors. I was also given a certain amount of leeway. For example, I was allowed to wear glasses. This final aesthetic effect was very successful: in the words of one hostess, I looked like a real nerd *(shudaizi)*.

Despite all this, some clients still chose me. I asked hostesses for their advice on how to thwart customer's sexual advances. I exercised each of the following tactics while I accompanied the clients, and they turned out to be very helpful. One, invite customers to sing songs and play drinking games to divert their attention. Two, compliment customers on their civilized manners. Customers feel the pressure to live up to the standard that is set. Three, enlist the help of other hostesses. If there are other hostesses in the private room servicing the same or other customers, I would say to the overaggressive customer, "Aren't you embarrassed to behave like this in front of so many people?" Four, if all else fails, use physical force to extract myself from the immediate danger and run for help.

Despite these precautions, I became embroiled in several conflicts with customers. One, hearing that I had gone abroad to the West to study, invited me out to converse in English with him over tea. At that time it was 2 A.M. I politely declined, but the customer was very insistent. Sensing an imminent confrontation, a hostess called for the bar manager. While the owner and customer negotiated, I slipped into the back of the bar. Hostesses told me that I should make a run for it. They warned me that if I went out with the man, "I would be raped before I knew what hit me." Hearing these words, I slipped out the back door. After a couple of hours, I called the bar to check if the situation had calmed down. The bar manager told me that the client had waited two hours for me to return before being ejected by the bar bouncer.

On another occasion, a customer selected me to wait on him. While we were singing in the private room, he asked me to "go out" with him. I declined by saying that I had a "red light signal," meaning that I was currently menstruating. The customer was unsatisfied with my excuse and refused to pay the obligatory, minimum 100 *yuan* tip for the service. Although the term *tip (xiaofei)* is used to refer to the sum of money that customers pay to hostesses, it is not a tip in the Western sense of the word as a voluntary payment. Regardless of my special status in the bar as researcher, I had accompanied the man by singing songs and drinking just like a hostess. His refusal to pay was thus construed as an assault on the very system of operation. The bar manager and several male servers (all experienced criminals and street fighters) blocked him at the entrance to the bar. This show of muscle was enough to scare the customer into handing over the tip. However, as he exited, he left several threatening remarks: "Just you wait. I'll be back for you!" Quite scared, I asked the hostesses to warn me of his presence in the bar so that I could escape his future assault.

I hope this gives the readers some idea of how safety was a central concern in my fieldwork. This was especially true during my fieldwork in Romantic Dream, a bar located in Dalian's crime-plagued, red-light district. Living in the karaoke bars, hostesses and I had to maintain constant vigilance against police raids and attacks by thugs from competing bars in the city (including other bar owners and some frequent clients). At night, three hostesses and I slept on the couches in one of the private rooms rented by customers during operating hours. Every morning before going to sleep, we pushed a couch against the door in case gangsters attempted to break in. In times of danger, we held our breath and turned down the lights, making the room look unoccupied. We escaped danger several times. Experience of common adversity gradually brought us together.

Thankfully, the official friend who introduced me into the bars placed responsibility for my safety with the bar owners. As he put it: if anything were to happen to me, their hides would be on the line. Bar owners, however, spend only a small fraction of their time in the bars. Thus, the final responsibility for ensuring my safety fell on the bars' bouncers (dashou), mostly ex-convicts with experience in street fighting.

On one occasion, gangsters walked into the bar, grabbed me by the arm, and started dragging me up the stairs toward a private room intended for hostesses' sexual encounters with clients. The women were also sometimes raped there by gangsters. I quickly realized what was going on—that I was in real danger. I riveted my eyes on the bar manager, and then the bouncer, appealing for help. The gangsters were stopped by the bouncer and the manager, who said, "She is not a hostess here. She is my friend." This saved me from imminent danger, but the fear remained.

In practice, it took the combined efforts of bar owners, bouncers, and hostesses to keep me out of harm's way. I am indebted to them for their advice and, at crucial moments, direct interventions. To extricate me from precarious situations, owners and bouncers incurred the wrath of more than one irate customer whose outbursts disturbed regular business operations. Likewise, hostesses redirected their attention and energies, which would otherwise have been expended on profit-making matters, in order to look after my well-being. Without their sacrifices, my research in the bars would have been too dangerous to continue.

Whereas safety was a major issue, hygiene was another. Living in a filthy karaoke bar room without bathing facilities, I had lice in my hair and over my whole body. However, by living and working closely with hostesses in the bar, I gained their recognition and friendship. We shared the same danger, bitterness, and jokes from hostessing experiences. Once when we celebrated a hostess' birthday at 2 A.M. in the bar, we were singing songs and playing games until we were all drunk. I drank so much that I could not stop vomiting. Some hostess friends carried me to a sofa upstairs and brought me a basin. While I was throwing up, I felt an unfathomable sorrow inside and I began crying. At that moment, hostesses beside me also started crying. One of them said, "Whenever I am drunk, I cannot help crying and crying because of all the pent-up bitter feelings from hostessing clients. Now I can see that you feel the same way." That was the moment when I felt my heart closely connected to theirs, and we became emotionally bonded. That was the moment when their previous disbelief in my ability to understand their feelings was dispelled. That was the moment when they accepted me as one of them. Between sweetness and bitterness, we shared countless such moments, and they bonded us together as time went by.

From that moment on, my relationship with the hostesses developed from a straightforward researcher-subject relationship into genuine friendship. The hostesses began confiding in me their hopes and fears about their professional and private lives. In good faith, I could not do much more than lend a sympathetic ear and offer my advice. As I became more familiar with their life conditions, I grew increasingly concerned about the violence, abuse, and police raids to which they were routinely subjected. Even now, living in the United States, I still maintain frequent contact with many hostesses to remain updated on their changing life circumstances. Working and living with them, witnessing, experiencing, and writing about their everyday struggles have been emotional and disconcerting for me. Much of my writing has been accompanied by weeping, lamenting, smiling, and laughing.

Although denied legal rights as rural migrants and sex workers, these women struggle in a patriarchal environment for survival and legitimacy. My fight against patriarchy is restricted to my written works; their fight involves everyday painful and bitter negotiation with, and resistance against, their exploiters. To me they are the most ferocious fighters and heroic feminists I have ever encountered. While I realize that it is unrealistic for me to advocate for a system of decriminalization for these women, I hope my book can help us understand the hostile world within which they struggle for survival and a sense of identity.

One

PATRIARCHY, PROSTITUTION, AND MASCULINITY IN DALIAN

WAS THERE COMPETITION between Dalian men and Japanese men? My interviewees denied that they felt competition with Japanese businessmen, but a client confided to me that once when a karaoke bar hostess curried favor with his poor Japanese business partner but ignored him, he felt so emasculated that he immediately applied for an American passport. The access to an American passport symbolized for him a higher status than the Japanese businessman. Other stories also confirmed the competition.

Why would Chinese businessmen define their masculinity against Japanese models? How did their long history of subordination to Japanese authority contribute to this phenomenon? To understand the underlying reason, this chapter explores the uniqueness of prostitution and masculinity in Dalian, given its distinctive colonial history as a Russian and Japanese concession during the past century.

COLONIAL DALIAN

Dalian is a seaport city situated at the southern tip of Liaoning Peninsula in China's northeast (Manchuria). Before czarist Russia took over Dalian, the city had been a fishing village comprising sixty hamlets and one thousand households. In 1898, Russia negotiated with the Qing court a twenty-five-year lease for Dalian, making the center of the Guandong (Kwantung) Leased Territory a Russian province.

The Russian regime invested 30 million rubles to develop Dalny (meaning "far away" or distant) as an international free harbor and an industrial and garden city during the brief time they occupied it.[1] After the

Russo-Japanese War in 1904, Guandong Leased Territory was formally transferred to Japanese rule in the Treaty of Portsmouth.

The following year, Dalian became the key administrative and commercial center in southern Manchuria. Dalian was intended as the key Japanese military base for the conquest of Manchuria. The Japanese regime designated this place as their "mainland" *(bentu)* and referred to Japan as the "motherland" or "hinterland" *(neidi)*. In other words, the Japanese envisioned Dalian as part of Japan. They encouraged and even forced Japanese immigration to the city.

The colonial government gave more power to the local Japanese immigrant community with the first municipal elections in Dalian in the fall of 1915.[2] It was not until April 1919 that a civilian-controlled colonial structure was formally established with the creation of the Guandong government (Kanto-cho). In the period between 1905 and 1935, Japan invested more than 1.9 billion *yuan* in building Dalian's economy. The first decade of the Japanese regime saw a tremendous growth in population and in the economy. By 1919, the population of Dalian was more than a hundred thousand.

As a military base for Japan, Dalian's infrastructure was excellent, even exceeding Japanese cities such as Hiroshima and Kawasaki.[3] Many old generals in the Maoist era, after traveling the whole country for many years, wrote that they "finally understood the meaning of industry after coming to Dalian in south Manchuria and seeing large areas of high-voltage electric networks and densely constructed railroads."[4] As a colony, Dalian's economy soared because of the enormous influx of Japanese investment.

PROSTITUTION IN COLONIAL DALIAN

In 1905, General Tanaka obtained permission from the government to build the first brothel located in Fengban Street (currently Wuchang Street), which was called Smoke Flower Alley *(yan hua xiang)*. After dislocating thirty Chinese families, General Tanaka built eight brothels to house Japanese prostitutes. Hence a wilderness area with wolves and foxes was turned into a flourishing street. As a result, Fengban Street became the most economically developed area in the city.

From the beginning, the Japanese imposed a racially based class system on prostitution in Dalian. Japanese brothels were referred to as *you kuo* (tourist contour) on Fengban Street and Xiaogangzi (currently Xigang) as the first class; Chinese brothels located in the Shahekou, Ci'ergou (currently Pingkangli) district and Hongyi Street were relegated to second and third class.[5] Brothels within these two districts were further ranked based on building size and how elaborately they were furnished.[6]

Consistent with the history of prostitution in China, prostitution in Dalian was an integral part of the entertainment industry.[7] A unique feature of prostitution in Dalian was the separation between residences, entertainment hotels, and brothels.[8] Living in separate quarters, courtesans met their customers in entertainment hotels to converse, play music, and sing, and then often proceeded to the brothels to enjoy food and sex.[9] The relationship between the courtesans and the owners required that the owners advertised and provided the clothing for the courtesan; for this, the owners received 30 percent of the profit. The courtesans responded to the demands of the customers, including their demands for music, and received 70 percent of the profit. Not all prostitutes enjoyed the benefits of courtesans; prostitutes of low status in the hierarchy worked in dance halls, opium shops, and teahouses that spread all over the city and were subject to police harassment and other dangers.[10]

Prostitutes were viewed as both victims and perpetrators. Newspaper articles demonstrated a sympathetic attitude toward the prostitutes.[11] They asserted that it was impossible for these poor women to find a normal job and that they should not be allowed to starve to death. Pressured by their family, these papers insisted, these women turned to prostitution. This victim discourse paradoxically coexisted with the perpetrator rhetoric. Newspaper articles charged that prostitutes had become addicted to this kind of decadent life and their sexual desires.[12] Thus it was impossible for them to stay in an ordinary family. The articles enumerated countless examples in which customers were victimized by prostitutes. Some customers were so infatuated with the prostitutes that they paid their body price and married them, even though after several years it usually ended with a divorce. For instance, a thirty-two-year-old man named Zhang Qiwu took a twenty-six-year-old prostitute as his wife. Life was happy until Zhang was unemployed. The prostitute's desires could not be satisfied. She pondered leaving Zhang. Later, Zhang found a job but the monthly wage was not handsome. She secretly prostituted herself and quarreled with Zhang every day. Fights and brawls were so boisterous that the neighbors were being disturbed. These stories, many of which ended in suicide, were used to make the case that men were often the victims of the prostitutes.[13] While the government attempted to regulate prostitution, the popularity of the institution doomed this attempt to failure.[14]

Echoing the sentiment of the Republican government in mainland China, the Japanese government in Dalian came to consider prostitution a potential problem that might disrupt social order. Beginning in the 1920s, the Japanese government limited the outing attire of the prostitutes.[15] In September 1926, the government standardized the contract between employers and prostitutes to prohibit operators from obtaining a high percentage of the profit. The government considered it important that brothels were run by respectable people. In September 1934, to protect the young, the government set a minimum age. Prostitutes could not be younger than fourteen years old and hostesses could not be younger than seventeen years old.[16]

During the 1930s, we see a kind of pendulum swinging back and forth between regulation and tolerance of prostitution. On the one hand, both Japanese and Chinese authorities were concerned with good social order and trying to regulate prostitution, particularly new venues of prostitution such as opium shops. At the other extreme, there were many complaints about regulation and the damage it caused business interests. As a consequence, we see an inconsistent pattern: sometimes opium shops were raided and closed, other times they were tolerated; sometimes street prostitutes were picked up, while other times they were left alone. This tension between good social order and a flourishing economy resonates with the current situation in China, as we will see in the next chapter.[17]

THE CONSEQUENCES OF THE DEPRESSION

Japanese imperialism, the war, and the collapse of world economies as a result of depression, natural disasters, and gender inequity all had a profound effect on China.[18] In Manchuria, as well as the rest of China, there was a return to previous practices whereby families sold daughters into prostitution for the survival of the family. The Japanese government responded to this phenomenon in Manchuria with approbation and blamed it on Manchuria's "bad social customs." It is certainly true that the instance of trafficking in Manchuria increased dramatically in this time, but one should recognize the devastating impact of the depression in Manchuria and elsewhere.

Every year millions were starving to death in the countryside. The trafficking of rural women into prostitution in Dalian followed the same pattern as elsewhere in China. The *Shengjing Times* disclosed cases where husbands forced wives into prostitution in opium shops.[19] Husbands were unemployed and depended on their wives for support. The press urged the authorities to scrutinize household registrations to locate those vagrants who depended on wives as hostesses.[20] In order to control prostitution, they believed, these men had to be controlled or banished. There were instances where wives had to flee their husbands to escape prostitution. Even though abandoning one's husband was a crime in China, the press believed that these women were the victims.[21] An example of this: twenty-two-year-old Xiaohong from Yingkou in Liaoning Province was coerced by her husband to work as a prostitute. In spite of her sacrifice, her husband often physically abused her. Later, she escaped with a man who paid for her train ticket and other expenses. In Dalian, she pawned herself for 200 *yuan* to the man who had helped her escape from prostitution. After this man deducted the cost of the ticket and other expenses, she had only 70 *yuan*. Her husband later pursued her to Dalian and sued her in court. The court mandated that Xiaohong follow her husband home, in spite of her protestation that she would rather die.

The above quotation accusing China of "bad social customs" was typical of the attitude of Japan toward China at this time. Japan owed a great cultural debt to China, having borrowed from her their culture and most notably their written language. Japan, like the rest of East Asia, had regarded China as the "Middle Kingdom," the source of common East Asian culture. However, Japan had learned from the failure of China to respond to the West with modernization and had undergone a dramatic modernization revolution on her own, the Meiji Restoration. During the 1930s, Japan would use the rhetoric of Confucianism against China to justify Japanese aggression. The following quotation from Matsuoka Yosuke is a good example of this:

One thing is clear even to a donkey running along an Asian highway: constant and hearty cooperation between the peoples of Japan and China . . . alone can work out the destiny of Asia. . . . China and Japan are two brothers who have inherited a great mansion called Eastern Asia. Adversity sent them both down to the depths of poverty. The ne'er-do-well elder brother (China) turned a dope fiend and a rogue. But the younger (Japan), lean but rugged and ambitious, ever dreamed of bringing back past glories to the old house . . . and worked hard to support the house. The elder . . . sold him out to their common enemy. The younger in a towering rage beat up the elder—trying to beat him into some sense of shame and awaken some pride in the noble traditions of the great house. After many scraps the younger finally made up his mind to stage a showdown fight.[22]

Yosuke had brilliantly redefined China's military defeat by Western imperial powers into a moral failure that justified Japan's own colonization of China. Abduction by criminals and the sale of women by families into prostitution and concubinage were prevalent issues in Dalian.[23] The *Shengjing Times* even listed the names of hostesses of opium shops with biographical details, which included stories of abductions from the countryside of Hebei and Tianjin.[24] The reason for the rampant abduction, sale, and pawning of women was social change. Japanese imperialism, the war, and the depression displaced many peasants from their land. In the city, many people lost their jobs. Natural disasters such as droughts and hail and government-levied heavy grain taxes also drove displaced peasants to the city.[25] Earlier in 1920, Japanese capitalists had forced the peasants off their land and had occupied their paddy fields. Because it had taken the peasants three years in a lawsuit to regain their land, many women were sold or pawned to the city to work as prostitutes in brothels and opium shops.[26] In 1927, peasants from Shandong migrated to Dalian in large numbers due to natural disasters. This included many women abducted or pawned into prostitution in Dalian.[27] By 1928, the population of migrant laborers from rural areas of Shandong and Hebei had reached 574,087.[28] These migrants were too poor to afford a wife in the marriage market.[29] Others were too far away from their hometown wives. This was the beginning of a lopsided gender ratio that by 1948 had reached 194 men for every 100 women, the most severe inequity in the entire country.[30] Gender inequity and heavy immigration greatly increased the demand for prostitutes. Poverty and dislocation supplied the demand for prostitutes.[31]

Concerns about the large numbers of vagrants and vagrant prostitutes once again caused heavy governmental and nongovernmental involvement. The solution was to provide them with useful training. This was accomplished through the reform institute, which taught printing, sewing, and textile skills.[32] In addition to the labor education program initiated by the government, nongovernmental associations helped fund the return of these women to their homes. The Dalian Shandong Native Association *(Shandong tongxiang sui)* was established in 1926 with more than a hundred thousand members for this purpose.[33] The association, made up of mostly merchants, reached out to roaming Shandong refugees and trafficked women.[34]

FEMININITY IN COLONIAL DALIAN

In spite of the power of the New Culture movement, which advocated that women free themselves from the oppressive grip of family patriarchy, deeper cultural values continued to work in Dalian as elsewhere in China, where women continued to sacrifice themselves for their parents and husbands. One might think that since Dalian had been outside of the embrace of the motherland for forty years, they should be long divorced from the Confucian ideals of female virtues. The reality, however, was just the opposite: because Dalian was under imperialist rule, the desire to grasp the essence of Chineseness was even stronger. During Japanese colonial rule, Chinese intellectuals felt the pressing need to revitalize Confucian ideals to assert their Chineseness.[35] They were concerned about the loss of morality and the deteriorating social ethos. They considered it their task to reinforce Confucian moral values by organizing classes to educate society. In 1935, they established the Manchu Morality Organization *(manzhouguo daode zonghui),* previously named Wanguo Morality Organization Guandongzhou Division. Its role was to propagate morality by way of newspapers, radio, public lectures, and so on.[36] They published excerpts from the morality lectures in installments in the *Shengjing Times.* The government also encouraged the organization to promulgate morality through the radio every Sunday for twenty minutes. To expand their influence, the organization built four hundred instruction halls. They posted advertisements to attract potential teachers who were trained for three years to conduct classes in morality. These teachers were dispersed throughout counties and towns of Dalian. The county heads were responsible for ensuring that the great masses and officials received this instruction.

Later on, other Chinese would accuse Manchuria of being disloyal to China and being too solicitous to the Japanese invaders. It is important to remember that while Manchurians were torn between their loyalty to China and the benefits derived from Japanese investment, there was an intense nationalist response to the Japanese as well.

What we see in Dalian in this time is a dual response to the growth of nationalism. On the one hand, we have a return to traditional values; on the other hand, there is a contrasting model of new womanhood. We should note that this dualism is consistent with the past responses to colonialism beginning with the self-strengthening movement. The Manchu Morality Organization embodied traditional Chinese women's virtues. It instilled in the minds of the people meticulous moral teachings about female virtues, including the Three Obediences and the Four Virtues.[37] Specific virtues were related to different social roles. An example of a designated role is that of a daughter. Among a long list of virtues required of her would include obedience to her father. The morality book taught that "women are born with filial famine and ethical debt. So the purpose of their lives is to clear that debt."[38] It instructed women to recognize their fate and accept it *(zhiming renming)*. For instance, if they are taken as a concubine, this is their fate and they should happily accept it. It was indispensable to the good order of the state that women should perform their proper role. A virtuous daughter will become a virtuous wife. A virtuous wife will be a virtuous mother. A virtuous mother will bring up virtuous sons and daughters. Hence a virtuous nation will be created. A strong country is concomitantly established. Women were again considered expendable and expected to sacrifice their freedom and happiness for the family and state. The revival of traditional values competed with the values of the New Culture movement, which continued to argue for strong educated women who were partners to their husbands.

MASCULINITY IN COLONIAL DALIAN

The colonial impact on gender concepts was very complicated in Dalian. In Dalian, the colonial experience shaped a unique form of masculine identity. Chinese schoolboys were subjected to a brutal program of calisthenics by their Japanese military overlords.[39] While this treatment was justified as an "Asian brother" rehabilitating his sick brother (China) for the good of all East Asia, it was experienced by Dalian boys as brutal and humiliating subservience to Japanese authority. To rehabilitate their subjugated identity, Dalian boys sought relief through competition in soccer. In contrast to calisthenics, which subjected the boys to rigid Japanese authority, soccer allowed free and creative expression. By playing soccer, Dalian boys in essence rejected Japanese control over their bodies. The success of Dalian boys against Japanese opponents in soccer became the central narrative in Dalian's resistance and was essential in shaping the identities of Dalian men.[40]

This masculinity was manifested not only in soccer, but also in the re-institutionalization of Confucian values based on sacrifice and the subjugation of women. The Wanguo Morality Organization reinforced and extended Qing discourse on female virtues of filiality, chastity, sacrifice, and subservience. Women's sacrifice and obedience became a foil against which men recovered their masculinity. While the dominant force during this time in mainland China was influenced by the New Culture movement, which aspired to support the liberation of women, in Dalian, sports and the revived Confucian doctrine were pushing against this trend.

JAPANESE OCCUPATION AND
TREATMENT OF WOMEN

Part of the exploitation of China involved the Japanese military government mobilizing Chinese women and men to contribute services through several organizations. The All-Manchu Women's Union Organization, an outfit led by Japanese women, was established in 1931 to provide Japanese male soldiers with "feminine warm feelings to encourage a masculine strong will."[41] The chief of the Japanese army advocated that all Japanese women should express their sincere love and support for the "sacred philanthropic, just, and peaceful worldly cause" by leading Chinese women to wholeheartedly serve the Japanese soldiers with their "motherly, womanly, and sisterly warmth and love."[42] This organization had eighteen divisions in various cities of Manchuria that served twenty-four "soldier families" *(shibing zhijia),* that is, rest homes for Japanese soldiers. It also trained

Chinese and Korean women to be "good mothers"—to care for the basic needs of Japanese soldiers such as washing their clothes.[43] Chinese women in these organizations provided free services such as raising funds for the colonial war; collecting money for refugees; consoling the families of injured and dead soldiers; rewarding soldiers with food and drinks; tidying up their rooms; sending them newspapers, magazines, and books; lifting their spirits and emotions; boosting their morale; and so forth.[44] Through these organizations, Chinese women were organized by the Japanese to serve as obedient subjects *(liangmin he shunmin),* submissive to the Japanese military regime and its male soldiers. At the same time, forty houses with more than a thousand Chinese and Korean "comfort women" *(wei'anfu suo)* were established. These comfort women either volunteered or were abducted or tricked into military brothels to offer sexual services to Japanese male soldiers.[45]

The use of comfort women as female slaves of the Japanese soldiers echoed the theme of camp prostitution in Chinese history. Comfort women accompanied and served the army camp essentially performing like sexual machines.[46] The premise of the system of army comfort women was that men could not control their sexual desires. Therefore, the military government provided means to satisfy their soldiers. The Japanese army managed the comfort women and the comfort houses and expanded their numbers over time. The comfort women's system was established for two reasons: to prevent venereal disease and to guarantee security.[47] Japan's military government learned a lesson from its previous experience of occupying Siberia, where the high incidence of rape led to the outbreak of venereal disease throughout the army.[48] One unit completely lost their fighting power. This situation shocked the government, and to prevent repeating this history, military leaders later on decided to equip the soldiers with women under the supervision of the military camp. The military thus unified the management of hygiene and sexual desire. Another goal of the system was to safeguard the security of the occupied area, which was important because Japan intended to permanently occupy the region. Widespread occurrences of rape would only irritate the Chinese people and ignite anti-Japanese passion; supplying the soldiers with comfort women could prevent them from raping local women. Providing for the sexual needs of the soldiers was considered the best way to raise the morale of the soldiers. It also prevented soldiers who visited prostitutes in occupied areas from leaking military secrets.

There were four sources of comfort women: Korea, Japan, China, and Southeast Asia. The first comfort women came from Japanese brothels. During the war, quotas were established for Korean, Southeast Asian, and Chinese women. Because during the war Japanese women could not meet the demands, the other three groups were coerced into prostitution.[49] Tactics such as false job advertisements for maids were used in addition to coercion. Captured Chinese female soldiers were also turned into sexual slaves. Korea was officially incorporated into Japan in 1910, so it was convenient for Japan to use force or inveiglement to mobilize large numbers of young women as comfort women.[50] From 1938 until 1940, Japanese policemen recruited young unmarried women from poor peasants' families in the villages of Korea and Manchuria. Japanese women were coaxed into prostitution through slogans encouraging them to serve the holy war. Such was the intensity of nationalism in Japan that many of the Japanese women, including prostitutes, were willing to serve the soldiers and demonstrate their loyalty to the country.[51]

CHINESE WOMEN IN MANCHURIA

What is lost in the above discussion is the manner in which Chinese women in Manchuria took advantage of the nationalistic clash to press their own agenda. The result was a classical case of unintended consequences. Chinese women have always been the "invisible men" of China. Both the Maoist and Manchurian separatists failed to foresee that Manchurian women, like other clever human beings, might use the occupation for their own purposes. By feigning acceptance of Japanese authority, these women actually launched their own rebellion against patriarchal dominance.

The dichotomy between loyalty to China on the basis of nationalism and loyalty to Japan on the basis of economics was finessed by the Chinese women, who cooperated with the Japanese for their own reasons. The women joined Japanese-sponsored segregated women's organizations designed to control and penetrate society by extending domesticity into the public sphere.[52] While the Japanese regime exploited the women for its own purposes, the women were able to appropriate its resources—both the ideology and institutions of the organizations—to carve out a space to fashion their own lives as independent and autonomous women.

Many of these strong-willed women, aspiring to an independent income, went outside of the home to lecture despite their husbands' disapproval.[53] Some used the discourse of filiality to parents to trump unquestioned obedience to their husbands, leaving their men to set up new lives.[54] Some even found merits in remaining unmarried. In a nutshell, they subverted while reconfiguring the pedagogy of family values to seize the opportunities offered by the sponsoring women's organizations. The independence of these Manchurian women anticipates the flexible approach to loyalty of modern-day hostesses in Dalian trying to navigate an equally complex and dangerous social and political structure to achieve their own ends.

Ambivalence toward Colonial Rule

As Wang Yanhui, deputy director of the Dalian foreign trade and economic cooperation bureau, put it, "Because of history, the Japanese are very familiar with Dalian." Dalian's friendliness toward Japan contrasted sharply with the antagonistic response of many Chinese elsewhere. "Dalian residents were largely spared the brutality of Japan's imperial army that many areas of China suffered between 1931 and 1945," said a former city official and amateur local historian. "People in Dalian were making the goods that Japan was using to kill other Chinese, so they don't feel the same way as other Chinese. And young people don't hear the same kind of stories from their elders as they do elsewhere." He added, "People in Dalian had close contact with the Japanese; they learned Japanese at school, and they felt familiar with Japanese ways."

Japanese investment had helped develop Dalian. Even today, Dalian's industrial parks bulge with big Japanese corporate offices, and sales to Japan account for more than 40 percent of the city's exports. Although Wang Yanhui dismisses suggestions that Dalianites were any less outraged than their compatriots at Japanese wartime misdeeds or more recent disputes over territory, she made it clear that city officials saw no reason why politics should get in the way of business: "We in Dalian will not forget history, but we cannot hold the grandfather's war against the grandchild." The rewards of such pragmatism were that about twenty-five hundred Japanese companies invested $5.6 billion, accounting for 40 percent of foreign investment in Dalian. That investment meant the introduction of world-class industrial management and new opportunities for suppliers.[55]

Postwar Dalian under the Russians

In 1945 the Soviet Union took over Dalian and returned it to China in 1954. However, they allowed the local Communist Party to govern Dalian beginning in November 1945. When Japan surrendered, there were two hundred Chinese brothels in the city, housing thousands of prostitutes, as well as numerous Japanese and Korean brothels.[56] In 1945, Japanese and Korean brothels were closed and then in 1946, all Chinese brothels were eliminated and all prostitutes were sent home. Those who did not have a family, including those roaming in the street, were sent to reform institutes. But even after the brothels were abolished, some prostitutes turned to dance halls and teahouses to pursue their profession. There were eighteen privately owned dance halls and 225 female dancers in Dalian. In order to address this problem, the municipal government set a deadline for the owners to register with the social bureau. Using this strategy to identify the prostitutes, dance hall owners were intimidated and immediately closed down in the following month.

While one kind of prostitution had been eliminated, 184 teahouses continued to hire hostesses and practice prostitution. The city government began by licensing the three hundred hostesses who were working in teahouses and restaurants, half of whom were Japanese. The municipal government mandated that operators register with the civil bureau and receive certificates for the hostesses. They were required to prove that the hostesses did not have syphilis or other venereal diseases. In 1947, the civil bureau went a step further, intervening to persuade the hostesses to change professions and participate in economic production, punishing those who did not comply. After the intervention, most hostesses changed jobs and returned to their families; and in 1951, the municipal government terminated the registration of hostesses. Brothels and opium shops were closed down, and prostitution was almost completely eliminated.

The Chinese Communist Party Takes Over Dalian

The reform movement under Mao combined labor and ideological education, with the intent of eliminating "parasitic sloth" and providing workers with useful labor skills. The former prostitutes were indoctrinated in CCP ideals that cast the party as the savior of the poor people in the struggle against feudalism, capitalism, and imperialism. The indoctrination process lasted from one to three years, and only on Sunday were they allowed to visit with relatives. Those whose attitude and performance were satisfactory were the first released, and those who were resistant to reform were publicly sentenced and sent to the public security bureau.

As we have seen, the majority of the prostitutes were rural migrants who were sold, pawned, or abducted into prostitution in Dalian. While Maoist Dalian classified rural migrants as vagrants *(you min)* and targeted both vagrants and prostitutes in the reform program, they also set out to cut off the source of prostitution by severing the rural-urban connection.[57]

The Maoist state transformed Dalian from a port and garden city into a chemical manufacturing center. Although racial apartheid no longer existed during this period as the local government transferred people from the slums to houses formerly occupied by the Japanese to eradicate racial hierarchy,[58] the Maoist regime instituted a new kind of apartheid. The Communists had raised the status of peasants and workers to that of masters of the nation and vanguards of the revolution. However, by using the household registration system to prevent peasants from escaping the hardships of the countryside, they relegated them to a permanent status of second-class citizen. As a result of the 1958 household registration system, 156,000 people were driven back to rural areas. By 1960, 2,402 migrant households had been expelled to rural Shandong. Paradoxically, a revolution built on peasants ended up victimizing the same peasants.[59]

COMMUNIST RULE: ECONOMIC MARGINALIZATION INCITES CRIES FOR INDEPENDENCE

Although Dalian was politically liberated by the CCP, the economy went sluggish, and Dalian men felt marginalized and emasculated. An article titled "Northeastern People Claim Angrily: We Want Independence" narrates the history of economic marginalization and backwardness as a result of the CCP rule.[60] The anonymous author is an official in a heavy industrial city in Liaoning Province. The author, who has access to numerous government documents in his work, asks, "How did we get into this situation?" His answer: the "backwardness and nonindustrialization" resulted from the CCP's prejudiced policy toward Manchuria. According to the author, at the beginning of the Maoist state, the central government published a lengthy document about industry that included only one sentence about the northeast: "Chinese industry is mainly accumulated in Shanghai and another marginal area *[pian ju yi di]*." The marginal area referred to, according to the author, was the northeast. While Shanghai accounted for 35 percent of national light industry, Liaoning Province alone accounted for 70 percent of the total national output of heavy industry. Liaoning also produced more than 80 percent of major products such as steel, electric power, and military hardware. Even in coal and handicraft industries, Liaoning accounted for 55 percent.

At the beginning of the People's Republic of China (PRC), Dalian had the largest heavy chemical industrial base in China. The author corrects what he considered a historical wrong long done to Dalian by emphasizing the contribution of Dalian in the victory of the Communist Party in China. The author also corrects a general who contended that the Huaihai battle was won with the use of small go-carts. The reality was that the triumph of the battle was dependent on cannon cast in Dalian's factories. Political leaders eliminated the crucial function of Dalian in the battle because Dalian used to be a colony. There was no doubt that people at the highest level of the government were aware of the importance of the northeast; otherwise they would not have made statements like this one: "As long as we have the solid base in the northeast, even if we lose all the other bases, the Chinese revolution will still succeed." The northeast shouldered the heavy task of liberating China, and northeastern soldiers shed their blood in the Korean War. The author emphasizes that the dense railroad network in south Liaoning allowed materials to be transported to the front. The author was very angry that the party distorted history to make Sichuan, Shandong, and Shanghai appear to be the areas that had shed blood and sacrificed the most for the war. All the Chinese armies from the northeast and all the war materials produced in Liaoning were erased from history, he contends. It is clear that Communist Party leaders were embarrassed by the key role played by the northeast, particularly Dalian. Most Chinese were eager to forget Dalian's tarnished history as a colony.

During the construction that was part of the Maoist planned economy, the products of the northeast were exported to other parts of China. More than 89 percent of the products produced in Shenyang were exported. During the Maoist era, the only railroads constructed in Liaoning in the 1970s were funded by the province. The author asserts that the golden era of 1960s railroad construction was made possible only by the selfless contribution of the northeast. More than 30 percent of Liaoning's technology was exported to other parts of China, and Liaoning's managerial talents were sent to the western part of China.[61] Huge numbers of the province's factories were dismantled and also shipped to the west. Even today in many countrywide factories and military enterprises, you can still find Shenyang and Dalian managers and workers. Many of them died without ever being able to return home. A friend of the author's father was sent to southern China, and his family did not hear of his death for six years.

Even in agriculture, the contribution of the northeast was considerable. For example, soybean output accounted for 44 to 57 percent of China's harvest from 1962 to 1977. Although Beijing produced no soybeans, it received an average of 6.67 times more soybean oil per person than the northeast during the three years of natural disasters from 1959 to 1961. The situation in the northeast was not good, but the region was still able to sustain itself because of its two natural granaries in Jilin and Heilongjiang Provinces.

As China turned toward capitalism in the early 1980s, the risk of opening economic zones in the southeast of China was shouldered by taxes collected in the northeast. Of the ten most heavily taxed cities in China, four of them, including Dalian, were from Liaoning Province. Because of the sacrifices made by this province in the late 1980s, Guangdong's gross national product had reached 70 percent of Liaoning's. Although the northeast was already having severe difficulties, the government continued issuing policies designed to build economies in the southeastern provinces. The government was oblivious to the appeals from the northeast to reduce their burden and treat them equally. Li Guixian, the vice chair of the National Political Association, has said that the Northeast had become "the place to take responsibility for the cost of opening China to the outside world."

We can see the roots of Dalian's current unemployment problem in the policy of overtaxing the northeast industrial base. Heavy taxation prevented the northeast from renewing their capital equipment in the late 1980s.[62]

Because government policies heavily favored cities such as Shanghai during the 1990s, they developed rapidly. The northeast became a "caged tiger constricted by the state planned economy." By this time, Liaoning's industrial output had fallen behind Guangdong, Shandong, and many other provinces. The northeast that had been the vehicle for Chinese industrialization was now left to wither. The area that had once led China had become a backwater of Chinese industry. This is hard to understand on economic grounds since the coal and iron resources that were necessary for making the steel existed most abundantly in Manchuria; the railroads and ports necessary to export steel were also strategically located in Manchuria. One can only surmise that this decision was based on politics rather than economics.[63] The author sums up the problems of the northeast by saying, "When your sisters and relatives had to prostitute themselves, have you, a northeastern person, ever thought, 'What on earth was the reason?'"

The author blames the central government for prostitution and backward development of the northeast. His article elucidates the ambivalence that Dalian men came to feel toward the CCP, which had marginalized and emasculated them while at the same time liberating them from colonial rule. Their anger toward the central government culminated in demands for independence. Although Japan colonized Dalian for forty years, some Dalianites apparently did not feel as marginalized by the Japanese as by the central government. The Japanese treated Dalian as a legitimate and important city of Japan and made large investments in the city, turning a small fishing village into a prosperous industrial city. In other words, Dalian prospered economically under Japan but declined economically under China. Illustrating the importance of economics, it is interesting to note that Nanjing, the scene of Japan's worst wartime atrocity, is now competing to attract Japanese investment. Although some officials admit that the peak of investment has passed, it is important to acknowledge that Japan was the primary force in creating modern Dalian.

Due to its distinctive colonial history, Dalian has had to manage a complex system of prostitution and cope with diverse ethnicities. When Dalian was under Japanese control, specific locations were designated for Chinese and Japanese brothels, each having its own separate red-light district. One office controlled the three separate functions of residences, entertainment places, and brothels. When the conflict with China began in 1937, another category of prostitution was established—comfort women. This system echoed the ancient Chinese form of official prostitution, by which female captives were taken as sexual slaves.[64] After a brief postwar nationalist interlude, Maoist Dalian eliminated prostitution but did so by creating a rural-urban divide. The Maoist state deprived peasants of all mobility they may have had during the Japanese period and used them to support and serve the needs of the urbanites. Moreover, during the post-Mao era, the rural-urban boundary became increasingly hard, and rural migrants were regarded as criminals to be severely prosecuted, regulated, and denied their due legal or human rights. While this treatment stopped the flow of prostitution for a period of time, isolating peasants in the countryside and exploiting them laid the foundation for the resurgence of prostitution in the 1980s and 1990s. It was the intense poverty and desperation of peasants that broke the floodgates in the 1980s and filled the cities with an estimated ten million prostitutes.[65]

It is easy to understand the ambivalence that Dalian men have felt toward the Japanese, the Maoist state, and even the post-Maoist state. On one level, they were politically liberated by the Maoist state; on another level, they inclined to favor the Japanese rule because the city had been treated as a major center of Japan and had received heavy Japanese investment. Dalian was also spared the plundering and atrocities committed by the Japanese in other Chinese cities. While the citizens of Dalian as Chinese people also resented Japanese colonization, some Chinese women were not hesitant to take advantage of it for their own benefit. Coming full circle, as we will see in the next chapter, we witness a new form of Japanese influence on Dalian—the karaoke bar.

Two

FROM BANQUETS TO KARAOKE BARS:
A NEW SEXUAL AWAKENING

KARAOKE BARS AND MARKET REFORMS

In Dalian today, it is difficult and unusual to find entrepreneurs and officials who are building business networks and negotiating contracts without engaging in entertainment offered in karaoke bars. Helen Siu and Wang Gan both argue that these sites in China provide the necessary networks in a post-Mao society where civic organization is lacking.[1] Entrepreneurs and officials alike routinely partake in the "coordinated sequence" *(yitiaolong fuwu)* that consists of luxurious banquets in expensive restaurants, singing in karaoke bars, and massages in sauna salons. Blue-collar urban and migrant male workers with limited wages emulate the lifestyle of their socioeconomic superiors by patronizing karaoke bars, albeit low-tier ones.

"Singing-and-dancing" ballrooms *(gewu ting)* reemerged with the initiation of economic reforms in the late 1970s after being banned for nearly thirty years. Although officially tolerated, they came under severe supervision both nationally and locally.[2] Shanghai, a city famous for its dance halls, saw the first reappearance of Western-style ballrooms in 1979.[3] Even in the relatively open environment of Shanghai, dance parties were organized by labor unions and youth leagues and had to be endorsed by the work unit's letter of introduction. The events were closely supervised by monitors whose job was to keep men and women from dancing "too close together."[4] In Dalian, the first dance hall appeared in 1984, featuring a band of six singers and a capacity of three hundred people.[5]

Karaoke bars did not appear in China until the early 1980s. The components of karaoke technology—audio, video, and laser recording; storage and retrieval technologies—were originally invented in the West and later spread to other parts of the world.[6] It was not until after World War II that Japanese inventors reconfigured these components into a "new and hybrid technology form" for the purpose of communal singing.[7] The karaoke bar culture has since radiated from Japan to Korea, Hong Kong, Taiwan, the south of China, and finally to China's northern regions.

In Dalian, new karaoke bars mushroomed throughout the city starting in 1988. With the rise in popularity of karaoke bars, a red-light district sprang up in the center of Zhongshan district. Around the end of the 1980s and early 1990s, a number of karaoke bars were opened on Stalin Road (currently known as People's Road). The scope of business was considerable. Hostesses were recruited by the hundreds, and bars and hostesses prospered.

Drastically different from the previous dance halls organized by work units, karaoke bars aroused tremendous social curiosity. They used Western audiovisual technology, splendid exterior and interior furnishings, and neon lights, and featured high prices and beautiful hostesses. They suited rich people's desire for "modern" consumption, allowing them to display their talents in singing, and their power and wealth. One could argue that the karaoke bars symbolized a shift from the old bureaucratic culture to the new entrepreneurial culture. They provided a venue for young entrepreneurs to demonstrate their sexual prowess before colleagues, through singing, bragging, and seducing hostesses. They quickly became the site of the most fashionable recreational and commercial activity for men.

In the 1980s, state corruption had taken the form of large banquets. Susan Brownell contends that the 1980s obsession with food derives from widespread malnutrition in that decade, a constant sense of scarcity, and vivid memories of hunger during the Maoist era.[8] The ration system reinforced the state's superior position and made its recipients "beholden to and dependent on it."[9] Mayfair Yang even suggests it possesses the recipient.[10] "Food is one of the main ways in which the Chinese state is symbolically constructed as provider, superior, and incorporated part of the self," according to Brownell.[11] In the 1989 student demonstrations, the hunger strike symbolized rebellion against state authority.[12] The central position of food as a symbol of state power, represented by the political importance of banquets, was eroded during the 1990s by the end of the food rationing system. However, the basic principle that power is symbolized by one's ability to more than satisfy bodily needs was established by this practice and extended to more varied forms of food consumption and to sex in the 1990s. Simultaneously, the economic reforms that gave rise to the private sector began to create an opening for emerging businessmen to redefine their masculinity. The karaoke bar provided a means whereby they could not only redefine themselves sexually but also contest the importance of the banquet and food as a symbol of state power.

Initially under the reforms, the growth of karaoke bars and entertainment venues was largely (by some estimates 80 percent) supported by state funds spent by officials doing "state business."[13] In the 1990s, in Fujian, prostitutes were discovered in a hotel run by the People's Liberation Army; in Guangzhou, prostitutes were discovered in a guest house run by the provincial Women's Federation; in Shanghai in 1994, both the Public Security Bureau and the People's Liberation Army were intensely involved in operating karaoke clubs and brothels.[14] Although the first karaoke bar in Dalian was established by Japanese businessmen, now many establishments in the city are run by party officials. In addition to the customers paying with state funds, the other large constituency has been the local police force, which is allowed free entry in exchange for securing the proper permits and ignoring legal violations.

After the mid-1990s, increasing amounts of private funds were spent at karaoke bars by businessmen. This transition might be attributed to the Japanese influence in Dalian, Chinese men's emulation of the previous state practices, and the model provided by Japanese businessmen, their economic superiors. The rising importance of karaoke bars marked a rebellion by the emerging Chinese business class: by embracing the karaoke bar, Dalian men challenge the monopoly of state power as represented by the banquet. By appropriating the new karaoke bar, they had created a new venue within which they could contest the dominance of the old state order and reestablish their masculine identity.

Erotic Services in Entertainment Establishments

Erotic services take place in various establishments that include karaoke bars, hotels, sauna salons, hair salons, disco and other dancing halls, small roadside restaurants, parks, cinemas, and video rooms. Among those who run these establishments, karaoke bar owners are the most selective in evaluating women's height, facial beauty, figure, and social skills such as singing, dancing, flirting, drinking, and chatting techniques. Unlike many other establishments where the service is nothing but intercourse, karaoke bar hostesses' services are far more encompassing. Only a few of the karaoke bar hostesses I observed would accept male strangers' request for intercourse, for which they charged twice as much as those in other environments except for a few five-star hotels targeted at Japanese clients. Because only the beautiful and skilled can be chosen as company for the night, numerous young women do not survive in the karaoke bar and skid to other places such as sauna salons.

The karaoke bar hostesses often expressed their contempt toward women in other establishments whose work involved nothing but sex. At one time when all sauna bars were closed in Dalian due to lack of water in the city, sauna hostesses flocked into karaoke bars. Karaoke bar hostesses commented to each other in low voices, "Look at their gray faces! It's from every day's sex work *(dapao)*." Sauna hostesses told me that they could not compete with the karaoke hostesses because "here clients are too particular about your looks and figure. It's different at sauna bars. In sauna bars, appearance is not that important because the clients' goal is simply to have sex." Karaoke bar hostesses were aware of this difference. They rated their own status second only to foreign hostesses (Russian) who worked in renowned hotels.

In karaoke bars, the duration of each service could range from one to four hours. Hostesses had to keep their clients satisfied through conversing, flirting, singing, dancing, and drinking with them. If a hostess's service failed to please a client, the client had the right to replace the hostess in the middle of the service, in which case the hostess had no choice but to leave without compensation. Therefore, to gratify clients, hostesses would start by surmising the likes and dislikes of the client and acting accordingly. It was also imperative that hostesses consumed a huge amount of alcohol with the clients to fulfill the consumption level set by the bar owner. Thus the bathroom was crowded with hostesses vomiting into the toilet and filling the room with suffocating smells of alcohol and vomited food. Besides drinking, other things such as singing, dancing, and carrying out flirtatious conversations were expected during the service. Beyond this standard service package, some hostesses offered sexual services at the request of clients for an additional fee. Their monthly income ranged from a low of 6,000 *yuan* to tens of thousands of *yuan*.

JAPAN AND THE RISE OF KARAOKE BARS IN DALIAN

The popularity of karaoke bars in Dalian was linked to its close economic relationship with Japan. According to my interviewees, the opening of karaoke bars was a means through which the Japanese introduced their products into the Chinese market. My interviewees attested that in the middle of the 1980s, the Chinese government tried to protect Chinese products and put strict restrictions such as tariffs on imported goods. Due to the conservative Chinese market and the prevalent boycotting of Japanese products, Japan found it extremely difficult to open the market and export their products there. To change this situation, Japanese leaders chose Dalian as the base to open Chinese markets, just as in the colonial past they chose Dalian to be the military base for controlling East and South Asia.

Whether an accurate depiction or not, my interviewees consistently argued that toward the end of the 1980s Japanese businessmen came to Dalian to corrupt Chinese government officials, just as they had used the Dalian-Chinese "traitors" *(hanjian)* who willingly served the Japanese colonialists to control the Chinese. The means they used were the karaoke bars. In 1988, they established the first karaoke bar in Dalian and started inviting officials to enjoy the pleasures of prostitutes and technology. Named Tokyo 898, the bar was financed by a Japanese businessman and run as a Sino-Japanese joint venture. It is said that the bar's karaoke equipment was imported from Japan and brand-new—an almost unheard-of extravagance at that time in China's economic development. Eventually, the use of prostitutes between businessmen and government officials in karaoke bars so penetrated Dalian society that it became accepted as a legitimate way to conduct business.

According to stories told by my interviewees, Japanese businessmen first formed relationships with officials in these establishments and then tried bribing them with cash. However, these officials were afraid to accept these bribes. So the Japanese businessmen changed their tactics by offering to send the children of these officials to Japan and the United States to study. The officials' income was very low at this time, but it was safer to receive wealth in other forms such as education benefits for their children. Also, the Japanese businessmen targeted the wives of these officials, giving gifts such as Japanese cameras, TVs, and refrigerators. Through these gifts, study opportunities, banquets, and prostitutes, the Japanese businessmen conquered the officials who changed the rules, offered them the official seal—"the green light"—and allowed large quantities of Japanese products to flow into the Chinese market. As Japanese products made their way into the market, the Japanese government lowered the price to encourage sales. Because the quality was better and the prices more acceptable, only slightly higher than Chinese products, they gradually became more and more popular. There were even issues of smuggling. Japanese businessmen eventually used the expanded market to begin dumping their obsolete products such as old-model washing machines, refrigerators, and so forth. Although they were old in Japan, they were seen as new and popular in China. In addition to products, production lines for obsolete goods were also facilitated by the corruption of the officials. Chinese factories that purchased the rights to produce these obsolete goods were once again exploited by the Japanese, as these products were of such poor quality that they were rejected as junk by Chinese consumers.

In spite of Dalian men's persistent denial of their emulation of Japanese businessmen, stories from my interviews did suggest that Chinese businessmen, with their long history of subordination to Japanese authority, could not help but define their masculinity in terms of Japanese models, at least subconsciously, it seemed. Events in the 1990s echoed and reminded Chinese businessmen of the enslavement of Chinese women by the Japanese soldiers and the loss of face this involved for the Chinese men. Although competing with Japanese businessmen and remembering with outrage the Japanese practices during the colonial period, Chinese businessmen demonstrated their masculinity by emulating Japanese violence toward Chinese women. This was best exemplified by the Japanese Military Flag Incident, which involved Zhaowei, the hot Chinese female movie star. While making an ad, Zhaowei wore a dress printed with a Japanese military flag. It ignited a national fervor against her all over the country. Internet forums cursed and condemned her conduct. Under huge social pressure, she publicly apologized. This happened in 2001, but it is still a hot issue online today. At the time of this writing, there have been forty thousand Internet hits this year on the articles attacking her—on just one Web site. Male nationalists condemned her for selling out and saw her as no better than a volunteer comfort woman. "If the Japanese army could fuck this famous actress, why can't we patriots?" they protested. In a column titled "Strong Country" in the *People's Daily,* some men spent a long time discussing how to humiliate Zhaowei by desecrating her body. They debated whether they should cut her breast first or her nose or ears, to punish her for serving as a "Japanese army prostitute." In the debate columns of other popular Web sites such as sina.com, netease.com, and sohu.com, many people were contemplating what kind of male animals should be used to rape Zhaowei. Male nationalists were not satisfied with thinking of raping Zhaowei herself; they fantasized traveling back in time to "fuck her female ancestors eight generations back." Interestingly, nationalism here took the form of emulating the Japanese once again and raping a woman whom they thought had already been raped by the Japanese.[15]

AMBIVALENCE TOWARD THE JAPANESE

In spite of all the anger created by the incident, the attitude in Dalian toward the Japanese was clearly very ambivalent. My interviewees ascertained that Dalian was chosen as a port to enter the Chinese market because of the success of cultural colonization during colonial rule and because Japanese is commonly spoken in this area. The stories told by my interviewees were verified by many sources. Wang Yanhui, deputy director of the Dalian foreign trade and economic cooperation bureau, said that when Dalian started to open its economy in the early 1980s following market reform, Japanese companies were the first to arrive, drawn by its proximity, port, and pool of Japanese speakers.[16] Fumitaka Kashii, president of Toshiba Dalian, claimed that location and cultural links—and even a local cuisine catering to the Japanese palate—made Dalian the ideal place for new investment. This Japanese influx resumed the economic relationship from the four decades after 1905.

Kenichi Ohmae, one of the world's leading business strategists, claims that during this time Dalian was becoming a center for software development and businesses requiring fluency in Japanese such as insurance

processing and call centers.[17] Japanese companies have benefited tremendously from this relationship. Fumitaka Kashii said his factory made its
first annual profit within three years of starting business in Dalian in 1993
and had paid back its investment by 2000. Kashii said that the Dalian
company was one of the Toshiba group's first two in China and was currently assembling advanced medical equipment for the Chinese market.
He asserted that the success of Japanese companies in Dalian was a result
of effective negotiations with local bureaucracies in the mid-1990s that
clarified confusing commercial policies.[18] Although it is left unsaid exactly
how these negotiations were carried out, the history of the first established
karaoke bars by the Japanese in Dalian and the provision of prostitutes
to Chinese officials were no doubt connected with the corrupt nature of
these dealings.

The ambivalence of Dalian people toward Japan is evident. While
on one level the city was politically colonized, on the other level, it economically prospered. It grew from a fishing village to a garden city with
advanced technology. The CCP had liberated it from Japanese rule, and
yet the economy suffered. The political and economic aspects of the city
were in conflict.

An incident happened in Dalian that aroused nationwide anti-Japanese
and anti-Dalian fervor. On May 8, 2004, two women living in Dalian's
Victoria Apartment Complex were awakened by a racket next door. At
midnight, they banged on the wall to quiet the neighbors. Shortly after
this, two Japanese men and a Chinese prostitute knocked on the door of
the two women. When the Chinese women opened the door, the Japanese
men beat them severely. The two women were later diagnosed with cerebral concussions, nose fractures, and severe injuries to their eyes, knees,
arms, legs, and lips.[19] The two Japanese perpetrators were the manager and
assistant manager of Dalian Entian Metal Company. After the event, one
was sentenced to fifteen days' detention, and the other was found innocent. Chinese outside of Dalian saw this attack on Chinese women as an
insult to the entire nation.[20] The Internet overflowed with angry diatribes
against the people of Dalian:

> Aren't there any righteous officials in Dalian? Is everyone in Dalian a
> traitor *[hanjian]*, flunkey *[zou gou]*, and wimp *[wo nang fei]*? Are Dalian
> police the fucking Japanese security team? I think so! All these traitors and

quislings *[mai guo zei]*, may your ancestors eighteen generations back and your descendants eighteen generations forward lead a life worse than dogs. All the Chinese people who have blood despise you![21]

Others angrily claimed that the Dalian police were not Chinese. A Guangdong commentator wrote, "People of Dalian, aren't you aware of this event? Do you know who was responsible for this outrage? If this had happened in Guangdong, that pig [Japanese man] would not dare stay in China. In Guangdong, we would rather suffer a devastated economy for another twenty years rather than being humiliated in this way!" He went on to express his rage toward the Japanese because of their condescending attitude toward the Chinese: "I think the Dalian police and government are against justice. These officials are willing to accept national humiliation in order to beg investment from the Japanese."

Some charged that Dalian government officials and police were "bastards" left by previous Japanese colonialists. They referred to them as the dogs of the Japanese. A Zhejiang commentator wrote that the Zhejiang people had pride enough to attack the Japanese colonialists in their province. They burned their stores and blasted their factories. Now all Japanese have left Zhejiang. This commentator wrote:

> Don't curry favor with the Japanese. Don't depend on the Japanese to develop our economy. They have enriched us but bullied us. Only Dalian has accepted this bullying by the Japanese. Here in Zhejiang, the Internet forum is boiling, yet it is so calm and peaceful in Dalian. Are you Chinese? If traitors came to Zhejiang, we would kill each of them. There are too many traitors in Dalian. I kill them, I fuck them. Such an event will never happen in Zhejiang. Zhejiang does not depend on Japan, but our economic development is good. Kill the Japanese. Dalian people's apathy really makes us hurt. We really grieve at their misfortunes but are angry at their passivity!

The prevalence of sexual metaphor in expressing male anger in these diatribes once again reminds us of the desperate need of Chinese men to recover their damaged sense of masculinity from the colonial period and the Cultural Revolution. This theme was continued by other critics: "You servants to the Japanese: did you forget who raised you? It's your own people! You were subservient and servile to the foreigners and cruel to your own people, you fucking trash, traitors, and dogs! Even dogs know to protect their own people. You are worse than dogs. You have put shame on the Chinese people. Shame on you, Dalian people!"[22]

The failure of the people in Dalian to respond to the Japanese as other Chinese had is to a great extent because of Dalian's strong historical links with Japan. In the era of reform, Japan had meant prosperity for Dalian. Those links encompassed the colonial-era buildings in its center, the inclusion of some Japanese vocabulary in the local dialect, Japanese dress styles (for example, the scarf worn by female street sweepers and the uniform of female equestrians on the street), Japanese restaurants, and even hotels with special "Japanese floors" for visiting businessmen.[23] A good number of hotels offered sex workers especially for the Japanese businessmen (as I will discuss in the following section). Besides such hotels, Dalian also had a street called Japanese Street that was lined with karaoke bars specifically serving Japanese customers. Some hostesses left Chinese karaoke bars to work in hotels exclusively serving Japanese businessmen. They told me that they could learn the Japanese language from clients and look for ways to migrate to Japan. One hostess hired a tutor to teach her Japanese during the daytime; she practiced at night with her Japanese clients. She commented that Chinese clients were too chauvinistic and that Japanese clients were much nicer and used condoms. She took me to the hotel for several nights. It was a four-star hotel, very luxuriously furnished. Sex workers were waiting in a hotel room to be chosen by Japanese customers. There was no singing or dancing involved, only the selection of sexual partners from twenty to thirty sex workers.

CULTURAL STRUCTURE OF KARAOKE BARS IN THE POST-MAO ERA

Since 1989, with the appearance of karaoke bars, the state has maintained a permanent nationwide antipornography campaign to ensure security and state control. The campaign is aimed at cultural purification and the creation of spiritual civilization (jingshen wenming). The erotic company of hostesses, pornographic TV shows, erotic performances, and prostitution within karaoke bars is condemned as cultural trash that destabilizes state rule and the socialist system. These erotic activities are also in stark contrast to Maoist ideology that culture should serve the polity. Mao, in his Yan'an speech in 1942, argued that "art and culture serve politics."[24] According to him, culture is a powerful revolutionary weapon for uniting and educating people and for eradicating and annihilating enemies. Culture also mirrors the social and economic situation. It should therefore support the interests of the Party, that is, the proletariat and the masses. It should also be national with Chinese characteristics, scientific instead of superstitious, and democratic for the proletariat masses.[25] Thus according to municipal government officials, the crackdown on karaoke bars was an attempt to reassert Maoist values, even in the face of the contradictions created by the demands of the new capitalist society.[26]

Mao's theory of culture has persevered into the post-Mao era. In the post-Mao era, throughout the country the CCP has been propagated as the "three represents": the representative of mass interest, the representative of the most advanced productivity, and the representative of the most advanced culture. This last item, meaning socialist culture, was meticulously explicated in the Bureau of Culture's operating principles: "Culture serves socialism and the masses, adhering to the four basic principles—Marxism–Leninism and Maoism, CCP leadership, socialist system, proletarian polity. Let a hundred flowers bloom; let a hundred schools of thought contend. We must preserve our values from China's past but take what is practical from Western culture." Bulletin boards with these words were hung up on the walls of the Municipal Bureau of Culture when I was conducting interviews there in 2001. The twenty-first century, as a government official claimed in an interview, "is the century of knowledge, information, economy, and culture."[27]

The fifteenth CCP conference in 2001 stated that the emphasis of state policy was to stress prosperity on the one hand and management on the other, and to improve the healthy development of the culture market. It was the task of local officials in the Bureau of Culture to implement this state policy. One high-level official told me that people now did not have any beliefs in life. Therefore, to prevent people (for example, *Falungong* practitioners)[28] from going spiritually astray and doing harm to the socialist system, it was essential to occupy every space and time in their lives. That would distract them from group gatherings, where they would play cards and chess and talk about topics harmful to the socialist regime. As one official told me, "The socialist ideology is to love the country, love the CCP, love socialism, and love one's hometown. Our job is to make sure that this main ideology infiltrates every nook and cranny of society, occupies this battlefield, and eventually wins the battle."

The multiple levels of cultural administrative units served as the vehicles through which socialist themes and state policy were disseminated and permeated. The cultural administrative units included the culture ministry (central), the culture department (provincial), the culture bureau (municipal), the culture center (district), and the culture station (residential, street, and community). Every culture station at the community level had a propaganda room with a newspaper and propaganda bulletin. Two propagandists from the culture station were responsible for indoctrinating each household and every member of the community. Collective activities were organized to penetrate every conceivable public space as well as the private space of households and to fill people's leisure time with educational and instructive public activities and performances imbued with socialist themes. Dalian was famous for its square culture. Numerous public squares, such as Zhongshan Square, Youhao Square, and Shengli Square, were sites for performances and activities designed to indoctrinate the public in socialist ideology.

The culture bureau head told me that the state guided and indoctrinated the mass culture through recreational programs. For instance, the library head in Xigang District organized the district-wide activity called Ten, Hundred, Thousand, Ten Thousand. They selected ten model winners in political and scholarly contests, selecting "a hundred reader backbones, a thousand readers, and ten thousand households reading good books in every community." Officials evaluated every household's library and awarded those who collected the most and "best" books. *Best* here was defined as books that embodied socialist values. Through these activities, the state policy of "socialist education and learning revolution" was channeled into each household through the library.

Other public activities included inspiring talks eulogizing CCP model members who had contributed to the lives of the people; poem contests eulogizing the CCP; and a large number of thematic recreational programs celebrating nationalism, the CCP, the People's Liberation Army (PLA), socialism, the hometown during National Day, Labor Day, PLA Day, CCP Day, and so on. On these occasions, only songs that praised the CCP, its leaders, and socialism were allowed. These educational public activities were, as the officials told me, important legacies of past communes and the collectives. The aim here was to inject and blend state policy and ideology into the mass culture so that healthy socialistic morality could filter into everyone's mind and life. As one official summed it up, "Everybody can see, hear, and feel socialism and communism, and it is our job to use it to form a coherent community around the CCP."

The Complexity of Targeting and Supporting Karaoke Bars

The main responsibility for administering state policy regarding karaoke bars was divided between the Bureau of Culture and the Bureau of Public Security. These two agencies represented the government's dual strategy of soft and hard administrative measures. Restrictions stopped short of an outright ban; rather, they intended to bring karaoke bars in line with a state-defined socialist culture. This is because the state and the sex industry are not separate entities. As we have seen, in response to Japanese maneuvering, state funds were used to support the early rise of the sex industry.

The state has profited from the sex industry's stimulation of the local economy and its attraction of foreign investment. A significant example of this is the annual fall fashion show in Dalian that has become an international event attracting models and celebrities from around the world. Important American officials such as Henry Kissinger regularly attended this event. According to a high-level official I interviewed, the successful growth of this event was based on the use of Dalian hostesses to entice and entertain important foreign investors and celebrities. According to this official, the hostesses were instrumental in making Dalian an important center of the fashion industry. She related that after the Dalian officials helped foreign investors and celebrities settle down in hotels, the foreign men and the hostesses, who were strangers to each other at that time, after talking for an hour or so at the hotel bar walked hand in hand to hotel rooms to engage in sex. She said that the Dalian officials were watching these scenes with both amazement and amusement. They all came to the conclusion that they should respect the foreigners' custom (*waiguoren de fengsuxiguan*) and "facilitate their habit by taking them to karaoke bars." Hence they launched a process in karaoke bars to train the hostesses to be more "civilized" (*wenming*) in walking, talking, and singing styles to cater to foreign tastes so that they could serve outside investors well. While this perception is largely based on the myth of the hypersexuality of foreign men, it is nevertheless an important factor in the government's unofficial support of prostitution in Dalian.

In addition, hostesses' support of rural development through remittances has promoted social stability and in fact ensured the survival of hard-pressed rural economies. It was reported that in China, the contribution of the sex industry to the gross domestic product in 1998 and 1999 came in between 12.1 and 12.8 percent.[29] Paradoxically, like the Maoist state's prostitution reform campaign in 1951, the post-Mao state enforced its "socialist morality" by criminalizing sex work as a capitalist vice and the result of Western spiritual pollution.

Municipal government officials stated in interviews that the government has brought many charges against karaoke bars in their zeal to affirm Maoist values. First, according to party ideology, karaoke bars have failed to live up to the standard of socialist business ethics. They claimed that China's market economy is not just a market economy but also a socialist market economy. Unlike capitalism's exploitation of the working masses in the pursuit of riches, socialist business should prioritize the needs of the people over profit making. The driving force behind the socialist market is not the profit motive but, rather, dedication—to the party, nation, and people. Bar owners' actual behaviors, however, have fallen far short of these ideals. They have exploited customers by levying hidden costs and purposefully misrepresenting the price of goods and services. What's more, they have used erotic services to play on men's weaknesses and attract more business. All these behaviors exhibit an overemphasis on making money to the detriment of the socialist market's stability and development.

Second, the "erotic service" (seqing peishi) offered in karaoke bars goes against "socialist spiritual civilization." The exchange of sexual services for money is an "ugly social phenomenon" associated with capitalism and should be wiped out to maintain a healthy socialist cultural environment and "civilized consumption." The third charge against karaoke bars is that, unlike the healthy, collective recreational activities promoted by the government, karaoke bar entertainment is centered on the individual. The Dalian municipal government, through the Bureau of Culture and its subsidiary organs, has directly supported and organized a variety of free, public events.

These activities were organized around particular educational themes. For example, a 1995 film festival held in Labor Park commemorated the fiftieth anniversary of the "global victory against fascism," "the war of resistance against Japan," and "Dalian's liberation."[30] Karaoke was seen as the antithesis of these healthy pastimes. Karaoke pandered to the desires of individuals to show off their performing talents. This focus on the individual is thought to bring out the ugly aspects of human nature, such as vanity and self-centeredness.

The fourth charge is that the extravagance of karaoke bars clashes with the government goal to downplay social differences. Since the economic reforms, Chinese society has witnessed a tremendous growth in economic disparities. In the urban centers, what used to be a relatively homogenous population of state-owned enterprise workers has become stratified and differentiated. Karaoke bars highlight these trends by encouraging excessive and conspicuous consumption as a way to show off wealth and social status.

THE ADMINISTRATION OF KARAOKE BARS: THE BUREAU OF CULTURE AND THE PUBLIC SECURITY BUREAU

The Bureau of Culture

The Bureau of Culture (BC) was responsible for managing karaoke bars according to socialist standards of civility and morality. It accomplished this task through a variety of administrative and regulative measures. First, the BC maintained detailed records on the business locations, store names, proprietors, exterior and interior designs, audio and video machines, and other information about the bars. This was the basis for the rest of the bureau's administrative efforts to regulate and manage the city karaoke bar scene. Second, strict approval procedures had been introduced. On the surface, the purpose behind these regulations was to ensure the quality of bars, but in reality they were mostly designed to reduce the number of karaoke bars. Prospective bar owners were discouraged from submitting an application by a circuitous approval process that wound its way through a total of five government bureaus: the Environment Bureau, Bureau of Culture, Public Security Bureau, Tax Bureau, and Industrial and Commercial Bureau. In addition, applicants were required to hand in a detailed and comprehensive description of the bar's project, including a diagram of its exterior and interior designs. Even minute details of the structure of the bars were required to meet government specifications. For example, suite doors had to have transparent windows no less than 50 × 80 inches in size and be installed with locks that could not be locked from the inside. Inside, suites were required to be brightly illuminated and without inner rooms. (Some karaoke private suites include a small inner chamber separated from the main room by either a thin wall or curtain. These spaces were often used to conduct illegal sexual services.) If approved, a cultural operation license would be issued to the owner for one year.

Third, bar owners were required to attend monthly classes organized by the BC to study state policy and law. Those achieving high test scores were awarded Civilized Karaoke Bar plaques that could be displayed inside their bars. This policy was designed to hone the bar owners' sense of pride as contributors to the socialist cultural market. Inculcated with this new thought, bar owners would take the initiative to transform their bars into civilized spaces where the lofty sentiments of clients could be nurtured.

Fourth, it was required that karaoke bars should have Chinese and socialist characteristics. In particular, they should provide mainland Mandarin songs, "healthy and inspiring" revolutionary songs, Chinese-style mural wallpaper, Chinese paintings, Chinese-style bar names, and Chinese food and snacks. Lurking not far beneath these regulations was a palpable sense of crisis that Western and Japanese influences had begun to erode Chinese culture. As an official of the Bureau of Culture explained to me: "Imported Western culture in China is like an aircraft carrier—high quality, durable, and powerful. Chinese culture, however, resembles a small sampan, only able to float a hundred miles. We need to develop a singing-and-dancing business with Chinese characteristics to attack the foreign cultural market in China."

The Public Security Bureau

The Public Security Bureau (PSB) served as an "Iron Great Wall" *(gangtie changcheng)*, providing the muscle behind state policy. The main vehicle for PSB intervention was the antipornography campaign *(saohuang dafei)*, itself a part of a wider, more comprehensive attack on social deviance known as "crackdowns" *(yanda,* literally, to strike severely). These campaigns lasted for spurts of three months at a time to be repeated three times a year, strategically centering on important holidays (for example, National Day and Army Day) and events (for example, the Asia-Pacific Economic Cooperation conference). Crackdowns targeted a number of social ills, ranging from unlicensed video game arcades (said to corrupt the minds of the youth) to undocumented rural migrants (said to disrupt urban management).

Pornography was a mainstay on the list of crackdown targets. It included a wide range of illegal behavior, such as pornographic media (for example, magazines, laser discs) and performances (striptease). The behaviors that received the most organizational resources and manpower, however, were the "erotic services" conducted in karaoke bars and other commercial establishments (saunas and hair salons). The PSB employed a complex system of raids to attack karaoke bars. Their techniques were self-described as "guerilla warfare" (da youji) in reference to the heroic efforts of Communist revolutionaries against Japanese invaders and nationalists. Raids were divided into several types, including "regular raids and shock raids, timed raids and random raids, systematic raids and block raids, daytime raids and night raids." Those PSB units and individuals who performed well, measured by the number of arrested hostesses and amount of fines levied, received high honors and cash bonuses from the municipal government.

Elaine Jeffreys, in her book *China, Sex, and Prostitution*, defends China's antipornography campaign and argues that the campaign-style policing—launching short, sharp strikes against selective activities—has successfully amended the "deteriorating public order" and that fines and administrative detention are exercised as "soft ways" and "lenient approaches" to offenders in order to avoid "the stigmatization associated with criminal sanctions."[31] Thus the relationship between local police and older prostitutes is "amicable," and prostitutes support the empowerment of the police "to patrol the street so as to provide them with protection and surveillance."[32] Jeffreys's book is entirely dependent on "translations" of secondary sources, making it appear that these translations reflect reality in China. My ethnographic research reveals a completely opposite story. In fact, as I will demonstrate, the antipornography campaign directly targets hostesses and severely aggravates the violent, exploitative, and risky working conditions of these women.

Although hostesses fall into a gray area—the law does not clearly identify them as either illegal or legal—in everyday practice it is recognized that hostesses provide illegal erotic services and hence are the major target of the antiprostitution campaign. As I argue below, police raids make them both legally and socially vulnerable. If their sexual services were disclosed by their clients to the police, they would be subject to extreme humiliation, arrest, fines, and incarceration. Indeed, in their everyday lives, local police constitute their daily fear and terror. Because the police wield arbitrary power, hostesses find it obligatory to obey their sexual demands without monetary compensation. Local officials not only sexually and economically exploit hostesses but also keep "spy hostesses" as their personal harem.

The antipornography campaign also allows bar owners to severely regulate the hostesses who otherwise would operate in a more laissez-faire manner. Because the state's antipornography policy is manipulated and usurped by local officials and bar owners for their own ends, leading to a violent working environment for the hostesses, the women do not disclose their real identities, which makes it more convenient for men to be violent toward them, sometimes even to the extreme of murder. It was reported that in the city of Shenyang in 1999, more than one hundred hostesses were murdered.[33] In Dalian, hostesses' bodies were found murdered on the street, but police could not identify who they were.[34] When I accompanied my closest hostess friend, Dee, to her rural hometown, I asked her mother if she was worried about Dee's safety in Dalian. At my question, her mother's face sank with distress. She kept silent for a long time before plucking up the strength to tell me that at one point she had thought Dee had been murdered in Dalian. She said, "I did not hear from her for three months. She did not call me. I did not have her phone number. . . . I really thought she was dead. You know, it's so common in Dalian. I have often heard of hostesses' dead bodies found there. I believed Dee was among them. I was worried sick. I got so sick that I could not get up from bed. I thought I was never going to see her again."

CONTEST, COMPLICITY, AND NEGOTIATION

It was difficult to translate state policy into practice. The complex interactions between sex industry participants on the one hand and state agents on the other led to a gap between the theory of policy and the practice of enforcement.

State policy was distorted and even derailed by the interest-seeking behavior of local officials. Karaoke bars were an important source of extralegal income. As one PSB official candidly remarked, "Karaoke bars and hostesses are our sources of livelihood. We basically cannot live without them." Officials extracted economic benefits from karaoke bars through a combination of bribes and fines. As the same PSB official explained:

> Soldiers [read: police] and bandits are always from one family *[bingfei yijia]*. We depend on the bar owners for extravagant food and recreation. Without them, we could never live so well. As a matter of fact, in confidential police meetings, whenever high-level officials declare a police raid for the next day, immediately almost all of the policemen stand up and ask for permission to go to the bathroom, where you can hear them calling their bar owner friends on their mobile phones, saying "Hey, tomorrow at this time you have to be very careful." Then the next day when the police launch the surprise raid, only those bar owners who did not offer sufficient bribes or misbehaved get caught and heavily fined. But there are also times when we are ordered to make immediate bar raids in districts not in our charge. In such cases, nobody has their own network at stake, and there is an incentive to arrest and fine as many hostesses and clients as possible. You get a considerable percentage of the fines, which makes up the better part of your monthly income.

This quotation shows how state policy was hijacked in the service of officials' personal economic interests.

Local officials' exploitation of hostesses was not limited to economic benefits. PSB officials maintained a group of spy hostesses *(xiaojie jianxi)* who reported on bar conditions as well as acting as the personal harem for these officials. In exchange for these services, hostesses gained immunity from police sanctions. I was told how to tell who was a spy after mass arrests. Hundreds of hostesses were herded into police station cells. After an hour or so, some hostesses would ask for a break to go to restrooms and then never come back. These hostesses were the spies. The other, less well-connected hostesses had to call friends to submit the fine of thousands of *yuan* before being released.

Hostesses might not be only a way for corrupt officials to get rich but an essential ingredient of regional economic success and hence political career advancement.[35] There seemed to be substantial pressures that pushed local government into at least tolerating if not outright embracing the karaoke bar sex industry. One official told me a story of how a subregional leader profited from the sex industry. In the story, the leader had originally taken a hard-line stance against the sex industry and ordered a string of very harsh and ultimately very effective police raids. The backlash to these measures was swift and devastating. As hostesses fled the area to safer ground, they withdrew their savings from local banks, bringing about a sudden shortage of capital that threw the subregion into financial crisis.[36] More seriously, the male customers who used to frequent the karaoke bars began their own exodus. Investors pulled out and tourists stopped visiting. Under the effect of these severe sanctions, the local economy fell into stagnation. Facing political ruin, the leader reversed course and started secretly promoting the local sex industry. Having learned his lesson well, he not only restored the former sex industry but also turned the place into what became heralded as the "largest pornographic subregion in the province." He built an extravagant mansion and hired hostesses to entertain visiting officials. Each weekend on Friday night, the city officials would arrive to appreciate the sea views from the mansion, enjoy the banquets, and then lock their rooms and enjoy the company of hostesses. These orgies lasted the entire weekend. His "brilliant achievements" eventually satisfied his superiors and gained him awards, reputation, and promotion. Valid or not, this story offers a glimpse of how some officials benefited tremendously from the sex industry.

COPING MECHANISMS OF BAR OWNERS

The state, by making erotic services in karaoke bars illegal, created a market for corruption on the part of local officials who were among the greatest beneficiaries of the bar system.[37] While local officials were manipulating state policy to exploit bar owners and hostesses for their own gains, bar owners were forced to develop counterstrategies. The three bar owners with whom I worked improvised creative maneuvers to counter local officials, while still having to share profits through bribery.

The owner of the upscale bar in which I conducted fieldwork was a well-known local gangster. His karaoke bar had opened in 1998 and had become the most prosperous bar in the city. During the strong antipornography campaign in July 1999, however, a hundred hostesses were scared away, which severely curtailed his bar business. That was at the beginning of my research, when I did not know about the antipornography campaign. I went to work as usual on July 1, 1999, only to find a handful of hostesses in the hallway. While I was baffled by the scene and wondered where the hostesses were, the madam came up and ordered us to go to the fitting room upstairs. Wondering to myself, Why do we need to go to the fitting room? I walked up with the others. The madam instructed, "To anyone who comes in the room asking who you are, say you are a saleslady for Kirin beer." We nodded. When she left, other hostesses told me that this was the time of the crackdown. They agreed that it would be dangerous to come the next day. Fear pervaded the whole night. After midnight, while I was riding in a taxi with a hostess to stay over at her place, she instructed me to bend over under the seats because the police were raiding hostesses on the street. She said the police would stop the taxi to catch the hostesses.

A couple of days later, we were called over to the bar for a meeting by the madam. Sitting in the hallway with 130 other hostesses, I was taking notes on the bar owner's speech. He was furious at the receding business and local officials' restrictions:

> I strongly urge all of you to return to the bar and resume working! As you may have already heard, many hostesses have been imprisoned nationwide. This relentless campaign spread from the three big cities of Beijing, Shanghai, and Guangzhou to Dalian. However, despite this awful situation, we have to continue working; otherwise we will starve to death and nobody will care. Besides, if you are not working here, what else can you do? Go back home and farm in the field like peasants? I know none of you would like to do that. What other skills do you have? None! There is nowhere else you can work. With little money, you cannot even find yourself a husband. Rich men will terminate their relationship with you, too. You have been enjoying the urban lifestyle and have developed the habit of spending money like water. Habituated to such a high level of consumption, there is no going back. You have no choice but to continue working as hostesses. If the police arrest you, that means they arrest me. You have me as your boss—you don't need to worry about a thing! Just

remember, how do you think I could have opened such a flourishing and famous bar in the city center without a strong tie with the city government? There is nothing to be afraid of. We always learn in advance about the police's "secret" raids. I was just informed that officials in the Bureau of Industry and Commerce would inspect our bar secretly one of these days. The officials have their state policy; we have our countermeasures. You will be completely transformed into waitresses in form and hostesses in nature. In that case, you are part of our legal staff, and there is no way inspectors in plain clothes can find any reason to arrest you. They in no way can control customers from coming for hostess companions. . . . Here are our concrete countermeasures to fight against their policy. First, starting August 1, all of our titles will be changed. The madams should be addressed as "Directors of Public Relations." You will be addressed as "waitress" instead of "hostess." After all, the social status of "hostess" is too low. Remember, we will not have "hostesses" from now on, but "waitresses." Second, you will be grouped in tens and assigned to different sections of the bar (ten karaoke rooms in each section). In the future, instead of standing together in the entrance hall, you will only gather at your designated sections waiting to be chosen. Third, every one of you will have to wear the uniform dress with a name card on the chest, different colors for different sections. At the end of this meeting everyone should hand in 100 *yuan* and register your dress size. We will have the dresses made by this weekend. In the future no casual dresses are allowed. Fourth, from August 1, the state will levy a tax on bar revenue. So be sure to receive clients' tips privately. If your clients offer the regular tip of 200 *yuan,* they will leave it at the front desk where you can pick it up. If they offer more money, it should be conducted privately between the two of you. Fifth, the three directors (madams) will handle your business. You will have to report to the directors (madams) if you are going offstage with a client. If the director does not know this client, he may be an undercover inspector, in which case you are forbidden to go with him. In case you do go and run into trouble, we will not take any responsibility. Sixth, every one of you has to have your hometown identity card (ID) and Dalian temporary residence card (TRC). Those of you who have not yet purchased or renewed your TRC have to do it soon. Otherwise you will be easy targets for the police. Here is a form for you to fill out and hand in afterward. I will compile a book with a record of your picture, name, and photocopy TRC, through which you will be transformed into our formal employees protected by law. When the police come, I will show them this book and assert your waitress identity. Who the hell will dare to arrest you! After all, men cannot dance with men, and there is no way to prevent men from coming for hostesses. Meanwhile, make sure that you serve your police clients well; otherwise they will raid our bar without giving me prior notice. Once such an incident happened, and I was furious. I said, since you people working in the government are utterly unreasonable, we people in society will fight against you to the death [*huopin*]! Why do you people in the government think you have the right to do whatever you want? I am a common man, but I have enormous social power. Don't ever mess with me!

The bar owner contrasted his identity as "a common man" with the "people working in the government." He expressed his anger and antagonism toward the "unreasonable people working in the government" and listed his tactics to cope with the state policy. In several instances, we saw the conflict between the officials and the bar owners escalate to the point where the owners vowed to "fight against . . . [them] to the death." While it is questionable that the bar owner would actually confront the authorities in this way, it does illustrate his anger and frustration. More realistically, he utilized nonconfrontational maneuvers, that is, converting illegal bar hostesses into legal employees through shifts of title, dress, identity, work sections, and so on. Such a strategy plus his strong official ties not only gained him some leverage at this critical point of the political campaign but also allowed him to impose more severe regulations and discipline on his hostesses, who were used to operating in a more laissez-faire manner.

To secure his bar business, he tried to persuade the hostesses to return to work reminding them of how they had become used to high-level consumption and reassuring them that he had good ties with officials. He also extorted profit from the hostesses by charging more for their uniforms than they actually cost (like the other two bar owners). Later he insisted that all hostesses be present at the bar at precisely 7:30 P.M. every day and not leave until 12 A.M. unless they went offstage with clients. Hostesses coming late or leaving early were to be fined 600 *yuan*. Hostesses had to request a leave or a night off from the director, which in principle was not granted. He also planned to train and discipline the hostesses' walking, speaking, and singing skills to attract more clients. The bar owner used this moment of crisis as an excuse to impose new demands, controls, and restrictions on the hostesses.

The owner of the bar Prince, a graduate from a local university with a B.A. in geography, also displayed much contempt for local officials. He told me that he and other bar owners never listened to the political lectures at the monthly meeting run by Culture Bureau officials. He did not know and would not like to know anything about law or politics, because "as long as you develop profound ties with officials by distributing bribes well, you are all set." There were numerous police raids that took place in his bar during my research there, but every time we had been informed beforehand. Bribery was the main avenue through which he maneuvered around the state policy.

A low-tier bar owner, an entrepreneur who owned another private enterprise, talked to me with great indignation: "I have really had enough of dealing with officials! Loads of bribes to them every month, plus I have to show deference. I actually provide them with so much money each month that sometimes they even invite me to dinner! I am so fed up with it that I cannot wait to get out of this country!"[38] Several times during my research in this bar, upon the news of a sudden police raid, I quickly followed everyone upstairs and hid under the beds in a small, locked dormitory room. This bar owner was often very angry and complained to the officials about not having been informed of such sudden police raids. However, there was really nothing she could do about it except provide more bribes. She told me that because she bribed so well, for several months officials waived her taxes and electricity fee, which was a large sum of money.

Later, she sold her bar to Bing. When I saw her again, she appeared much happier, although she still complained to me and another official:

> I finally got liberated from those damned people! I hate them. Think about it: who would need to go to karaoke bars to do business if officials were not involved with their political power? We entrepreneurs could definitely live without karaoke bars and conduct business by offering each other the lowest price. However, the state system is such that you have to deal with the officials and entertain them to prevent them from harming you or imposing injustice. The business of karaoke bars would never have been this prosperous had officials not participated in their growth. Now when I see them on the streets, I feel so much hatred inside of me that I am too tired to talk to them. They complain that I disregard them when they are not useful any more. But I am just too exhausted.

These three bar owners' accounts, filled with resentments, negotiations, and compliance, attest to their efforts to manipulate hostesses and maneuver within the restrictive state system. At the same time, they have to systematically bribe and show deference to local officials, who, as state agents, usurp and manipulate the state policy for their own interest and profit. Thus, the interaction of such fragmented power among these three levels of state law, government officials, and entrepreneurs is central in the evolving history of the karaoke bar industry.

While the karaoke bar has thrived as a result of market reform, it is important to remember that it was central to the Japanese strategy to open up the Chinese market. The karaoke bars served as a beachhead into China for Japanese businesses. It stimulated and solidified the economic relationship between Dalian and Japan. Japanese investment in Dalian is the highest in China.[39] It is estimated that Dalian has ten thousand foreign ventures, more than two thousand of which come from Japan. Dalian has also built a strong high-tech park and foundation for firms with Japanese operations.[40]

We are faced here with a great irony: in order to recover from the colonialists' emasculation, men in Dalian embraced an aspect of the Japanese culture—karaoke bars. The karaoke bar was part of the tactic Japanese businessmen employed to open the Chinese market. By emulating their economic superiors in their consumption practices, the emerging Chinese entrepreneurs carved out a new niche to defy the monopoly of state power as represented by the banquet and to reclaim their masculine identity.

However, this new venue of freedom was under constant attack by police raids. The state oscillated between targeting and supporting this particular sex industry. Indeed, the state was connected with the sex industry in both official and unofficial ways. Officially, the state repressed the industry in the form of regulation. Unofficially, the state promoted the industry to foreign visitors for foreign investment, and state officials supported it through patronization. These seemingly contradictory relationships both worked together and conflicted with each other. They worked together as state officials appropriated the repressive policy for their own benefit. They conflicted with each other as state officials suppressed while at the same time patronized and supported the industry.

As a result, the antipornography campaign not only failed to achieve the goals proclaimed in state propaganda but further aggravated hostesses' working conditions. Different actors manipulated state policy for their own ends by controlling and abusing the hostesses. An exploitative and violent environment was established in the sex industry through the interplay between state administrative and cultural power, the agenda of local officials, and the maneuverings of bar owners.

Three

Fierce Rivalries, Unstable Bonds: Class in the Karaoke Bars

Loud Western music filled my ears as I stepped into Romance Dream, a karaoke bar in Dalian. I was accompanied by a high-level official in the municipal government and a businessman, both regular customers. At the door, a beautiful woman dressed in a cheongsam greeted us with a bow and ushered us inside. As I made my way into the main lobby, my nose tickled from the pungent odor of cosmetics. Images from an American X-rated video flickered on a wide-screen TV. More than a hundred *zuotai xiaojie* (literally, women who sit on the stage) stood poised in eager anticipation of the male customers. The women were heavily made up and fancily dressed, their heads topped with elaborate coiffures. The *Mami* (madam, or mother), clad in sheer black tights, pointed at a dozen of the women with the antenna of her walkie-talkie and led them into VIP rooms located on the second floor. There, a lucky few would be chosen by customers as escorts for the night.

What are the economics of the karaoke bar industry? What is the hierarchy of karaoke bars in Dalian and how does it signify post-Mao social stratifications? In describing the economics of karaoke bars, I examine the exploitations of the hostesses by the bar owners, madams, waiters, and bar bouncers. I argue that what prevents the hostesses from collective action is their unstable coalition (or complete disaffiliation), the incentive to select noncooperative strategies, and the costs and risks associated with such collective action.

The Hierarchy of the Bar Industry

Karaoke bars were the most expensive bars in Dalian, with prices far exceeding the level at other recreational spots, such as coffee bars, pottery bars,[1] soft-drink bars, music bars, and so forth. Within the karaoke bar industry, bars were ranked vertically according to city locale; exterior and interior furnishings and facilities; organization and management; the number, beauty, educational level, and turnover rate of bar hostesses; its clientele; and its spending level. I conducted field research in ten karaoke bars. Most of my time and effort, however, was concentrated on three bars: Colorful Century (high tier), Prince (middle tier), and Romantic Dream (low tier).

AN UPPER-TIER KARAOKE BAR

Colorful Century was housed in a four-story building just off Zhongshan Square. Zhongshan Square was the financial heart of Dalian where the most important banks were located. The city of Dalian was composed of six districts, three county-level cities, a county, and three special administrative zones. In the eyes of the Dalian urbanites, only four centrally located districts were considered the "city" of Dalian, and the rest were adjacent "countryside." These four districts were classified hierarchically according to their locations in the city—from the center to the periphery as Zhongshan, Xigang, Shahekou, and Ganjingzi. Karaoke bars in Zhongshan district had the highest status.

As we entered Colorful Century, its façade was draped with strings of small and colorful blinking lights that fanned out like the train on a Western wedding dress. The words *Colorful Century,* in large, electrified Chinese characters hung over the entrance. The doors themselves were fringed with plastic ivy and more flashing lights. Two security guards stood at either side of the entrance gate. The heavy thud of techno music drums rumbled from the entrance. Three tall, beautiful young women dressed in identical red cheongsams made elegant bows at the entering customers and ushered them inside the bar. The entryway spilled out into an expansive lobby of glossy marble and ceiling-tall mirrors. Two golden God of Wealth statues surveyed the scene from atop their perches on pedestals in the middle of the room. Their grinning visages were enshrouded by thin ribbons of fragrant smoke that rose from incense sticks sprouting from a sand-filled porcelain pot at their feet. A few hostesses quietly tended to the small garden of incense sticks, plucking out the old ones as they withered and collapsed and planting new ones. These hostesses made little, repeated bows while clasping their hands. They prayed for good fortune that night.

More than 150 seductively dressed women were gathered on the left side of the lobby. They sat on three rows of benches like the audience to an unseen performance. In fact, however, they themselves were the observed. A camera hung from the ceiling fed to monitors installed inside each private room. Customers could select their escorts from the comfort of couches while sitting in these suites. The stairs leading to the upper-floor private rooms were lined with two teams of waitresses, all the same height and with the same hairstyle, dressed in the same dark embroidered miniskirts, their breasts half exposed, and their hips scarcely covered. They simultaneously saluted customers, "Good evening!"

The upper stories of this bar were divided into five sections (A, B, C, D, E) of ten karaoke rooms each. There was also a fitting room for hostesses that could serve as a hideout during police raids. The karaoke rooms provided privacy. Each room was equipped with karaoke equipment, including a twenty-nine-inch TV that continuously played excerpts from erotic Western videos. Each karaoke room was furnished with an air-conditioner, rosewood furniture, beautiful window drapes, wallpaper, carpeting, magnificent dim ceiling lights, a big couch, and an end table. There was a space between the TV and the end table where clients could dance with hostesses. They could dance either to each other's singing or to the dance music chosen from a song booklet. The couch could be unfolded into a bed at the request of clients. Many karaoke rooms had adjunct secret bedrooms separated by a curtain camouflaged to look the same in texture and color as the wallpaper. This was designed to prevent discovery in case of a police raid.

Colorful Century was on constant alert for raids. Equipment was provided to ensure the safety of the bar and all its habitants. An alarm button was set up in each karaoke room so that if police made a surprise visit, the alarm could be activated to alert everyone, allowing them to hide and destroy any evidence of illegal activity (for instance, refolding beds into the couch position). In addition, each staff member carried a walkie-talkie with a long antenna that could be used to communicate with others during raids and facilitate the coordination of emergency measures.

Organization and Management

Organization and management were the most complicated in the high-tier bars. There were three madams, a manager in the entertainment section, three female receptionists, ten security guards, one hundred and fifty hostesses, twenty-five waitresses, four bartenders, a woman who checked coats (called the coat lady), a female janitor, and the bar owner. The three female receptionists were fashion models from outside of Dalian. The coat lady who used to be a hostess in the bar became the bar owner's mistress and was promoted. She sold hostesses the stage cards, essentially their onstage fee (20 *yuan* each) and stored their purses (1 *yuan* each). Everyone knew about her identity as the owner's mistress, but no one dared to gossip about it.

Hostesses in this upscale karaoke bar were taller with greater facial beauty and more shapely bodies than those in lower bars. They were also better educated; four of the hostesses from this group had graduated from high school. They ended up at their current karaoke bars in various ways. Some were introduced to a bar through their friends, previous coworkers, or hometown friends. Many brought their sisters to work in the bars. Some simply called a taxi when they arrived in Dalian and had the driver take them to the red-light district. A few were bought by the bar owners from pimps.

Hostesses did not necessarily stay in one bar forever. In fact, there was a high turnover rate. Certain unattractive hostesses in high- and medium-tier bars were rarely chosen by clients. These hostesses ended up moving to other bars at similar or lower levels. During my research at this high-tier bar, some hostesses who had never been chosen, after a week or so, simply vanished. Later, I encountered some of them in the medium-tier bar described later.

Security guards wore green, pseudomilitary uniforms. They all had certain connections with the boss or the entertainment manager. Their main job was to keep the hostesses from leaving before 12 A.M., ensure that clients paid hostesses' tips, and maintain bar security. Occasionally a team of the security guards rushed upstairs like soldiers to quell fights in the karaoke rooms. The suppression of disturbances always involved violence and blood. Unarmed or armed (with beer bottles, knives, and glass) fights between drunken clients or clients and hostesses were daily occurrences in the bar.

Violence against and Exploitation of Hostesses

At Colorful Century, hostesses often came downstairs, crying from their injuries: their legs, arms, and breasts black and blue from the hard pinches of some clients. Some hostesses chose to endure whatever abuse they were subjected to, but some opted to quit and, consequently, received no tips for the time they endured. Those who clenched their teeth to see it through with smiles held back their tears and complaints for later when they sent off the clients and returned to the community of hostesses.

Not only clients, but also madams, the bar owner, the entertainment manager, and security guards inflicted violence on the hostesses. Once, a hostess came into the fitting room to change from her dress into slacks because her client had been pinching her legs. While she was changing her clothes, the madam came in, furious. The madam slapped her face very hard and hit her in the head with her phone, yelling at her, "Don't you know that your client is looking for you? Why are you hiding here? I have looked for you everywhere! I am now ordering you back to your client right away!" The poor girl tried to dodge the madam's blows, as her face reddened from the madam's slaps. In an anguished voice, she agreed, "Sure, sure, I will go back right away." Fleeing the madam's blows and harsh words, she quickly slipped out of the room.

Hostesses not only obeyed the bar staff but also were responsible for ordering enough beer and snacks to meet the minimal expenditure. Some bars required that, in addition to other fees, customers consume snacks and beverages at a certain monetary level. Known as the minimum charge, these requirements created an onerous burden for hostesses. Hostesses were held responsible for ensuring that customers' expenditures reached the mandated level. To stimulate customers' consumption, hostesses themselves had to continuously consume, especially alcohol. At Colorful Century, the minimum charge was set very high at 400 *yuan*. Here the bathroom was always filled with vomiting hostesses, who then returned to their clients to continue drinking. Because of this daily alcohol overuse, most hostesses not only put on weight (which led to other self-destructive, weight-loss practices) but also developed stomach problems, which in severe cases resulted in hospitalization.

Hostesses were often urged to attract returning clients. In one assembly, the bar owner said:

> Those hostesses in Shanghai not only are extremely flirtatious, but also spend 1,000 *yuan* on their dresses. Such high-quality clothing always assures them high tips. You should follow their example: raise your dress quality and change often. Thus you can maximize your chance to be chosen. Your dress expenditure will eventually be covered. No investment, no gains. In addition, you have to exercise singing and dancing, walking and speaking skills. You have to develop returning clients. Then you will gain profits not only for the bar, but also for yourselves. As a man myself, I know that a man easily gets bored with a hostess after she goes offstage with him. So if you are smart, you will not do it for the first few times. He will then have to come back here more often to try to get you to bed. That will give you more opportunities to earn his tips before finally consenting to go offstage with him. By then you will have profited a good deal from him. You also have to learn to drink a lot and toast the clients. Clients here are very vain. Say to them, "I wish you a successful business!" They will be really happy. You have to be open enough to strip his pants off. Meanwhile, you have to give him face. All in all, you have to make the karaoke room titillating and inviting!

Not only the bar owner, but also the three madams managed and disciplined the hostesses. The three thirty-five- to thirty-nine-year-old madams—"heads of the group" *(lingban)*—called on a team of hostesses and led them into clients' karaoke rooms for selection. The hostesses told me that the whole process depended on whether the madam presented you to the clients or not. Clients generally sought a hostess with a beautiful body and face, big breasts, and one who was able to drink, sing English songs, sing and dance the best, and so on. After inquiring about their preferences, the madams either strongly recommended several hostesses who "fit their tastes the best" or directly pushed some hostesses to those clients' side. So it was very important for a hostess to bribe one of the madams. Once I saw a hostess secretly handing 400 *yuan* to a madam at the entrance gate. The latter accepted it after feigning refusal several times. If the hostess did not bribe the madam, she would not call on her or recommend her to clients. Eventually, the hostess would be left with minimal chances to be chosen.

This kind of bribery produced three factions. Each faction was led by one madam, who would call only the hostesses in her faction to the clients' karaoke rooms. New hostesses had to decide which madam seemed nice before bribing her to be accepted into her faction. However, during my research period, several strikingly beautiful new hostesses, without bribing the madams, did manage to "sit on the stage" (*zuotai,* accompany clients) because they secretly followed other hostesses into the karaoke rooms without being noticed by the madams, or clients watching the monitor were struck by their beauty on the TV screen.

Each time hostesses sat on the stage, they received a minimum tip of 200 *yuan* from the clients, 20 *yuan* of which was paid to the bar as the "stage fee" *(taifei).* When hostesses went offstage, the minimum tip was 400 *yuan* and hostesses had to pay 50 *yuan* for the "offstage fee." In each karaoke room, madams and waitresses each received a tip of 100 *yuan* from the client.

Madams and waitresses sometimes crossed over occupational lines to serve as hostesses. For madams, acting as a hostess often reflected the abuse of power. Madams often used their gatekeeper role to reserve the best customers for themselves, even going offstage with them. During my research, I witnessed several times when the madams, instead of leading hostesses to karaoke rooms, volunteered to personally serve "good clients" as their hostesses. A *good client* was defined by his high social status and more civilized manners, only staying for an hour at the most and giving higher tips. In such cases, hostesses suffered the least, for the shortest time, and for the highest tips. Clients who were thus deprived of an opportunity to choose between hostesses had to either awkwardly protest or settle for the madam. According to the bar owner, many of these clients never came back again because they were fed up with the madams. Instead, they visited other bars to look for new hostesses.

A MEDIUM-TIER BAR

Similar-scale karaoke bars like Colorful Century but located in the other more peripheral districts were rated medium level. The medium-category karaoke bar was less extravagantly decorated both on its exterior and interior. It was still quite upscale, with three one-story buildings respectively named Prince Branch 1, Prince Branch 2, and Prince Branch 3. The three branches were built next to each other. Each branch had eighty to a hundred hostesses and twenty-three to thirty karaoke rooms. Hostesses were housed in a big dormitory building behind the bar. A much smaller percentage of these women, only three, graduated from high school, the highest degree in their group.

The entrance doors were adorned with electric lights, but less extravagantly than at Colorful Century. As we entered the bar, the first thing we saw was the counter of the bar. The hallway had a wooden floor instead of a carpet as in the high-tier bar. The hallway led to a long corridor, each side of which was lined with a series of karaoke rooms. Hostesses were sitting, standing, or wandering in the corridor. Usually they gathered in two karaoke rooms watching TV until newly arrived clients were ushered in and they were evicted. The interior of the karaoke rooms was decorated in a fashion that was similar to those at Colorful Century, except that there were no foldable couches or adjoining bedrooms. The karaoke equipment was manufactured in China. There was no minimum charge, and the spending level was 50 percent lower than the high-tier bar but 50 percent higher than the low-tier bar. The karaoke room rental fee was also 50 percent lower than in the high-tier bar.

Organization and Management

The organization and management were much less complex. The bar owner was in charge of the second branch where I conducted my fieldwork. The other two branches were under the command of his wife. The staff in each branch besides hostesses included two bartenders (one male and one female), four waiters, one madam, and a female janitor. The staff members were either related by blood or possessed other close connections to the bar owner. There were no security guards or segregated factions. There was no requirement of a stage fee. Hostesses were not allowed to leave the bar before 12 A.M., but some did slip away.

Hostesses working here had to meet four requirements. First, they had to have worked as hostesses before; experience was very important. Second, they had to be able to consume a great deal of alcohol. Third, they had to dress well. Fourth, they had to be sexually open-minded. Hostesses were expected to lead customers in their consumption of beer, hard liquor, and snacks to boost bar revenues. However, there was no fixed minimum charge, which alleviated some of the pressure that forced hostesses in the high-tier bar to daily gorge themselves on liquor and food.

The abuse of hostesses was relatively less serious than in the high- and low-tier bars. The madam at this bar was male, and he sometimes showed preference for some hostesses, whom he called more often and recommended more vigorously to customers. However, the favoritism and factionalism found in the high-tier bar was much less severe here. On average, hostesses' onstage tips fell into the range of 100 to 400 *yuan,* according to the quality of service and their clients' generosity. Their minimum offstage tip was 300 *yuan.*

The bar owner was very proud of his bar's advantages over first-rate bars such as Colorful Century. There were no security guards at the door. According to him, guards were intimidating and served only to frighten clients away. Also, as he commented, because he was an intelligent bar owner who offered no drugs or private rooms for sexual encounters, this assured the clients of the bar's quality and attracted clients with high morals.

A LOW-TIER BAR

The low-tier karaoke bar Romantic Dream was located in an enclave of twenty-six karaoke bars in a seedy neighborhood huddled under a suspended railroad in Shahekou district. It was known as the red-light district and was notorious for its polluted conditions, low-quality clients, and aggressive hard-core thugs and criminals. While thugs and criminals could be seen in upper-class karaoke bars, their numbers and the level of violence were much greater in lower-class bars. As I discussed in the first chapter, gangsters were involved in attacks on hostesses, plundering and theft of bars, the sale of drugs, and even murder. This red-light district street was first built in 1996. For the first three years of its existence, dead bodies were found lying in the street almost every morning. The police could do nothing about it. During my fieldwork there, I witnessed many bloody fights and saw gangsters roaming the area.

The gangsters of Dalian were tough street fighters who were members of numerous criminal organizations *(tuan huo).* Government officials told me that there were close connections between gangsters and the local government that fueled crimes and violence in the city. Gangsters were scattered throughout the sex industry working as owners and bouncers of karaoke bars, disco bars, sauna bars, and other places. They also were involved in the abduction of women from other provinces,[2] and sold ketamine powder, ecstasy, and other kinds of soft and hard drugs in entertainment venues. During the period of the World Soccer Cup, they organized illegal underground gambling activities. These activities were less bothered than protected by the police.

At times conflicts between different cliques in the underworld escalated into violence. One such incident occurred between two cliques in a hotel in Sanba Square in Dalian in October 2004. One person was knifed to death, one was shot to death, and a number of people were seriously injured. When the police arrived, gangsters resisted arrest and attacked the police with knives. In self-defense, the police shot one person to death. After the event, the remaining gangsters escaped. It was these kinds of gangsters that hostesses were dealing with on a daily basis.

When you entered Romantic Dream, the open doors pulsated with electric light bulbs. One or two hostesses in sexy clothes and heavy makeup sat at the entrance doors, smoking. The open doors gave every passerby a very clear view of the hostesses who were sitting inside. The bar had two floors. Upon entering the bar, one immediately encountered the hostesses in the hallway, sitting on the couch in front of the bar counter or on the chairs around the hallway, watching TV or making themselves up. The hallway floor was tiled, and the couches were very dark from grime.

There were two corridors of karaoke suites on each side of the bar counter. There were twenty karaoke rooms on the first floor. Three karaoke rooms on the second floor consisted of a waiters' dorm, hostesses' dorm, and a private room for sexual encounters *(paofang)*. The private room was specifically prepared for clients to sleep with hostesses. The lights in these karaoke rooms were as dim as those in the upper- and medium-tier bars. The interior was decorated similarly except that it was filthy. Beer, tea, water, crumbs, and leftover food were spilled all over the floor. The walls were plastered with discarded dark chewing gum, and the couches were filthy and oozed a strange and unpleasant odor. The bathroom was also very dirty. Romantic Dream provided not only a room for private sexual encounters but also a strip dance show by the hostesses in the karaoke rooms. The bar staff and hostesses tried not to spread the word too widely, lest these two items, which were illegal, attract police raids.

At Romantic Dream, prices were negotiable, including hostesses' tips. There was no karaoke room rental fee. The snacks and fruit plates were of much lower quality. Like the other two bars, this bar endeavored to develop steady clients by offering discounts. They utilized hostesses to attract returning clients and raise the spending level of clients. They tended to exploit new clients, foreigners, and clients from outside the city.

Organization and Management

The staff at Romantic Dream included three multifunctional waiters (madams/doormen/janitors), two bar managers, approximately twenty-seven hostesses, and a barkeeper/security guard *(kan changzi de)*. As with the high- and medium-tier bars, blood ties linked the bar proprietor and management into a relatively cohesive group. The two bartender-managers were the bar owner's brother and sister-in-law. The barkeeper-security guard, Bing, was one of the owner's distant relatives. The other staff members were introduced to the owner through other connections. These pre-existing ties allowed ownership and management to maintain a united front in relation to hostesses.

The three waiters also worked as doormen and janitors. Because of the high competition among the twenty bars along this street, each bar needed several doormen to block cars, stop passersby, and push them into the bar. The aggression was so intense that cars and people avoided the area at night for fear of being harassed and pulled into the bars. Doormen stood on the street shouting at the passersby about their "exceptionally beautiful and sexually open" hostesses at a low cost. There were twenty-seven hostesses at Romance Dream. Only one hostess had graduated from high school, the highest degree in their group. Hostesses in principle could not leave before 2 A.M. However, some hostesses left a little earlier without being reprimanded.

Each bar on this street had connections with several taxi drivers, who offered to drive hostesses home every morning and bring outside tourists (including foreign tourists) to patronize the bar. The benefit to taxi drivers was just one more example of the economic importance of the karaoke bars.

Each bar also had to hire a thug as barkeeper. This barkeeper had to be good at fighting; otherwise, the bar would be forced to close down due to the harassment of roaming gangsters and other thugs on the street. During my research in the bar, I witnessed numerous bloody fights between Bing and bar waiters and gangsters, clients, and passersby. I saw Bing and bar waiters throw heavy stones and chairs at clients and some passersby until blood streamed down their faces. The bar owner told me that Bing, after having killed and severely injured many men in previous fights, was once sentenced to death. The bar owner spent a great deal of money to finally get Bing out of prison before hiring him as the bar guard. The mere presence of Bing in the bar kept many gangsters and thugs away. According to the owner, if Bing were not in the bar, it would definitely be a mess: all of the hostesses would flee in fear, and everything would be plundered away by gangsters. She trusted Bing and the bar managers to take care of my safety.

Violence against Hostesses

Hostesses at Romantic Dream were often discontented with the slack business and their low status. They were encouraged to go elsewhere by clients and hostess friends. However, the bar bouncer Bing warned everybody that he knew everyone in the karaoke bar circle throughout the city. He said that if anyone dared to leave for other bars, he would have them beaten to death. Hostesses who did manage to switch bars had ties with one or more gangsters as their protectors; otherwise, no one dared to leave.[3]

Gangsters and other bar owners often came to visit. When they saw pretty hostesses, they dragged them upstairs and raped them. When they saw less pretty hostesses, they slapped them and beat them up. Hostesses were extremely scared of some of the toughest gangsters and thugs. They would run as fast as they could to escape them. Once I fled along with the other hostesses. We climbed up the back wall to the railroad tracks behind the bar, losing our shoes and cutting our feet in the process. It was a very unpleasant experience. Most of the bar hostesses have been raped one or more times by the gangsters. Almost all of the hostesses, to protect themselves, were connected with one or two gangsters. They frequently joked, "We hostesses are relatives of the underworld."

Waiter Li served as the "madam." His girlfriend was May, one of the bar hostesses. There were times when Li led only May and her close friend into the karaoke room while leaving the other hostesses outside. This was unfair to the other hostesses, especially when many hostesses had not earned any money for several days because of the lack of customers. Business at Romantic Dream was less prosperous compared to the other two bars.

Once, waiter Li again led only May and her friend into the clients' karaoke room. Quite upset with it, the other hostesses were sitting together in the hallway, drinking hard liquor and complaining in low voices. Nobody dared to speak up. All of the staff members, as always, were eating together on the other side of the hallway. I wanted to comfort the hostesses; however, since many of them had not had any clients for several days, I realized how useless my comforting words would be.

Hostess Hui, a good friend of mine, had served clients that night. She appeared very indignant about the injustice done to the other hostesses. She downed several glasses of beer. Pretending to be drunk and given courage by the alcohol, she walked toward the staff circle and pleaded with waiter Li on behalf of the other hostesses. "Didn't you know that some hostesses have not had any clients for several days? Why did you just push your wife and her friend into the room without informing the rest of the hostesses, especially when your wife has already had clients tonight! Why didn't you lead the other hostesses into the room to be chosen?" As she spoke, her voice trembled with fear and tears rolled down her face. The bar managers and the barkeeper tried to calm her down, but waiter Li jumped up and began punching her in the face and head, kicking her severely in her chest and belly, yelling at her, "Didn't you already have clients? Why are you minding the other hostesses' business? None of the others complained. So why are you complaining about me having my wife sit in the karaoke room?" Hui collapsed into a chair from the impact of the kicks and blows. She did not dodge at all but screamed, "Ok, you beat me! You beat me! Beat me hard! Beat me hard! Beat me good! What I said was true!" The other hostesses tearfully threw themselves in front of Hui to protect her from the blows, crying and huddling around her, deflecting the blows and kicks onto their own bodies, while pleading to Li, "Stop! Don't beat her anymore. Don't beat her anymore! Please don't beat her anymore!!" Seeing this scene, I could not help crying myself.

I wished I could have done more than just help Hui to her bed and take care of her afterward.

Such struggles against the madam's injustice never ended well. As Bing told other hostesses, "Had it not been Hui but any other one of you who spoke up [Hui was the "bar mainstay," *tai zhu zi*], I would have broken your legs and driven you away." Bing always beat up the hostesses who did not obey him. At times, when other bar owners came to borrow hostesses, he ordered some hostesses to go. Once when a hostess did not want to go, he shut her in a room and beat her up. Other times, when some hostesses slipped away to other bars to sit onstage, they always received a good beating when they returned. Bing yelled at the hostesses, "If anyone does not listen to me, I will beat you to death!"

Bing had raped almost every hostess in the bar, but no hostess dared to utter a word about it. As Dee once said:

> They beat us up anytime they want! You think this [profession] is so easy? Who are we? Hostesses! The bar boss and managers belong to the upper class, and we belong to the lower class. I know that. Bing can rape us any time he wants, and we cannot utter a word! Sometimes I fought with Bing, but the other hostesses just tolerated it. I think if we could unite together, we would be in a much better situation. However, some hostesses like Lynn fell in love with Bing and flattered him all the time! They get pushed to the clients by Bing and earn handsome tips every day.

Hostesses' Intrarelationships

Dee's criticism of the lack of collective action among the hostesses resonated with other hostesses in the bar. This criticism is at odds with previous research that highlights the centrality of native place for migrant workers' political alliances and networks. Numerous significant ethnographic and historical studies of migrant workers in Tianjin, Shanghai, Subei, Hankou, Guangzhou, Shenzhen, and Beijing document the crucial role that native-place networks play in providing mutual financial and emotional support and organizing protests and strikes.[4] Calling this alliance a "localist network," Ching Kwan Lee illustrates its significance in the lives of women workers in Shenzhen. This network assists women in securing jobs, teaching them work skills, and offering them emotional and financial help. Similarly, Pun Ngai's research on women workers in Shenzhen emphasizes kin-ethnic enclaves developed in the workplace in a "honey-comb" pattern, that is, with the core kin in the middle and the family members and relatives on the periphery.[5] She elucidates how kinship and ethnicity intersect in cementing group formation and in providing the best type of assistance in a hostile city. In fact, migrant women's informal ties are so strong that they project the possibility of labor resistance. As Ngai states, it "silently render[ed] support to the social revolution from below by migrant workers in the city."[6] To control production, managers find it necessary to break up kin-ethnic groups by inserting outsiders into the work group.[7]

What made the Dalian hostess group unique from nonhostess migrant workers in the previous studies? The failure to mobilize collectively was not because they had succumbed to the persuasive patriarchal powers. Rather, as I came to conclude, it was because collective mobilization was severely inhibited by two key factors: one was the possibility of breaking out of the subordinated group (in game-theory terms, there are incentives to defect rather than cooperate); and the other was the potential cost of cooperation.

There was constant tension between the hostesses' loyalty toward their subordinate group and the allure of potential benefit that could be reaped by defecting from the group. For many hostesses, it was their aspiration to break out of the group and subvert the current hierarchical social order. As long as a portion of the people had the prospect of defecting from the group, they would not be able to mobilize together. They would not jeopardize their chance of defection by submitting themselves to the group too much through mobilization. Thus, the interest-maximizing choice of individual group members ultimately resulted in the loss of interest of the whole group. For instance, in the above-mentioned scenario where some hostesses tried to mobilize together against exploitation by the bar owner, a couple of hostesses stood by the owner for fear of losing their status and interest in the bars—and thus their chance of upward mobility.

Hostesses' group-identification was highly mercurial and context-sensitive: it changed as circumstances changed. At times of collision or conflict with urbanites, hostesses with rural backgrounds temporarily united to confront the threat. In one instance, an urban hostess "stole" a rural hostess's client by displaying her urban ID and denigrating the other hostess's rural background in front of the clients. The rural hostesses responded by collectively criticizing, cursing, and threatening violent retaliation against the group of three urban hostesses in the bar. It should be noted, however, that this alliance was transient and did not precipitate cooperation in other areas of endeavor.

At other times, rural hostesses disidentified with their rural relatives when they came to visit them. For instance, hostess Lin's cousin sought her help to work as a hostess in the bar. Lin brought her over to the bar around 6 P.M. to chat with everyone and explore job opportunities. The next day Lin said that her cousin was too *tuqi* (unsophisticated, like a hick) to work as a hostess there. Everyone else agreed that there was simply no way to cover up her rural aura. Lin said, "Whatever she puts on, she still has the *tuqi* taste. She is just not suitable for this job." Lin's use of words and tone of voice sounded exactly like an urban woman denigrating a rural woman. In the end, through her network with a client, Lin found her cousin a job at a restaurant. On other occasions, hostesses ruthlessly commented on rural people and their village folks as stupid *(ha le)* with "peasant consciousness" *(nongmin yishi)* or "small peasant psyches" *(xiao nongmin xinli)*. Under these circumstances, hostesses emphasized their cosmopolitan attributes over their rural backwardness.

The possibility of collective action was not only impeded by hostesses' incessant repositioning between groups (and outright denial of group affiliation) but was also curtailed by internal group competition. As I was told, their main competitors were other hostesses. They struggled to discard their rural roots and competed with other rural migrants to break out of the subordinated group and attain upward mobility. For instance, because it often happened that hostesses stole each other's clients, hostesses learned to guard against each other (for instance, they did not introduce their own clients to others). Meanwhile, they competed with each other over onstage times, clients' status, and benefits earned from their clients.

Hostess Hong and I were very good friends. She invited me over to her rented apartment to stay many nights when we confided to each other about our personal lives. However, as close as we were, she never introduced her boyfriend to me. When her boyfriend rented an apartment for both of them, she asked me to help her move to the new apartment. She told me to come at 8 A.M. Sunday morning, adding casually that her boyfriend would join us as well. I went at the requested time but never saw her boyfriend. Around 9 A.M. when the moving was over, she asked me to leave because her boyfriend was coming soon. Only then did I learn that she had arranged for her boyfriend to come at 9:30 A.M. so that he and I would never meet. Hong's cautionary attitude was well justified in the hostesses' group where snatching each other's clients and boyfriends was common.

Hostess Shi and Ying were both from Anshan in Liaoning Province. They came together to the bar as very good friends, and they were always together. Like everyone, I thought they were best friends. One night Ying was crying in a karaoke room alone. When I asked her why, she said,

> Everyone thought Shi and I were best friends because we are locals
> *[laoxiang]*, but in fact, I am better friends with Dee and the others than
> I am with Shi. Shi and I are just not compatible because we have different
> characters. Shi has always cheated and hurt me. Yesterday Shi's client
> *[laogong]* asked me to go to a sauna bar with him. I can assure you that
> I was just sitting there in the hall with him and did not do anything. In
> fact, I was trying to say good words about Shi because he was criticizing
> her. Later, Shi heard about our excursion and came over to the bar. She sat
> beside the man and tried to irritate me. She was talking with the man
> loudly and laughing all the time, totally ignoring me. I did not have any
> interest in that man, and now she is doing all this to irritate me. In the
> end I said I am leaving.

Ying was crying the whole time when she was telling the story. In another room everyone was gossiping about Ying and Shi: "If Ying did not do anything with that man, how could Shi be angry with her? That man is Shi's client and loved Shi so much. How come Ying intruded and went with him to the sauna bar? She is crying so much, but nobody has any sympathy for her! Ying has all the schemes *(xinyan)* in her heart." Others continued, "Yes, you can make good friends with Shi because she is very easygoing, but not Ying at all. Remember when she first came here? She looked like an old grandma *(lao da ma)*, extremely ugly. Now she looks much better than before. When they first came here, she always spent Shi's money. Remember every time when they had meals? It was always Shi who paid the bill. But when Shi borrowed money from Ying, Ying immediately demanded a return." Apparently the hostesses were used to the scheme of friends stealing each other's men and felt indignant about the fact that Ying went out with Shi's client, regardless of her original intention. In spite of the emphasis placed on localist networks in the literature on migrant workers, my research of hostesses showed that although Shi and Ying appeared to be best friends bound by localist ties, these ties were always trumped by the possibility of gaining competitive advantage.

In addition, substantial costs associated with cooperation inhibited collective action. If hostesses mobilized together to defend their rights, the stigma on each as a hostess would be publicized. It would severely endanger rather than promote their upward mobility. Also, hostessing was only a springboard for them to move on to more respectable professions of entrepreneurship. Therefore, any kind of mobilization or unionization amongst hostesses could serve only as a barrier to their ultimate objective to stop hostessing rather than remain within it. Finally, because their work sites were subject to a series of police raids regularly each year, mobilization was highly circumscribed by political repression and hostesses' lack of political resources. In view of these significant costs, it was not surprising that hostesses evinced no motivation for collective action of any kind.

However, hostesses did ally themselves in small groups based on blood relations and exchange of benefits. Many hostesses either arrived in the city accompanied by relatives or were later reunited with relatives when they came to the city. It was not uncommon, then, to find sisters and cousins working as hostesses in the same bar. Hostess Huang and her cousin Ling bumped into each other on the street, and Huang learned that Ling was working as a hostess in a nearby sauna bar. Although the two of them had years of animosity and misgivings against each other in the village, in the city of Dalian they strategically formed a temporary alliance based on exchange of benefits. When Huang came back from Shanghai, she did not have a place to live. She contacted Ling for help. Ling's client lover Liu brought her to a nearby hotel where Ling made friends with May, the manager of the hotel and the second wife of Liu's colleague. Soon Ling and May became good friends and shared an apartment together. When Huang asked Ling for help, Ling introduced May to Huang and arranged for Huang to stay with them in their apartment. Huang stayed with them for two weeks while searching for another apartment.

While consanguinity served as a ready basis for an instrumental and temporary coalition, the number of relatives in any given bar rarely exceeded two or three, thus limiting the familial networks' impact on bar politics. Native-place associations were less common because of the threat of betrayal that other group members would divulge their identity as sex workers to the hometown community. Coalitions based on exchange of benefits were much more durable. Members of small groups not only offered advice and suggestions in dealing with clients and boyfriends, but they also provided emotional, professional, physical, and economical support to each other.

A good example of this type of coalition: when hostesses are abused by their patrons. Hua's client lover mistreated her, so Dee and several hostess friends admonished him together and demanded that he apologize to Hua. In the end, pressured by all these women, he did. In another situation, hostess Min was broken-hearted to catch her client lover sleeping with another woman in a sauna bar. Min's hostess friends took her out to a restaurant to drink the whole night, and then went to a disco so that she could forget him. Everyone told her that he was not worth it, and that she should pay all her attention and energy to earning money through going out with clients. Min followed their advice and went to hotels with clients.

What was the basis for small group formation, then? For instance, once hostess Cheng gossiped about hostess Hong in front of hostess Zhang without knowing that Hong and Zhang were friends. Cheng was severely beaten up by Zhang and a number of hostesses in Zhang's group. A hostess in one group not only supported the interests of her group members but also brought them to join her in her new job, perhaps in a more upscale bar. A hostess in an emotional crisis (for instance, abandoned or cheated on by her boyfriend) was often accompanied and comforted by members in her group. Hostesses in one group sometimes mobilized to rebel against wicked clients who had maltreated their members.

However, hostesses were often their own harshest critics. The biggest complaint that hostesses had of one another was the lack of loyalty. Hostess Di related to me how her friend of many years—a hostess in another bar—had abandoned her when she fell ill in the aftermath of an abortion. Di spoke painfully about how she was forced to ask a neighbor to help change the transfusion bottle that dripped medicine into the vein of her arm. Although Di swore to break off the relationship, she eventually had to resume it because she needed her friend's help to gain access to the madam who ran a Japanese bar. In this case, there was an instrumental reason for resuming the network.

Hostess Ling also told a story of betrayal, which she explained was a result of the often opportunistic mind-set of hostesses. When she had many clients and enjoyed a good relationship with the bar owner and management, the other hostesses tried to ingratiate themselves with her by paying her compliments on her clothes and buying her small gifts. Ling in return introduced clients to her closest friends. After Ling became ill following an abortion, however, she fell out of favor with many of her former clients and in turn her closest hostess friends.

The following example epitomizes the fleeting nature of all such coalitions. Hostesses Huang and Dong were best friends even though they came from different areas. They called each other sisters. However, the informal ties between Huang and Dong did not exist without rifts. To save rent, Dong moved into Huang's apartment, which was rented by Huang's client lover Yu, general manager of a shipment company. Dong promised that she would sleep at a sauna bar if Yu came back to stay with Huang. One day Yu called and asked Huang if she was alone at the apartment. Huang responded that three hostesses, Dong and her two friends, were there. Yu did not come back. After several weeks Huang called Yu, urging him to come back for a night, and paid about 200 *yuan* to settle Dong and her two friends at a sauna bar for a night. Although Huang treated Dong like her own sister, Dong did not reciprocate. In fact, Dong was quite jealous of Huang for her numerous lovers. Whenever seeing a man with Huang, Dong would ask the man, "Which one of us looks younger?" Because Dong was plump and looked older, men always politely commented that she looked a little older than Huang. Dong would immediately cry out, "Look at her! She is already a mother of an eight-year-old boy! How can I be older than her?!" Time and time again Dong made sure that every man Huang was with knew the fact that Huang was a mother.

Dong always asked Huang, "How come you always have good times, but I don't? Why don't you introduce me to some managers under Yu's leadership and see if we could become lovers as well?" To help her out,

Huang made Yu bring over three managers to meet with Dong and her three girlfriends. One of Dong's girlfriends hooked up with one of the managers, and another girlfriend stole Yu away from Huang. Huang was completely in the cold. Since Yu did not come back anymore, Huang decided to move out. On the day she was moving out, the woman living downstairs said to her, "You are too foolish! Do you know who has stolen your lover?" Huang shook her head with puzzlement, "Who?" The woman said, "The one you have helped the most." Huang was so angry that she confronted Dong immediately, "Do you know who has stolen *[qiaozou]* my husband *[laogong]* away?" Dong pretended that she did not know. Huang said, "You don't know? Stop lying to me! Your close friend is doing this to me. How can you treat me this way? Have you ever had a sister like me who offered you a place to live, money to stay in the sauna bar, and introduced you to men? I treat you better than your own sister, but you have totally betrayed me!" Dong had nothing to say but murmured, "I have warned you of losing him before, but you didn't listen." Huang said to her, "From now on, we are no longer friends. You have hurt me too much." Later, when Dong called up asking her to go to Shanghai together, Huang replied, "In Shanghai, I can be a good friend of yours, but in Dalian, we are not friends." Because they were going to work in Shanghai where neither had allies, they needed each other for support, causing their friendship to be at least temporarily reestablished.

As the example illustrates, regardless of the basis of clique formation, all coalitions were unstable. Competition between hostesses for scarce resources provided strong incentives to betray group members. For instance, hostess Fang found out that hostess May earned a tip from a client by promising to introduce him to hostess Fang. Another time, hostess Cheng sheltered and took care of hostess Hong for a month and a half during Hong's abortion period. Cheng was extremely unsatisfied with the low compensation fee of 200 *yuan* that Hong offered her. There were other cases of hostesses' snatching away each other's boyfriends and not looking after friends. When such betrayal outweighed cooperative behavior, the small group dissolved. Their networks existed in a constantly changing process caused by the tension of members' continuous betrayal and cooperation. Whether the group could maintain its cohesiveness depended on the overall proportion of members' cooperation vis-à-vis betrayal.

HOSTESSES' MANIPULATIONS

As Dee concluded, collective action among the hostesses was almost impossible, and individual struggles against rape and unfair treatment did not lead them anywhere. Rather, as one hostess told me, "earning tips is the most serious business." Customers were normally required to give a 100-*yuan* tip, which could be reduced to 50 *yuan* on slow nights. Out of 100 *yuan,* 10 were owed to the owner as the stage fee. This fee could be waived if the hostesses were able to bring in 240 *yuan* worth of consumption from their clients in the karaoke room. Dee told me:

> Once I was sitting with two other hostesses in the karaoke room. We agreed among ourselves to drink twenty-four big bottles of beer (10 *yuan* per large bottle) to have the stage fee waived. So we started drinking crazily to death. We almost gave up our whole lives for it. We went to the bathroom to vomit. When we could not throw up any longer, we used our fingers to help. We did not care about the severe stomachache but came back to the room and started drinking again. At last, only one bottle was left, but none of us could finish it. Just because of this one bottle, the managers refused to waive the stage fee. We were really upset and angry. We regretted what we had done and vowed to each other, "Ten *yuan* is nothing really! It's not at all worth giving up our lives." From then on, when we sat with clients, we seldom ordered a thing.

Hostesses were exploited by having to pay not only the onstage fee but also the offstage fee. The private room upstairs was prepared for clients to sleep with hostesses for a couple of hours or for a whole night *(baoye).* The price for a whole night was much higher than a couple of hours. However, it was always the barkeeper Bing who talked to the clients and negotiated the price. Hostesses working for the whole night only got half of the tip (400 *yuan*) the next morning. The other half was kept by Bing and the bar managers. No one dared to complain openly.

Later on hostesses developed ways to cope with this inequity. When clients came to the bar looking for hostesses to go offstage, few hostesses consented. It left the outsiders with the false impression that few hostesses in this bar went offstage. However, in reality, all the hostesses did, although behind the scenes, to save the entire tip for themselves. One hostess said, "Why should we earn the money for the bar managers? We have established a settled relationship with our clients. We schedule a time outside of the bar to do it. We keep the money in our own pockets. Who needs them as the mediators? Actually, everyone in our bar goes offstage, but secretly."

The bar managers and owner were stingy not only with the hostesses, but also with their steady clients. Dee told me, "Bar business should rely not only on us, but also the steady clients. However, the bar managers exploit these clients even harder!" Aware of this situation, hostesses on the one hand faced pressure to order more food and drinks in karaoke rooms, and on the other hand secretly established relationships with clients. As their connections were set up, hostesses requested that their clients take them out for dinner. In such cases, they not only earned the tip of 100 *yuan* but also helped their clients save money from the bar overcharges.

Some hostesses sat on several stages at the same time *(cuantai)*. For instance, Dee managed to sit on five stages at one time. As she explained:

> The key is: Do not let yourself be seen by your clients when you are sitting on different stages. Once I heard that five of my steady clients were coming on the same night. I was sitting in the first client's karaoke room until it was time for the other clients to come. Then I said, "I have been feeling really sick these days. I feel really uncomfortable now. Can you leave now and come back some other time?" He agreed and left, offering me a tip. Then the other clients came one after another. I went into the second client's karaoke room and said, "Look, my sister has just arrived here in Dalian with a friend. I really have to go to the train station to pick her up. It will take me about an hour or so. I will be back for sure." Then I left and went into the third client's karaoke room and said, "Look, my sister will come over to be a hostess. I need to rent her a room, buy her some clothes and merchandise for everyday use. When she starts working here, she will earn money and return the loan to me. Can you give me some money?" He gave me 200 *yuan*. See, the tip is already in my hands. "Thanks so much! I am sorry that I have to leave, but I will definitely be back in about forty-five minutes." Then I repeated the same story in the other two karaoke rooms and promised to be back in, respectively, forty and thirty minutes. After that, I returned to the first karaoke room and said, "Sorry I am back so late. Oh, I am feeling so exhausted and sick." Then I stayed there for a few minutes before asking them to leave. They gave me the tip. Then I returned to the other three karaoke rooms, in turn, and repeated the same story.

During my stay at the bar, I saw hostesses like Dee trying to accompany different clients at different karaoke rooms at the same time. One time, hostess Ping was caught doing this by one of her clients. He got so furious that he started swearing and throwing beer bottles at her. The waiters finally had to stop their fight. Apparently, Ping had sat in his stage for a while and he had already violated her body by touching and fondling. At first the client refused to give any tip. Eventually under the waiters' pressure, he paid 50 *yuan* (half of the regular tip) and left. Because Ping was the mainstay of the bar, she was only severely scolded by the bar manager.

CLIENTELE

The hierarchy of bars was closely related to the status of their clients. Among the numerous types of bars in the city, the karaoke bars, representing the highest status, charged the highest consumption fee.

Clients who frequented coffee bars, pottery bars, soft-drink bars, and music bars belonged to a social circle called "new people" *(xinxin renlei)*. These relatively young clients in their twenties had not yet established social status or wealth. Ranging from white-collar employees to university students, they pursued a "cool" bar culture at a much lower spending level. In Dalian, there was a well-known pottery bar across the street from the municipal government building. However, to my surprise, when I invited a political official to that bar, he had not even heard of its name. Eventually, when we entered the bar and ordered two drinks, he sat there restless and speechless, not knowing how to relate to the place. I tried to start a conversation, but he still appeared at a loss as to what to do. Finally, he suggested leaving for a karaoke bar and asked for the bill. It was only 12 *yuan* for two drinks. He threw 20 *yuan* at the waitress and told her to keep the change. The waitress pursued him to the door and insisted on returning his change, but he refused, complaining, "How come it's so cheap? How can the bar owner earn money, really!" The low spending level in such types of bars thwarted the desire of officials and entrepreneurs to show off their social status and wealth. Karaoke bars, however, offered a desirable space that suited such needs. It was a significant status symbol to be able to comfortably enter karaoke bars and feel at home.

Men who went to upscale bars varied from local government officials to nouveaux riches, businessmen, policemen, and foreign investors. For many young women, these men were ideal husbands because of their wealth and their high social class (for instance, having a prestigious profession).

A hostess hoped to be lucky enough to meet a nice man who would take her as his wife. During my research at the three karaoke bars, six hostesses were married to their customers and left the bar scene, setting an example for the remaining hostesses to follow. Karaoke bars offered them an opportunity to socialize with these higher-class men and even become a member of their circle through marriage.

A few high-tier karaoke bars in the city were especially renowned for serving high-ranking official clients. Clients in medium-tier bars fell into a wider range, from nouveaux riches and entrepreneurs to officials of all levels. During my research at Prince, I encountered corporate and enterprise managers, judges, police, and officials, among others. These clients were similarly recognized for their eminence and prestige.

During my research at Romantic Dream, only one official friend came to visit me, and only once. He told me, "I cannot come here anymore. It really ruins my reputation to come and visit here." Since I told him about my research in that area, the political official had been acting very distant. In his eyes, I was not only associated with this low-status and infamous place but was also a potential carrier of a sexually transmitted disease (STD). As a matter of fact, he constantly asked me to have my blood checked in the hospital because staying in that bar I might have become infected. This official knew that I did not sexually service customers. His view reflected not only his ignorance of how STDs were transmitted but also how the red-light district was viewed as dirty and contaminating.

This area of the red-light district was considered stinky and notorious. Its clients were regarded as men of the lowest quality. As the medium-tier bar owner told me:

> Only those who have earned a little money and have no idea how to squander it will go there to show off. They are the least educated men in the city. Some are even blue-collar workers. Hostesses there are of the lowest class. They are dirty and ugly. If clients here mention that they have visited that area, they will immediately be mocked and despised. People will think that they belong to the lowest class! The spending level there is really low. Here, if a client comes in inquiring about the karaoke room rental fee and fruit plate rate, he will be instantly looked down on. Clients with wealth and social status never inquire about price. They walk directly into the karaoke rooms before reading the menu. They know about the rate because they frequent such places.

It was true that clients tended to demonstrate their power and wealth by walking directly into the bar without caring or inquiring about the spending level. During my research, every time I followed a political official and his friends to karaoke bars, they never read the menu before ordering drinks, snacks, and fruit plates. The ability to march right in and order without consulting a menu indicated the clients' high social status and prestige.

By contrast, in the low-tier bars, many clients asked and negotiated the price (room rental fee, hostesses' service fee, and so on) with bar managers before entering the bar. The room rental fee was always waived with a big discount on the bill. At times the hostesses' service fee was even lowered to 50 *yuan*. Hostesses jokingly called the bars on this street "paupers' paradise" *(qionggui daleyuan)* because they catered to the poor.

However, a bar's infamous reputation was known only by the local people, not by outsiders. Therefore, the city's red-light district attracted outsiders visiting Dalian as tourists or on business trips. As a result, clients frequenting the area were very diverse: petty entrepreneurs (foreman and heads of construction companies, for example), foreign and Chinese tourists, foreign businessmen, police, a few white-collar workers, and such blue-collar workers as migrants, garbage collectors, construction workers, taxi, and truck drivers.

Karaoke bars reflect post-Mao social stratifications, as the patrons' social status was not only matched by the status of the karaoke bars but also indicated by their way of consumption. Blue-collar workers and migrants, while negotiating the price to emulate this lifestyle by paying for occasional visits to low-tier karaoke bars, could not hide their low social class.

Although ranked vertically, all karaoke bars coalesce in their exploitation and violence against hostesses. Hostesses are cognizant of their low position in the hierarchical relationships in the sex industry. Although victims of a hostile political policy and an exploitative sex industry, hostesses' chances and concern for social mobility thwart their collective action. Nonetheless, hostesses do form unstable small-scale group cliques and rely on these networks for help and security. These informal networks, facilitated and enabled by blood relationships, common rural background, native place, and mutual benefits, are transient and temporary due to the internal competition and the costs and risks of protests.

Four

TURNING IN THE GRAIN:
SEX AND THE MODERN MAN

THIS CHAPTER LOOKS AT THE LINK between the body and the economy. Once a Marxist political economy, the current Chinese economy has recently gained independence with the decline of orthodox Marxism and the rise of neoclassical economics. This independence from politics has made the economy available for metaphoric use. The metaphor works both ways: economy as body and body as economy. The former is evident when economists "diagnose" economic problems as cancers or other illnesses that hamper the operation of the economic system. The line dividing state and private spheres (for example, the society) has never been clearly drawn in Chinese history, applying even to private considerations such as sexuality, where the state has historically regulated prostitution. Therefore, it was easy to use sexuality in making the transition away from a state-planned economy. This transition was channeled through a new cultural form, the karaoke bar imported from Japan. In this chapter I will show that the system of Chinese state clientelism explains why it is the hostess's body that is employed to redeem or recover men's masculinity. My thesis is that because of the involved risks and social trust in the alliance between entrepreneurs and officials, sex consumption serves as an institution for the preselection test and bonding activity that ensure social trust in the alliance.

An economic understanding of the body sees the body as composed of various resources that, according to circumstances, require conservation, investment, and so on—in short, management. The brunt of the responsibility for this complex operation falls on the individual as the owner of the body. Although men in the Maoist era did not need to worry about allocation of resources or self-control, the post-Mao society gives them entrepreneurial freedom to manage their bodily assets and to assert self-control. My hypothesis is that the greater the subjective strain on the male body's sexual function, the more likely it is that an economic view of body will emerge. This is reminiscent of the somatization of social stress discussed by Arthur and Joan Kleinman.[1] Although I have not systematically researched the body perception of other male groups, my experience of interaction with nonclient men suggests to me that their view of the sexual body is less economic than most of the clients seeing hostesses at karaoke bars. It is not the case that clients have more sex than nonclient men but simply that the clients have to allocate their sexual attention between multiple objects—their wives and any number of hostesses.

In this chapter, I take issue with previous theorists who argue that men patronize hostesses to sustain their masculine power. Instead, I argue that in China the underlying reasons are far more complex. Clients conceived of their sex consumption as the embrace of a Western-oriented model of modernity and a rejection of artificial restraints imposed by a puritanical Confucian-socialist system. They made an analogy of turning in their *jing* (semen) to their wives just as the peasants turned in the grain tax to the state. I argue that clients perceived themselves as the managers of their bodily assets and exercised what I call "misappropriation," that is, they allocated their semen between their wives and hostesses as a mode of resistance to attain an independent body, just as *liang* (grain) was misappropriated by peasants who rebelled by cheating the government of their taxes.

Clients' "consumption" of hostesses becomes the criterion by which clients evaluate each other's moral quality and business competence in Chinese state clientelism. Male consumers strive to demonstrate a rational, "cool" masculinity by conquering the emotions of female sex servers, thereby proving their own emotional self-control and ability to manipulate the emotion of others. Such traits are highly valued among these men, whose activities often fall into gray or prohibited areas of the law. Success or failure at projecting a masculine image crucially determines participation and relative position within the elite, male-dominated circles of Chinese business and government.

AN ETHNOGRAPHIC VIGNETTE

Through an old classmate, Xie, I was able to experience a karaoke bar scene from the point of view of the patrons. This experience provided an insight into the complex reasons for the patrons' sex consumption. As with the courtesans in ancient China, who tested the mettle of young men, these modern courtesans of Dalian provided a testing ground for contemporary alliances of Chinese entrepreneurs and officials. As I would see during the evening, the pursuit of pleasure was entangled with a bonding and testing process. The men would share companionship and pleasure but would also attempt to demonstrate their self-control through their emotional detachment from, and control of, the hostesses. In this highly competitive jungle of modern capitalism, not all are fit. Capitalism asks, Are you man enough to make the grade? In the modern corporate world, one must not only be fit but fit in. Shared masculine values and shared striving create unit cohesion. One aspect of the karaoke bar is masculine triumph over women. Triumph in the bar prepares men for triumph in the market world.

Xie, a high-level official in Dalian, introduced me to his three friends. They were part of his social base that helped secure his official position and wealth. Their relationship illustrates that the lines between state and society, public and private spheres are not clearly drawn in China. Hu and Ren were owners of private enterprises. Jin was the head of a police bureau in the central district of Dalian. More than a thousand karaoke bars, hotels, restaurants, sauna salons, and nightclubs fell under his jurisdiction. Xie emphasized to me the importance and inherent danger of these connections. Nobody can rise to power without the help of one's friends, and nobody can maintain that power if one of those friends fails. Each "friend" contributes and receives, in what, if successfully cultivated, can develop into a long-term exchange relationship. Each of the friends had resources to offer the others: Xie, his official power; Hu and Ren, their economic power; and Jin, his legal and administrative power. To strengthen their ties, they often gathered in restaurants, karaoke bars, and sauna salons. The bill was always taken care of by the entrepreneurs Hu and Ren.

One night after a banquet at the most luxurious Korean barbecue restaurant in Dalian, I followed these four people to an upscale karaoke bar in the center of the city. On the way, Xie reminded everybody not to disclose his identity to the bar boss. Everyone agreed. We finally arrived at a splendidly furnished karaoke bar. The bar boss, a young and charming woman in a tight black shirt and funky white pants, warmly received us as we entered a large antechamber. She led us into a small rented room and served us beverages and tea. Sitting on the sofa next to Xie, the bar boss gazed at him through shining eyes. "I haven't seen you for a long time," she murmured. "Where have you been? You know, if one day I am laid off, I have to depend on you to help me find a job!"

"Oh," Xie replied with a very sullen expression on his face. "I've been busy lately. I went to the United States to study for an MBA degree and did not get back until recently." These words were uttered with such sincerity that no one would have suspected that this was in fact a lie. As Xie must have anticipated, the bar boss, upon hearing these words, immediately moved closer to him, her large eyes now getting bigger and shining with enthusiasm, "Really? How is the world out there? What is it really like?"

Xie put down his cup, not even looking at her, and said in a very impassive voice, "It's all right. People work under too much pressure there, not like us Chinese. We really know how to enjoy ourselves." These were the exact words I had told him earlier when he asked me what America was like. It amused me so much that I almost burst into laughter, but at the same time I was surprised that my offhand comment had been so quickly absorbed and reemployed in his performance of masculinity. Evidently, demonstrating an urban knowledge of the world, and in this case American life, conveyed potency.

Xie at this point stood up and said, "I think we should go." Puzzled and perplexed, we followed him out of the bar. As we were walking toward the car, Hu made the comment that this woman was kept as a mistress by a man named Liu. Jin immediately corrected him and said that Liu was already dead and that she was now kept by another man, Chen. Hu then acknowledged his mistake. Xie at this point asked cynically, "Who the hell hasn't she been involved with?" Seeing Xie was upset, the two men started teasing him: "See, Xie must have something at stake here." We finally urged him to disclose his story:

> It is so disgusting to meet her here. I got to know this woman originally in a bar where she served as a bar hostess. She came from the countryside. She served as my hostess and eventually we became involved in a "very close relationship." She soon became a madam with a handful of hostesses working for her. We were "very close friends." One night I was invited to a banquet to meet with the most powerful people in the city. The

moment I stepped into the room, I heard people teasing a very powerful city celebrity and his mistress. I turned around only to find that the woman in his arms was none other than she. It was not until that night that I found out that she had been that man's mistress for a long time. Ever since then I haven't wanted to see her. The mere thought of her makes me nauseous. I have made up my mind that next time, before I go to a dinner party, I will make sure that I ask first who the participants are before deciding to go. If I ran into her again, I would be too disgusted. Now she is already a karaoke bar boss. What a jump! Already she has climbed so high with the support of her powerful man! Such a worn shoe [whore]!

The other men soon chimed in, joking about his awful experience and condemning women such as the bar boss who exploit their beauty and sexuality to dupe men into giving them money and status. However, they soon started teasing each other for having slept with too many hostesses. One could sense the tension that they experience between real emotional attachments to hostesses on the one hand and a masculine ideal that requires cool detachment on the other. While Xie was attempting to treat the hostesses as an instrument for his own purposes, he resented their manipulation of him. He testified to his friends that he was able to see through the hostesses' deceitful façade and maintain a cool distance from them. Indeed, it is precarious to show a sign of succumbing to an emotional involvement with hostesses, which, according to the code of the patrons, signals moral weakness and potential betrayal.

This tension was also evident when we finally came to an adjacent bar. Everybody was teasing Hu because he was anxious that he might run into the hostess he used to keep as a mistress. The bar boss, apparently a friend of theirs, warmly led us into a karaoke room. "You know," Jin remarked to me, "what we hear here the most is, 'My parents are seriously ill,' 'My brothers and uncles are in debt.' . . . Men feel sympathetic and are willing to support them with money. For instance, Hu has been financing so many hostesses secretly." Everybody laughed. Hu added, "We men are just performing here because we all know hostesses only recognize money, not us. However, there are also cases where men fall in love with them and are eventually cheated by them. Jin is one of them. Jin, why don't you tell us about your previous experiences with the two hostesses you fell for?" Jin laughed. "You know," he said, "we police also play around. If we catch Hu in bed with a hostess, I have to let him go. After all, he is my friend, right?"

At these words, a team of heavily made-up and provocatively dressed hostesses filed in, facing us and looking at us eagerly and flirtatiously. Jin shouted at them, "Who loves me at first sight? Raise your hand!" No reaction from the group. Jin yelled again, "Nobody falls in love with me?" Hu directed his finger at a hostess and commanded, "You. Let me see you! You! Come over. You, the one beside the girl with the permed hair. You come over and serve Jin. You, come over and serve Xie." Then he pointed at another hostess to sit by his side. Three hostesses came over and sat beside each of them. Hu said to me, "What these hostesses dislike the most is to stand in line waiting to be chosen. Men point at them one after another, ordering: you, you, you, come over and sit here. What we men dislike the most is to take out money and offer tips." Everyone laughed. It is prevalent in this setting that patrons display their masculine power through pointing at hostesses and ordering them around. It is also evident that by asking hostesses if they have fallen in love with them, patrons try to prove that they are desirable partners.

I was sitting next to Jin's hostess, a young woman with long hair, wearing a transparent black shirt displaying her black bra and most of her breasts. Jin was holding her in his arms, asking, "Did you fall in love with me?" The hostess threw her head into his chest, replying with a tint of embarrassment, "Yeah!" Jin continued, "Then why didn't you raise your hand?" The hostess said, "How could I do that? I am a shy girl. Besides, if I had done it, how could I face the other hostesses tomorrow?" Jin asked about her age and hometown. She replied that she was twenty-two, from Jilin. Jin made the comment that she looked like a movie star. He said, "Look at the eyes. They are so deep and beautiful." Each man studied her eyes carefully. The hostess laughed coquettishly, "Don't tease me!" Hu turned to his hostess and said, "Look at mine. She has small eyes like Lin Yilian [a Hong Kong singer]."

Hu turned to Jin and his hostess, commenting, "I find that both of you actually look quite alike. You should become a couple. Hostess, this is really true: he is going to divorce tomorrow. So you need to grab this chance. His wife has eloped with a guy who sells sweet potatoes." Jin cut in, "I am a shoe repairman." His hostess laughed, "It is okay. I am willing to marry a shoe repairman." Hu followed, "Or I will get divorced for you as well. How about that? Are you going offstage *(chutai)* with us tonight? I will pay you a lot more." The hostess was laughing, "No." Jin asked her, "How long have you been doing this?" The hostess replied, "One year."

She stood up and said, "I have to put my bag away." She left the room, and we heard her talking on her mobile phone. Shortly she came back. Xie reprimanded her in a severe voice, "If you go out calling someone again, we will ask for a change of hostesses." She appeared quite upset. Jin said, "Why don't you go offstage with me tonight? I want someone to sleep with me." The hostess kept silent. Jin raised his voice, "Are you going offstage with me? If not, get out, and ask for another one to replace you." The hostess stood up and left angrily, shouting to the other hostesses, "The client wants someone who goes offstage!"

Soon another hostess with permed curly hair and scarlet lips came in. She was also wearing a transparent top exposing her bra and breasts. No sooner had she sat down than Jin started interrogating her, "Are you going offstage with me?" The hostess nodded her head, "Sure." Jin asked, "How much?" The hostess replied, "I don't know; the same as the market price." Jin continued, "What is the market price?" The hostess did not reply directly: "You have never been to the bars?" Jin replied, "No, I have never been to the bars." He turned to another hostess, who responded, "I don't know. Cost nothing." Jin's hostess uttered, "It costs a sack of potatoes." Xie cut in, "That's only 50 *yuan*." Hu asked, "Are you talking about Heilongjiang rotten potatoes?" She replied, "No, good potatoes, about 300 *yuan*. That's the regular price here." She then corrected herself, "Sorry, I meant two sacks. Sorry, I said it wrong." Jin said, "You mean 600 *yuan*?" Hu cut in, "Why don't you do it with both of us tonight? I will offer you double that price." Jin looked at his hostess, asking, "Will you?" She replied, "No, I would only go with *you* because you are my man. I am not the type of woman who follows any man who offers the most." Jin exclaimed, "Well said!" hugging the hostess even closer to him.

The three men started bragging about how they once spent more than 4,000 *yuan* on beer, French wine, ecstasy *(yaotouwan),* and the hostesses' strip performance. They were encouraging the three hostesses to perform a strip dance after taking ecstasy. Hu turned to Jin's hostess, "Last time when I was here, a guy took ecstasy and was totally drunk. When his hostess asked him to dance, he turned around and poured a whole bottle of wine onto her hair, face, clothes, and everywhere on her body. Now I realize that you were that hostess!" Jin's hostess said, "Right. At the time I was so angry."

Jin's strategy of eliciting from the hostess a confirmation of his own appeal to women, affirming his manhood and masculine charm, was a transparent use of the hostess as a vehicle to demonstrate his charisma and potency, and ultimately, his power, to his business partners. It is apparent that the power of the patrons is demonstrated both by their conspicuous consumption and by their capricious treatment of the women.

The clients and hostesses began telling off-color jokes. They laughed and the clients snuggled with their hostesses. I asked Jin, "Have you ever given the hostesses your name card?" Hu replied, "Never. Only foolish men will give out name cards. Once I distributed my friend's name card to many hostesses. I told them, 'If you ever want to open a business or change your residential status, call me anytime.' The next day my friend received numerous calls from the hostesses. He was confused. The hostesses said, 'Don't play around. You were with me in bed last night.'" Everyone laughed, but his story did make me realize that a certain amount of trust was entailed in going to the bars together with men who might be able to use it to cause trouble in the future.

As I was singing songs, I heard the hostesses playfully laughing and shouting behind me. I turned around and saw in the darkness that all three men were pulling their hostesses' heads onto their chests and trying to kiss and fondle their breasts and other parts of their bodies. The hostesses were flirtatious and coquettish, half-resigned, half-resisting. They were laughing and murmuring to each other. I quickly turned around to avoid embarrassing them and myself. After quite a long while, the three hostesses started entertaining the clients with poems, "On a spring night, sexual harassment is everywhere. Shouts from beds are floating in the wind. Virgins are turned into aunties. What is lovely about virgins? Hymen is the best. What is lovely about the aunties? Aunties' work is the best."

"Turning in the Grain Tax"

Clients used the phrase "turning in the grain tax" (*jiao gongliang*) to refer to having sex with their wives. Although grain taxes have existed in China since imperial times, the particular term used here—*gongliang*, literally "public grain"—is a product of the Maoist period. Early Communist rhetoric contrasted the voluntary and enthusiastic attitude with which peasants donated grain to the beleaguered Red Army troops with the coercive extraction of current (Republican) and prior (imperial) regimes. Peasants' willingness to hand in the precious, life-sustaining grain during a time of food scarcity proved their revolutionary consciousnesses, while at the same time legitimizing the Communists as the true representatives of the people. This idealized relationship of giving from peasant to state has been severely undercut in recent years. Peasants no longer (if they ever did) hand in their grain tax with revolutionary enthusiasm. Indeed, refusing to pay the grain tax has become a popular method of peasant protest against a range of perceived state abuses, from local corruption to unfair grain quotas. Rather than plant for the state, peasants would much rather take their crops to the market.

This grain tax rhetoric makes the body a microcosm of the state, a characteristic of the Confucian tradition. Here the state serves as the model emulated by the family. Conceiving the body as a state rather than conceiving the state as a body is unique to China. In her discussion of the relationship between body and the state, Susan Brownell suggests that the direction goes the other way in the Western tradition.[2] In the West, the body serves as the model for the state, not the state as the model for the body. It is interesting that in this metaphor, the well-run state serves as a model for the well-run male body, but it makes the male body subordinate to the female/state, a subversion of Confucian tradition. It shows that such metaphors can be used in complicated ways. Feeling subordinated when they believe they should feel privileged, men engage in compensatory masculinity with the hostesses. The root of it all may be that they have been taught that they should feel privileged and they do not.

Although I have never heard the expression used by nonclients in conversation, I have found several examples in Internet articles. For example, "turning in the grain tax" has also become a common euphemism for vomiting, especially when induced by seasickness. The verb *jiao* as it is used here means "to give" or "deliver." It differs, however, from other words with the same basic meaning (such as *gei*) in that it tends to be used more in situations where the giver is duty-bound to the receiver, usually a higher authority; for example, the Chinese phrases for "handing in homework" and "paying taxes" all use *jiao,* not *gei.* This unequal relationship of obligatory giving is counterpoised with the equal relationship of voluntary exchange reflected in the use of *jiao* in such compounds as "communicate" *(jiaoliu),* "negotiate" *(jiaoshe),* "trade" *(jiaoyi* or *jiaohuan),* and "social intercourse" *(jiaoji).* Many of these *jiao*-formed compounds are neologisms that were used to describe new types of modern relationships, especially in the rapidly expanding areas of international commerce and politics. *Jiao,* then, encapsulates two, very different relational logics: in the relationship of *jiao* giving, the social standing of the participants is likely to be uneven; the action is one-sided, from giver to receiver; and motivation is supplied by a sense of duty or imposed obligation. In contrast, *jiao* exchange occurs between subjects who, at least theoretically, are equals; there is a two-way give-and-take; both sides act out of self-interest.

LIANG

Liang is difficult to translate into English because it groups together classes of agricultural products—grains, legumes, and potatoes—that have no broader heading within the English-language food taxonomy. It is often translated as "grain" or "staple foods," but neither is very satisfactory: the former is a subset of *liang* and therefore cannot represent its entirety; and while the latter may be construed to cover the food types represented by *liang,* it also conventionally includes many items like salt and oil that fall outside the scope of *liang.* I therefore have eschewed the use of such English semiequivalents in favor of retaining the original Chinese term.

The symbolism of *liang* is deeply rooted in ancient Chinese culture. As K. C. Chang observes, a basic organizing principle in Chinese food is the distinction between *fan* (the semantic equivalent of *liang*) and *t'sai (cai)* (meats and vegetables cooked into dishes).[3] This division transcends the often considerable differences in regional culinary culture, indicating its fundamental nature. Based on his analysis of food sacrifice in Zhou mortuary ritual, Chang concludes that *fan-liang* occupied a more fundamental position than *cai* dishes in a Chinese hierarchy of foodstuffs.[4] The importance of *liang* is evident in everyday culinary life as well. *Liang* typically serves as the foundation of the meal: dishes are eaten on top of a base of *liang*; and, while the eating of dishes can be forgone in difficult times, it is impossible to become full without eating *liang*.

LIANG AND JING

Not all *liang*, however, is equal; nor are the consumers who eat *liang*. The type of *liang* one eats has historically served as an index of social standing within the community—more expensive, higher-quality *liang* flowing into the bowls of the wealthier social segments, while poorer families make do with inexpensive, low-quality *liang*. In an early 1940s Shandong village, M. C. Yang distinguished four classes based solely on *liang* consumption.[5]

Such divisions have not always been a product of unequal purchasing power but, rather, were imposed by fiat from above. Under Japanese rule, *liang* in Dongbei was divided into two grades: class A (rice, flour, and soybean) and class B (sorghum, corn, millet, and other coarse cereals). Only Japanese residents were permitted to consume class A grains. Even Chinese with the necessary economic means were forbidden access to these higher-grade types of *liang*. Manchukuo law made possession of class A *liang* by a Chinese an "economic crime." Who ate what kind of *liang* eventually became a way of identifying the two groups: the Japanese as rice eaters; the Chinese mainly as sorghum eaters. According to Y. N and L. K. Hsu, this distinction even seeped into everyday language: it was said that "a situation of desperation from which there was no pleasant way out" was "like a Japanese eating *gaoliang* [sorghum]."[6]

The above situation forms the hermeneutic background for interpreting the metaphoric use of *liang* by clients. It is perhaps not coincidental that the original meaning of *jing* (semen) in ancient Chinese was "high-quality, fine rice." The comparison between *liang* and *jing* implied in this expression has roots in the Chinese language. The later usage of *jing* retains this sense of food as a life-giving source. Compounds like *jingqi* (essence and energy), *jingshen* (spirit), and *jingli* (vigor) reflect this aspect.

The relationship between *jing* and *liang* is not only linguistic but also functional: the former gives or produces life; the latter sustains it. Beginning in the early twentieth century, these two functions were seen to be in competition with each other. The past of *jing* and *liang* is intertwined with the historical transformations of China over the past century. Expropriation of *liang* through exorbitant taxes was seen as a key expression of peasants' exploitation under feudalism. *Liang* was valorized as the condensation of peasants' "sweat and blood" *(xuehan)*. *Jing* is both semen and seminal essence. It was traditionally considered finite, and if excessively ejected it could lead to weakness and death.[7]

If the two halves of this metaphor are merged together, it reads: the husband/peasant pays his *jing*/grain to the wife/state. The similarity that enables this metaphor lies less in the nature of the resources *(jing/liang)* or the transacting principals (husband/peasant and wife/state) and more on the nature of the transaction in which the resource is transferred. Men feel emasculated by their wives just as they earlier felt emasculated by the Maoist state. This is clearly a self-indulgent misconception: women's sexuality does not represent a sexual demand on their husbands; rather, it is an attempt to hold on to their husbands by satisfying them.[8] Men have failed to understand the nuances of gender power relationships within the family.

JING

According to popular Chinese thought, men's bodies are fueled by a thing called *jing. Jing* is both a substance (sperm) and an intangible energy (as in *jingqi* or *jingshen*). To reflect this double meaning, I use the term *jing* throughout this chapter. These two states are often conflated in everyday practice: a man who has put in a hard day of work might tell his wife that he lacks *jing*, meaning both that he is tired but also potentially that he is not up to having sex.

Business prowess was indicated by sex consumption. Men tried to achieve sexual potency in various ways. Conservation of semen was one of them. Their conception of semen resonated with the Taoist ideology. Semen was the most essential element for sustaining men's life and vitality. Semen was also finite, whereas women's yin was infinite. Men could reach immortality by retaining their seminal essence, and any loss of seminal essence jeopardized men's longevity. Men's seminal essence could be nourished by women's yin. One of the classic books on yin and yang written in 168 B.C. preached that, "Men's vitality lies in the seminal essence. You have to take care of it, protect it, and nourish it with food and the correct sexual intercourse. Make sure that the penis is constantly erect without ejaculating the semen. Thus the seminal essence can be conserved and the body will be strong even if you are more than a hundred years old."[9]

According to this text, correct sexual intercourse is one kind of self-cultivation in the Taoist internal alchemy of mixing internal body fluids. It is accomplished through making the semen flow backwards to be transformed from *jing* (seminal essence) to *qi* (vital energy) and then to *shen* (spirit). Men should only ejaculate during a woman's fertile period, which can nourish men's brains. Other times men should absorb the maximal yin essence from the woman without ejaculation to mix female red vital essence with male white vital essence and nourish their seminal essence. Men should retain their penis in the women's vagina as long as possible because the longer it remains there, the more yin the penis will absorb.[10] It is said that men can achieve physical immortality by copulating with multiple wives and concubines. It is not good to absorb the yin from only one woman. In addition, men should sexually satisfy the women because the female red vital essence reaches its maximum at the time of orgasm. Thus men can absorb the maximum female yin without ejaculation. Also, men are encouraged to drink women's saliva after oral sex to contribute to their seminal essence. In everyday life, men should strengthen *(bu)* their yang from the "invigorating" food they consume, such as tortoise soup, sea cucumber, bird's nest, dear antlers, shark fins, ginseng, and the genitalia of male deer.

The clients' perceptions about their seminal essence seemed to resonate with this Taoist ideology. Men were very concerned about their seminal essence and intentionally strove to strengthen and conserve it. Men believed that copulating with as many women as possible, especially with virgins, helped nourish their seminal essence and life vitality. They believed that the number and age of their sexual partners determined how quickly the men would age. So they not only engaged in sex with as many women as possible, but also sought women as young as possible. They believed that copulating with young women would make them younger and more vital. Clients did not eat or drink anything cold after their ejaculation of semen. Clients told me that men's bodies were extremely vulnerable after expelling semen. Were they to drink or eat anything cold at that time, their health would be in extreme danger. Finally, clients are inclined to nourish their seminal essence through eating strengthening food. Such semen-nourishing and conserving processes were meant to strengthen men's sexual potency.

Emasculation during the Maoist Era

Clients blamed their dissatisfaction with their wives on the Mao-era revolutionary ideology that had robbed them of their unique status as men by extending equality to women. It is important to recognize the complexity of Chinese men's rebellion at this time. It begins with a rebellion against the stifling Maoist socialist state. This rebellion takes the form of sexual defiance of the values of the Maoist period. A second layer of this rebellion is a paranoid response to the perceived authority of their wives—especially the sexual demands made by their wives.[11] As post-Mao rebellious men, they attempted to recover their masculinity by establishing a more predatory sexual approach to women.

During the Cultural Revolution, men and women wore unisex clothing, and femininity was rejected as bourgeois. Mao's slogan "The times have changed, men and women are the same" was propagated. State-sponsored military training for women in school reached its height in 1964. The media extolled the female militant: Iron Girls, robust and muscular women taking the public role as proletarian workers and rejecting their former role as stay-at-home wives. They were represented driving tractors, trucks, and diesel locomotives or repairing high-voltage electric wires.

In reality, the Maoist revolution liberated neither women nor men. By creating a masculine iconic view of women, it subjected men to a competition that gave them very little latitude for self-expression. While supposedly men and women were equal, men, still carrying their traditional views, were confronted by the icon of women heroically performing male functions, such as working in the fields and defending the country. By introducing an apparent equality of dress and behavior, what really seemed to be happening was that men were forced to be supermen simply to maintain any kind of masculine identity. This robbed men of choice. They either struggled to achieve Mao's goals or faced emasculation. The efficacy of Mao's approach was demonstrated during the Great Leap Forward when millions of men nearly worked themselves to death. The Maoist state, by pretending to liberate women, had actually forged a tool to more fully control men. Once again, masculinity had been manipulated by outside forces, in this case by the state.

Body Symbolism under Mao

The Maoist intersections of body symbolism with the state-planned economy offered men security, but not freedom or social mobility. Ultimately, the lack of freedom and mobility were emasculating to men. The Maoist state-planned economy provided men with security through food. If people suffered from a chronic shortage of food in the past, the leaders of new China promised to fill their stomachs. Abundance of food—in particular, *liang*—became a core feature of an imagined communist paradise. This utopian vision reached fruition in the propaganda campaigns surrounding the establishment of public canteens in the People's Communes (1958–1961). The centrality of food to this vision can be gleaned from the visual rendering of the communes. A notable instance in this representational history is the Jiangsu Province National Painting *(guohua)* Exhibition held in Beijing in 1958. The People's Canteen was one of three themes selected for showcasing in the exhibition, indicating its high priority in the national agenda.[12] The painting—simply titled "The Canteen of the People's Commune" or, its slightly more elaborate alternate title, "Eat for Free at the Canteen of the People's Commune"—is as overstuffed as the stomachs of the peasants that it depicts. Every inch of the canvas is covered with images of material abundance: from overflowing grain bins to windmills, tree arbors, fishing boats, and so on. The visual focus of the painting, however, is centered on the idyllic walled courtyard of a traditional-looking countryside house. The courtyard is filled with people: some sitting and eating, others moving about. Just in case the idea of material plentitude wasn't obvious enough, the Jiangsu provincial committee member overseeing the project had the artists add a sign by the entrance to the canteen: "Today, three dishes and a soup, plus an additional half *jin* of pork for every person." Rather than distribute *liang* directly to rural households, it was instead collected and prepared by the canteens. Urged on by the massive overreporting of *liang* harvests, canteens opened their doors to commune members and nonmembers alike with names like Blissful Cafeteria.[13]

Although relatively short-lived, this experiment in collectivized food consumption is revealing in its explicit politicization of food and eating. According to mainland scholar Luo Pinghan, Mao had embraced the canteens as the "sprouts of Communism" or, as he is quoted as saying, actual

Communism.[14] The best way to the people's heart, the Communists concluded, was through their stomachs.[15] In this task, the Communists were
largely successful. Early reforms such as land redistribution and the formation of Mutual Aid Teams were intended to raise agricultural productivity and put more *liang* in the peasant's bowl. Under Maoism, peasants
continued to hand in *liang,* but this time to be deposited in the coffers of
a benevolent socialist state that guaranteed its equitable distribution.

Widespread famine made China's leaders realize that population growth
had seriously outstripped the lagging production of *liang.* Slogans promi-
nently displayed on the walls of public canteens exhorted citizens to conserve *liang.*[16] In the meantime, the initiation of the one-child policy in 1979
sought, among other things, to bring down the number of mouths need-
ing to be fed. This shift in population policy from pro– to anti–growth
meant that men's *jing,* if not worthless, had much more limited value. For
most couples, the birth of their first child signals the end of their reproductive careers. Any sexual activity thereafter becomes nonprocreative. The
value of *jing* plummeted. Although the Maoist state filled men's stomachs
and provided them with security, men were subject to the state-planned
economy that controlled their social movement and bodily functions.
This situation changed in the post-Mao era when men were given more
freedom and were able to self-manage and allocate their *jing.*

BODY SYMBOLISM IN THE POST-MAO ERA

Following this general economic symbolism, clients in the post-Mao era
are positioned as managers of their bodily assets. Unlike men in the Maoist era, men in the post-Mao era do enjoy a certain degree of freedom and
control. Men did not have to worry much about the allocation of resources in the Maoist era. It is the product of the same society that gives
them entrepreneurial freedom. In their sexual relationships as well as in
their economy, Chinese men are still trying to find the proper balance of
security and freedom. They do not seem to have found a healthy balance,
and in that they are representative of Chinese society as a whole.

Chief among a man's managerial duties is the allocation of *jing* assets
between his wife and the hostesses he visits. Clients' decision making is
powerfully shaped by the external constraints of state law and morality.
The phrase "The top has measures; the bottom has countermeasures"

(shang you zhengce, xia you duice) is commonly applied by clients to their sexual relationship with their wives, inverting the usual gender hierarchy of the Chinese family: the wife is on top in the position of the state, wielding power over her husband with her measures *(zhengce)*. The husband, however, is far from powerless: like other subjects of state power, he escapes his wife's control through countermeasures, freeing himself to do as he pleases. In truth, wives are anything but on top. By almost any socioeconomic measure, wives are disadvantaged in relation to their husbands: they are usually less educated and lack their husbands' social connections, wealth, and experience. This symbolic inversion of power relations places clients at the bottom. I have discussed how men felt dominated and castrated by the state's support of women's liberation during the Maoist era. This feeling of emasculation persists until today, explaining the anxiety that men feel about their relationships with their wives.

On the other hand, the state offers security in exchange for the tax. Even though clients complained that they could not tolerate their wives' "willfulness" ("She always yells at me"), none of these clients intended to divorce, as they told me in interviews. Indeed, family/wife/state offer not only security but also the constraint that comes with security. Commercial sex/sex worker/open market offer risk and the freedom that comes with risk. Maoism offered security but no freedom. As much as they might complain, most men probably would not completely give up security and are probably somewhat frightened by the insecurity of their current lives. Therefore, they undoubtedly experience some anxiety about losing this security, including anxiety about losing their wives. Proving to themselves that they are able to attract other women (not through money but through charm, as if she were another wife and not a bought woman) is one way of dealing with this insecurity.

WIVES

Clients' extramarital sexual conduct is rarely a secret to their wives. Clients are businessmen whose social interaction with associates is important to their prosperity. Much business, in fact, is conducted in karaoke bars. When confronted by their wives, clients justify their behavior as a necessary part of doing business. These men also, recognizing the economic dependence of their wives, feel free to impose an unequal code on their wives. As one client explained to me, wives were poorly positioned to directly challenge their husbands' infidelity. The comfortable lifestyle that wives enjoy—expensive clothes, frequent trips to the beauty parlor, and so on—is made possible by their husbands' earnings. Many wives do not work, and those who do would be unable to independently support themselves, much less maintain their current level of consumption. This economic dependence on their husbands rules out divorce or other strong tactics—for instance, demanding the cessation of extramarital activity—that might lead to the dissolution of the marriage. In addition, many wives seem to genuinely accept or at least cannot refute the need for such behavior. In the end, the financial security and material luxury that a wife derives from her husbands' business success may mean more to her than his sexual fidelity.

If a wife cannot prevent her husband from having sex with other women, neither does she passively submit to his philandering. Rather, a wife attempts to enlarge her "share" of her husband while reducing that of her female competitors. The organic integrity of the body, however, does not lend itself easily to such portioning. Instead, wives focus their claims on that most manly of male bodily products: sperm. As an object of contest, sperm—like hair and nails—belongs to a category of "detachable body parts"; while easily separated from the body, these objects' origin in the body grants them a special symbolic ability to represent the individual who produced them—for example, getting a lock of hair from a loved one before embarking on a long journey.

The scarcity of *jing* allows it to become an object of competition. The limited capacity of the male body to produce *jing* means that only a finite amount of it is available for sexual activity within a given period of time. This biologically imposed limitation enables an aggressive strategy of *jing* expropriation on the part of some clients' wives. For wives, then, the struggle to maintain some degree of ownership over their husbands takes the form of a contest for their husband's *jing*. In order to claim their husbands' *jing*, wives demand frequent sex from their husbands. Just going by appearances, an observer might interpret these women's demand for sex as a form of emotional consolation or, worse, an expression of sexual appetite. Both of these interpretations, of course, are incorrect: although some wives do experience a certain amount of distress over their husbands' extramarital sex, most accept it as normal. In fact, sex serves a managerial function as a way to both monitor and control their husbands. By appropriating her husband's limited store of semen, the wife limits his ability to consort with other women.

When clients leave their wives to have relations with hostesses, giving the semen to the hostesses rather than the wives, this misappropriation can be seen as a mode of resistance, just as *liang* is misappropriated by peasants who rebelled by cheating the government of their taxes. This misappropriation creates a dilemma for the client's wife. Through her husband's infidelity, she has entered unwillingly into a relationship with another woman. While this relationship is mostly indirect, mediated through the body of the man that they share, the possibility of a disease transferred from the husband to the wife may turn this relationship into a very direct confrontation. One strategy for avoiding this problem is to make incessant sexual demands on one's husband to reduce the threat of an external lover.

Client X's wife demanded that they have sex at least twice a week. Her reasoning, I believe, is typical of most clients' wives. First, a husband's ability to have sex proves that, if not completely faithful, he at least has not expended all of his *jing* on extramarital affairs. While this may seem meager consolation to those in (what they think is) a monogamous relationship, it should be kept in mind that most clients' wives do not expect total sexual faithfulness from their husbands. Rather, what counts to these women is not that they get all of their husbands' *jing* but that they get what they consider to be their fair share.

Second, wives demand sex to deplete their husband's reserve of *jing*. The reasoning here is simple: the *jing* her husband uses to have sex with her leaves him with just that much less *jing* to have sex with other women. Some wives may aim at preventing their husbands from having extramarital sex entirely. This intent is reflected in the declaration of one wife to her husband (later retold to me by the client-husband): "I'll fix you so that you can't mess around outside *[zai waimian hugao]*!" The hidden production of *jing* within the male body, however, makes it impossible for wives to determine with certainty whether they have successfully drained their husbands' *jing* supply. Most wives seem to recognize this fact and adopt a more moderate, managerial goal of keeping their husbands' extramarital sex within reasonable boundaries.

Several of my closer client informants confided in me that they had experienced impotence or erectile dysfunction *(yangwei)* in their initial or first several sexual encounters with hostesses. While these clients eventually succeeded in having sex with hostesses, the experience left an indelible impression on their perception of *jing*. The experience of impotence leads to a heightened awareness of bodily limitations.

NATURE RHETORIC

The concept of "nature" has served as a powerful rhetorical instrument in many social movements, most famously in the seventeenth-century bourgeois revolutionary's use of "natural law" to contest feudal hegemony. Its power lies in its appeal to an extrasocial "order of things" that embodies the qualities of goodness, harmony, and justice. Nature is how things should be, not necessarily how things are. Thus, the concept of nature provides social actors with a language through which to articulate their dissatisfaction with the status quo and make normative claims for social change.

In clients' words, it was the inculcated Confucian ideal that restrained and shackled them within the marriage that they were discontent with. Hence they craved a liberated Western mind and body. The "free" and "liberated" participation of clients in the purchase of sex demonstrated their dissatisfaction with, and defiance against, the socialist politics of the post-Mao era. Client Huang, a thirty-seven-year-old city cadre, expressed his contempt for what he called "perfunctory socialism": "Don't you think it's strange that China has so many nightclubs? This is a system with vast social stratifications. Socialism should not have hostesses. It's not allowed. China still wants to maintain a perfunctory socialism." Another client, Yang, general manager of a company, spoke indignantly about this issue:

> Our country needs the revenue from prostitution, but it still wants a layer of socialism to cover it up. We're fed up with it. It's by no means the natural way. Basic human nature is still forbidden, as in the Mao era. I want my basic human nature back. We don't believe in anything now. We just want to play and enjoy our life as it goes! What do we believe? Everything we were taught in school is such a huge joke and a lie! We feel cheated by the whole country. We need to enjoy what we have right now because there's simply nothing else worthwhile to do. We've been completely cheated.

The above quotation from Yang epitomizes the feelings of many men whose lives have been disrupted by the Maoist years. His statement is an understandable rationale for the freedom to enjoy an entirely hedonistic lifestyle. He is expressing the complete loss of belief in anything, the nihilism that follows the collapse of belief in Maoism. It is easier to rationalize hedonism than to respond to nihilism. However, I think it ignores the fundamental human drive that insists on meaning. What Yang is missing in his diatribe is the hidden drive for identity embedded in the new hedonism. As we discussed earlier, post-Mao men's identity is not just hedonistic, it is driven by the need to recover the masculinity lost during the Maoist era through the reassertion of male dominance over women who are being once again feminized for this purpose.

Client Yang's rationale is a complex statement on human nature and its relationship to political power and traditional morality. During my research, one of the most popular explanations of sex consumption held by both clients and the public at large is that men possess an innate and natural instinct for sexual pleasure. Most of my client informants explained that it is men's normal biological nature to crave sex just like food. If a man was satiated and warm, he could not help thinking of his sexual desire *(wenbao er si yinyu)*. "It's the man's nature." As client Jo said, "Sometimes I have to go to hostesses to release my pent-up energy. Man innately has the desire and impulse to possess women and achieve sexual power. Were Marilyn Monroe to come in right now, we would all stare at her and want to have her." Other clients pointed out that sex consumption helped stimulate their boring, mundane, and dull lives. Client Li contended, "I visit hostesses to look for stimulation and an emotional release. Stimulation from hostesses and peace with my wife form my life cycle."

Biological determinism suggests aspects of the new capitalism. Just as Adam Smith discovered the "natural" and immutable laws of economics, laws that overturned the old moral order in the name of natural law, biological determinism frees men to act with impunity regardless of the consequences. If it is natural, it is right. These ideas are appealing because they are black and white. There is none of the agonizing nuance associated with moral philosophy. Client Chang said to me, "Men release pressure and cleanse their soul by patronizing hostesses. Women are the toys because men earn money and women spend the money. Women cannot control their desires, but men can. Women are emotional and irrational animals, whereas men are rational human beings." Here client Chang expresses his rational control in sex consumption to earn his partners' trust. By reducing women to emotional toys and irrational animals, Chang elevates men as the more rational human beings. His assertion demonstrates his contemptuous attitude toward women, which indexes his eligibility as a potential partner in a business alliance.

Here, the client's rationale for his consumption of sexual services is linked to the general critique of socialism as violating basic human nature or instinct. This critique claims that socialism makes unrealistic demands on human conduct. It is "general" in that it is used to explain perceived failures of the socialist system in diverse fields of social experience. In the field of economics, the critique is used to understand the failure of the planned or command economy and the necessity for market reforms. Under the planned system, people were expected to selflessly contribute to social construction. Motivation was based on love of country and revolutionary fervor. The stagnation of the planned system and its eventual replacement by the market mechanism have led to a radical reconceptualization of human nature. This revised view has been critically informed by Western neoclassical economic thought, in particular the figure of economic man. By this view, humans are essentially selfish. The market economy, by relying on and promoting individuals' pursuit of self-interest, is therefore attuned to basic human instinct. In a word, it is natural. The opulence of market-based Western nations is seen to powerfully corroborate this thesis.

POST-MAO REBELLIOUS MEN

It is not surprising that men remembered the Maoist era as an era of emasculation. Men's feeling of political, economic, and sexual repression by the Maoist state patriarch caused them to search for their lost masculinity in the post-Mao era. Zhang Yimou in *Red Sorghum* met this need by portraying "the outlaws, drunkards, and rebels of Chinese legend" as heroes.[17] The male protagonist, a tough young peasant, demonstrates his manhood by kidnapping, ravishing, and impregnating the wife of a diseased older man whom he has killed. The old man represents the repressive state patriarchy. That he was diseased and old speaks for itself. Zhang Yimou, a post-Mao contemporary filmmaker, created this film in the 1980s, inventing a new model of Chinese masculinity. Even though he set the film in the 1930s, Zhang shows a set of figures who are defined not by passivity but by heroic action. They are free and liberated in every way, politically, sexually, and even economically. Even though Zhang Yimou has created an ideal based on the New Culture movement, it served during the post-Mao era as a model for a revitalized masculinity in China.

In the 1990s, expressions of gender differences allowed men to recover their masculine identity by reconstituting a feminine identity for women. Market reform and consumerism produced flourishing images of sexualized and hyperfeminine women. Some researchers argue that the market economy has appropriated women's bodies.[18] While Susan Brownell does not disagree with this, she argues that female images are also meant to serve the reformation of masculinity. Thus, the post-Mao era is not just about a refeminization of women, but even more about the recovery of masculinity. "We need to investigate the masculine identities that these images are appealing to," says Brownell.[19]

During the 1990s, men also required of their wives a new heightened sexuality as a means of enhancing their own masculine identity.[20] Women's sexuality became a backdrop against which men's identity was formed. The media blamed the growing divorce rate on the inability of some women to conform to this desirable sexual image. This new image of ideal women was critical in sustaining marriages. As throughout Chinese history, women once again were placed in the background, subservient to their men. What was new now was that they were supposed to be sexually provocative. In other words, women were expected to exhibit a more overt sexual desire for men. The ideal became a woman who is publicly attractive, even provocative, but who is clearly off limits to anyone but her husband. In this way she demonstrated the powerful masculinity of her husband who displayed her to others but monopolized her sexually. This epitomized "a modern hypermasculine sensualist: a superlover with special expertise in techniques and disciplines that both express and increase 'Chinese' superiority."[21] This new relationship between men and women resonated with the New Culture movement's support for a more independent, educated, and liberated woman. However, while this helped heal the bruised masculinity of the new entrepreneurial men, it came at the cost of once again objectifying women, turning them into trophy wives.

However, for the post-Mao rebellious men, the continued presence of socialist values limited their ability to express their sexual identity through a more free-ranging promiscuity. This rebellious attitude also held that socialist morality sets unrealistic standards for sexual conduct. Since Maoist times, prostitution has been classified as an "illness" of capitalist society. This definition transformed what would otherwise have been an embarrassing social blemish into a major theoretical crisis of socialist rule. Because prostitution is seen as fundamentally incompatible with socialism, prostitution's continued existence after the establishment of the New China could only mean one of two things: either China is not what the new leadership claimed it to be, that is, socialist; or, Marxist theory is wrong, that is, social phenomena are not a reflection of the economic system. Since neither conclusion was compatible with the political rhetoric of that time, the state was left with only one option: obliterate prostitution. In recent years, this hard-line stance has become considerably relaxed. This change in attitude has been made possible by Deng Xiaoping's repositioning of China along the Marxist development path. According to this revision, China has not yet entered the stage of mature socialism. Rather, China's socialism is still in a "rudimentary stage" *(chuji jieduan)* and needs to further develop its productive forces. The existence of prostitution, as with other social ills, is explained as a temporary byproduct of "social transition" *(shehui zhuanxing)* that presumably will disappear once mature socialism is achieved.

The contradictions between the official rhetoric about socialism and reality have led to the popular concept of a "moral vacuum" *(xinyang zhenkong)*, what Jian Xu calls "considerable confusion, dislocation and disillusion."[22] This sentiment was evident in manager Yang's indignant statement that they could only enjoy what they have now because they have been cheated by the lies taught to them in school. It was also articulated by another client:

> There is no future for this country! Nobody has any belief in life. Everything they consider is money and self-interest. No belief in life! What does the CCP promise the nation? What does socialism do for the people? No more than laid-off workers, too much corruption, unemployment, and increasing stratification between people! So we just want to numb ourselves by being addicted to something and do not want to wake up and face reality. The country has no future! The country also forbids people to have beliefs such as *Falungong*.

This client's rationale reflects the popular strand of thought that describes contemporary Chinese people as living in a moral vacuum because socialist ideals of self-sacrifice and cooperation have lost their legitimacy. As this client contends, socialism and the CCP bring people nothing but a sheer lie, control of belief, and social problems such as corruption, unemployment, laid-off workers, and drastic social stratification. Their criticism is directly targeted against the CCP and socialism.[23] Disillusioned by socialism and the CCP, they believe that there is "no future for the country." With nothing left to believe in, people are forced to turn to the hedonistic pursuit of pleasure and material wealth to compensate for the sense of emptiness and meaninglessness. Thus hostesses' bodies become the site on which they project their disbelief in, and defiance of, the socialist state.

PAN SUIMING

Pan Suiming, professor at the People's University at Beijing, offers several theories to explain the sex consumption of clients.[24] Pan is considered the most renowned scholar on prostitution in China. His works on the sex industry in China are so influential that they have been frequently cited by American scholars and published in various edited volumes in the United States. Pan states that the asceticism of the 1950s and 1960s when sex and pleasure were subject to total state control led to the post-Mao phenomenon of the unbridled purchase of sexual services. Men aspire to "revolutionize their ascetic lives of the past" and "prove their youth by being sexually active with young hostesses" so as not to "regret having lived empty lives in their dying moment."[25]

Sexually transmitted diseases under such conditions become "the proof of their sexual competence and potency." Pan observes that an "irreconcilable contradiction" as a result of a couple's "equal sexual relationship" also leads men to seek sex outside the home. According to Pan, in an equal sexual relationship, the husband has to selflessly contain his own sexual pleasure. Otherwise, his wife will not enjoy the sexual experience. Pan argues that many men cannot tolerate such conjugal sexual equality. Since the 1980s, countless sex booklets have instructed bridegrooms in foreplay details and methods for performance duration. As a result, unsuccessful bridegrooms have become increasingly frustrated, and sex has become a burden instead of a pleasure. Hostesses have thus become more intriguing because they never seek equality or sophistication in sexual encounters. They are servile without complaining. "Clients can, therefore, be completely selfish, lazy, and served by them."[26] Pan notes that this explains why the price of an act of fellatio and masturbation equals and sometimes exceeds that for sexual intercourse. The key attraction of these acts is that hostesses completely serve the men.

Pan also points out that, disillusioned with love, married men seek hostesses who "do not entangle them with love" *(sichanlanda)*. Such a "disillusioned love," Pan argues, is derived from the "worship of Western notions of romantic love." Single men, however, are not clients, because they "still believe in and pursue pure love, which hostesses cannot offer."[27] Pan states that some middle-aged men have been very conventional in their approach to sex. They are "not aware of sex techniques until exposed to porno videos." Their wives, however, are habituated to old ways and unwilling to try new things. So clients seek new experiences with hostesses. "Once clients enjoy sex with hostesses, they continue to seek it endlessly."

Pan divides the Chinese population into "two distinct classes" separated by a wide gap: "ugly men" and "beautiful women." Beauty is alleged to have been bestowed on the "superior class," "proud, pretentious, and most difficult for ugly men to attain." To "win the beauty's heart" and "override this class gap," men have to "cover up their ugliness with wealth," because no matter how beautiful a hostess is, "she cannot refuse a wealthy, ugly man."[28] Thus "class equality can be reached" through the consumption of sex.

Contra Pan Suiming: Importance of Social Factors

My research shows that Pan's simplistic emphasis on clients' enjoyment of sexual pleasure with hostesses fails to take into account the complex social factors behind their behavior. One could argue that it was our different research methods that led to our different research findings. While Pan based his findings on individual interviews, I based my conclusions on ethnographic research—participant observation. Compared with individual interviews, participant observation has been credited as a superior research method that allows researchers to immerse themselves in the studied culture, experience what the subjects experience, and establish long-term rapport with them.

Far from experiencing pleasure, the vast majority of clients included in my study reported that they experienced impotence the first few times they "went offstage" with hostesses. The most common reason cited for this phenomenon was excessive nervousness. In turn, impotence led to an intense sense of emasculation. After the first episode of impotence, clients continued to seek out hostesses until they were able to recover normal sexual functions. Thus, the driving motive behind sex consumption in these cases is not sexual pleasure but, rather, the interpretation of sexual impotence as loss of masculine power and dignity that can only be redeemed through the successful performance of sex with a hostess.

Other factors also relegated sexual pleasure to a minor role as the motivation for sex consumption. Because the purchase of sex was unlawful, clients wanted to prove their courage and liberation by patronizing hostesses. As some clients claimed, "It singles us out as more powerful, daring, and superior." Most important, clients felt that the purchase of sex effectively contested socialism and the politics of the whole country.

Some clients maintained that they wanted to be liberated from "Confucian ideals of human sensibilities" *(renqing)*. According to them, marriage in this ideal stressed obligation and responsibility rather than love. As one client confided in me, "In China, if a man feels indebted to his wife, he will devote his whole life to her to pay off that debt. Whereas the Americans by no means feel the same."

During my interviews, many clients attributed their patronage of hostesses to their unhappy marriages. They said that men older than thirty-six had not experienced love during their youth in the 1970s and early 1980s. This echoes the earlier discussion of the emasculation of men and suppression of male sexuality during the Maoist era. Clients claimed that most of their marriages had been arranged by relatives or friends, and thus patronizing hostesses constituted a kind of compensation for their "insufficient past" and "unsatisfying wives." Client Wang complained that his stay-at-home wife did not take care of the housework. "Like all other men," Wang said, "I expect my wife to assume her part of internal family labor—taking good care of the old and young in the family—so that I can work in the outside world. Otherwise, how can I compete well outside?" Other clients noted that their wives' constant suspicions were conducive to their visits to hostesses: "Husbands would do it just because their wives thought they did." They generally attributed their reluctance to divorce to family demands, for instance, their wives' financial dependence or their family members' (parents' and children's) love for their wives.

"My wife has a very bad temper," client Lin said. "Earlier, I would hug my wife so hard that I would not let her go. Now, I just pat her for a moment and leave. Touching her hands is no different from touching my own. This is how a thirteen-year marriage feels." There seems to be two aspects to the unhappiness of Lin's marriage. He tells us that once he was passionate about his wife, but that now touching her hand is like touching his own. He then suggests that this is simply part of having been married too long. His other complaint is his wife's willfulness. He wants a compliant wife.

Sex consumption is regarded as a form of resistance against the artificial shackles placed on human sexuality by an unnatural social system. For Yang and many other clients, Chinese Socialism and Confucianism are two parts of the same whole: an oppressive regulatory regime that stifles "human nature" and goes against the "natural way." Here, nature is defined according to the client's (and most mainland Chinese peoples') perception of the West—in particular, the United States—as a land of free and open sex.

The Chinese View of the West

The Chinese concept of the West plays a crucial role in the client's definition of nature. Here, the West does not denote a geographic region but, rather, a field of meanings. Local and global media, such as pirated Western products like video compact discs and digital video discs, form the ground on which Chinese conceptions of the West are based. These raw cultural materials are refined into complex concepts. The final product is only tangentially related to the raw materials themselves. Thus, the process is better described as the creative use of foreign cultural products rather than the direct impact of Western culture on Chinese society. Although the starting point is the unrefined foreign materials, they only acquire meaning through the reception-production process. In this sense, the West is "(re)made in China."

As this analysis demonstrates, perceptions of the West (and American society, in particular) play a critical role in shaping Chinese understanding of transformations in China's social and economic environment. Such an othering of the West—the appropriation of the West to critique the Chinese social and political system—resonates with the romanticization of the West in Japan.[29] The wealthy and leisurely Japanese women, so-called "yellow cabs," seek out white males with the alleged qualities of "kindness, sensitivity, sexiness, liberation, romantic, and erotic sentiment," which are claimed to be lacking in the Japanese male.[30] These Japanese women attempt to shift from a "backward and oppressive" Japan to what they see as "an exhilarating and liberating foreign realm," and "the inevitable destination in a unilineal tale of progress," explains researcher Karen Kelsky.[31] White men are commodified, packaged, and sold as romantic heroes and "the agent[s] of women's professional, romantic, and sexual liberation."[32] Kelsky argues that the racialized and sexualized meanings of white men are deeply entrenched in the "histories of modernity, colonialism and white hegemony in the west and globally."[33] Such an "international modernity is seen as offering them their very first chance at unfettered freedom."[34]

This theme of the West as the eroticized Other is also reflected in the banned Chinese novel *Shanghai Baby* by Wei Hui.[35] In this novel, the protagonist Coco's Chinese boyfriend Tian Tian is physically and emotionally impotent, leading her to a passionate affair with a married German businessman, Mark. Mark is virile, sensual, natural, and sexual, whereas Tian Tian is impotent and addicted to drugs, like the stereotype of the "Sick Man of East Asia" in the nineteenth century, who was effeminate and addicted to opium. Coco wants her Western lover to rape her "as a fetishist and a 'fascist' representative of Shanghai's colonialist past." Coco says, "Every woman loves a Fascist," and the greatest appeal of the Western lover is "his aggressive jack-booted sexual domination." Coco identifies with the Western ideology of materialism and liberation and seeks sexual pleasure and liberation. *Shanghai Baby* represents many Chinese people's dilemma between embracing the "liberated," "modern," and material West and clinging to the spiritual Chinese essence. Such ambivalence is grasped vividly in Coco's searching travail between sexual liberation with a virile Western man and spiritual entanglements with an impotent Chinese man.

GLOBALIZATION AND THE RISE OF ENTREPRENEURIAL MASCULINITY

China's economic success and increasing participation in global networks has led to its greater confidence and reduced anxiety about gender and state sovereignty. In the 1990s, the impotent men of the Communist state were replaced by wealthy male entrepreneurs. "Their reaction to the loss of Chinese women on the international marriage and sex markets was not so much to protest the practices of foreign men as to imitate them when they got the chance,"[36] states Susan Brownell, once again dramatizing the triumph of commerce over nationalism. Mayfair Yang observes that Chinese entrepreneurs, instead of taking offense to the Taiwanese and Japanese businessmen who had taken Chinese mistresses, simply emulated them and took mistresses themselves.[37]

While young entrepreneurial men recovered their economic and sexual potency, older, retired cadres were faced with impotence.[38] So devastated was this group that there was an upsurge in the market for tonics to reinvigorate their sexual life. Here again the link between politics, economics, and sexuality is drawn. Men with economic and political power become sexually potent, whereas men who have lost such power feel emasculated by the market reforms.[39] Thus Brownell attests that "masculinity is related to state power, nationalist ideology, the free market, and the marriage/sex markets."[40] The current situation has "unleashed an entrepreneurial masculinity that is apparently proceeding hand in hand with the return of male privilege and female disadvantage," the context within which the clients' sex consumption can be understood.[41]

Preselection, Bonding, and Trust in State Clientelism
Risks Involved in the System of State Clientelism

In the Chinese system where entrepreneurs need access to resources and where resources are controlled by an authoritarian political system, it is necessary, to facilitate business and to control risk, to form relationships between entrepreneurs and powerful figures inside the political system. Although state clientelism tries to reduce the risks involved, it creates its own kinds of uncertainty. These unpredictable factors go beyond normal business risks inherent in changing market conditions and competition from rivals. It includes risks emanating from the unenforceability of contracts, a mercurial legal-regulatory system, and state agents' arbitrary use of public power.[42] Selecting business partners that one can trust becomes an important challenge. How businessmen and officials conduct themselves in their illicit affairs with women is used as a standard to appraise their competence and moral qualities.

This special kind of network building was conceptualized by Mayfair Yang as a gift economy, which establishes personal relationships where the art of *guanxi* (social relationships) manifests its greatest efficacy and power in the post-Mao state distributive economy. The economic survival of businessmen depends on *guanxi*. In the post-Mao distributive economy, which relies on a bureaucracy of distributors to dispense resources and enforce the law, money is still not omnipotent, and *guanxi* is the road to success.[43] In this system, where it is office capital or political capital rather than money that controls access to resources, businessmen resort to gifts, banquets, and favors to express gratitude or save face, and create indebtedness and obligation. In practicing *guanxi,* officials usurp the power to grant businessmen operating licenses and a network of tax collectors, traffic and civil policemen, and wholesale or retail enterprises who could either supply them with goods or buy their goods. *Guanxi* thus personalizes an impersonal money transaction and substitutes market relations that are severely curtailed by "the redistributive and planned economy for state socialism."[44] It is in this process that *guanxi* has become instrumentalized into means-ends relationships and subverts state regulations and restrictions in the state redistributive economy.

Relations among entrepreneurs are full of risk because the nature of their transaction is extralegal. They thus involve the issue of social trust as to whether client A should include client B in the alliance, and whether client B is reliable and will not betray client A. For both sides, entering into client-patron relationships is fraught with danger. Here, the main risk is that at some point in the relationship the other party (or parties) will almost inevitably face powerful incentives to betray and terminate the relationship. Despite this fact, clientelistic links display considerable longevity. This can be explained by the fact that businessmen rely on a process of preselection, bonding, and trust, all of which are related to their sex consumption. *Preselection* refers to the process by which Party A appraises Party B prior to entering transaction relationships. *Bonding* refers to the affective ties formed between individuals while engaging in common activities. These bonds inhibit the individuals from betraying one another by imposing psychological penalties in the form of guilt or regret. *Trust* refers to expectation that others will adhere to the terms of agreement in spite of their incentives. I view trust as the outcome of preselection and bonding processes.

If a person seeks only his own personal interest or intends to maximize his self-interest, he will not work well with other partners. Thus the alliance will dissolve. So a preselection of transaction partners is critical.[45]

DANGER INVOLVED IN SEX CONSUMPTION

Patronizing hostesses was fraught with danger. Hostesses were seen as dangerous for a number of reasons, which varied to some degree by the social identity of the man—namely, whether the man was an entrepreneur or government official. The risks were much greater for the latter group as representatives of the Party and state. Patronizing karaoke bars, regardless of whether hostesses were present or whether there was sexual contact, was considered inappropriate behavior for a Communist Party member and might become grounds for stripping the man of his Party membership—effectively the end of any man's political career. While such political excommunication was a rare punishment in comparison with the prevalence of officials as sex industry consumers, the threat was real enough that officials attempted to keep a low profile in the bars. The government itself has taken measures to prevent its employees from becoming embroiled in messy scandals that tarnish the reputation of its leaders. For example, certain government departments and units began to forbid their employees from printing name cards after they were recovered from the purses of hostesses who had been arrested for prostitution.

Other dangers applied to male clients in general. Hostesses potentially had access through their job to a myriad of powerful men in business and government. It was impossible to determine exactly whom a hostess knew, as this was one of their best-kept secrets and also because of the benefits of claiming to know high-powered men even if one did not. Indeed, hostesses sometimes used this uncertainty to their advantage as a check against client prerogative ("I'll call so-and-so and have you thrown in jail!"). While fear of offending a well-connected hostess was hardly a perfect shield against abusive client behavior, most men could not afford to ignore the issue entirely and accordingly modified their actions, for example, by keeping their real identities a secret.

Part of this danger also stems from the media-constructed ominous and threatening image of hostesses. The media cautions city men that hostesses can destroy their careers because they are "red spiders"—sexually attractive but dangerous, poisonous, and evil. They appear in sexy, tight dresses and are charming and seductive. In truth, however, so the stories go, they are criminals who blackmail and murder male clients. A long tradition of fear of beautiful women precedes modern China. Men are strongly warned not to fall into the beauty trap because "beauties bring disaster" *(hongyan huoshui)*. They are reminded that past Chinese rulers in different dynasties lost their empire because of their indulgence in beauty. So they should not surrender to beauty at the cost of their careers. The media also cite true examples of how some officials' indulgence in hostesses has ended their careers and even lives. Thus, hostesses' "vicious brutality" and "evil, poisonous nature" are said to be detrimental not only to national morality but also to men's careers and lives. Reminded of the ominous power of hostesses, men are urged to better control the hostesses rather than being manipulated themselves.

QUALITIES PURSUED IN ALLIANCE MEMBERS

In karaoke bars, men are both the actors in their own performances and the audience for the performances of others. By observing how others conduct sex consumption, they assess each other's moral qualities and business competence. Only men who are able to demonstrate their deference, self-control, and sexual prowess in the consumption of sex can successfully prove themselves to be trustworthy, responsible, and capable business partners in an alliance.

Pierre Bourdieu points out that the ability to consume serves as a marker of the consumer's position on a vertical ladder of social stratification.[46] There are thus "right" and "wrong" ways of consuming. This conclusion is limited by the parochial roots of Bourdieu's analysis in classist French society. Although Chinese society displays vast vertical inequalities, it is also segmented along a horizontal axis into small groups or, in Chinese, "circles" *(quanzi)*. Aptitude for sex consumption indexes the consumer's membership in the business group.

DEFERENCE IN SEX CONSUMPTION:
BASIS FOR SELECTION OF ALLIANCE MEMBERS

During sex consumption in the karaoke bar, a host client must reveal his deference to his partner by serving him with the utmost enthusiasm, without reservations. This was accomplished through four avenues. The host client always made sure that he was the last one to select a hostess. When the hostesses filed into the karaoke room for selection, the host client urged his most important partner to start, followed by the less important ones. Often, when urged to start the selection, his partner declined the offer as a sign of courtesy. At this time, the host client took the liberty to order for him the most beautiful hostess. The less beautiful ones were selected for other partners. The host client always made sure that the least beautiful hostess was reserved for himself. The rank of the karaoke bar was meant to reflect the position of his partner. Choosing an upscale karaoke bar was a formal act that conveyed the host client's respect for his partner. Then, the host client instructed his partner's hostess to serve his partner with the utmost enthusiasm. He confided to her the importance of his partner and promised her a higher rate of payment if she served him to his utmost enjoyment. Finally, the host client urged his own hostess to walk over to his partner and propose a toast to him. Normally, he pointed to his partner and said loudly to his hostess, "This is my big brother. He is a very powerful, reliable, and responsible man. I respect him very much. Go propose a toast to your big brother for me!" His hostess would then approach his partner, express her respect and admiration, and drink up her toast. These were the four important avenues through which the entrepreneur host client conveyed to his partner, a government official, his respect and deference. It is important to understand that while a government official is being treated with deference here, the purpose of this deference is to corrupt the official and therefore is part of the defiance and rebellion against the state.

SELF-CONTROL IN SEX CONSUMPTION: BASIS FOR SELECTION OF ALLIANCE MEMBERS

In addition to deference, a man's self-control in sex consumption proves him to be rational, reliable, and trustworthy. These invaluable moral qualities index both his business competence and his reliability in a partnership.

In sex consumption, men were always at risk of losing self-control and plummeting over the edge by falling under the control of hostesses. Men were thus put to the test by being evaluated for their ability to maintain self-control. The rationale is that if one cannot control the hostesses (who are beautiful but poisonous snakes), one cannot be a good businessman. Conversely, if one can control the hostesses, one proves oneself to be powerful and reliable. Such self-control is described in Chinese as *xuanya lema*. It literally means to "rein in at the brink of the precipice." It suggests that hostesses are ominous like the edge of an abyss. How men face the danger of the hostesses demonstrates their moral quality and business competence. If they rein in their emotions and turn back, they pass the test and prove themselves to be competent and level-headed partners. If they fall over the precipice, they are considered suspect and unqualified to be business partners in the alliance.

While spending exorbitant amounts of money on hostesses could raise a man's status in the eyes of his friends by proving his wealth, it might also have the opposite effect if his actions are seen as driven by excessive desire. A man who was unable to control his desire was seen as a danger to himself and the group. Men were always careful about who they associated with and monitored each other's behavior for fear that the rash actions of a single individual would jeopardize their own well-being and the existence of the group. Men would express concern about a friend who seemed to be "losing it" and, if the behavior continued, would eventually discontinue relations with the individual in question. These self-defense mechanisms were set up to guard against the ultimate disaster: the risk of being sold out by a friend in trouble.

PERFORMING SELF-CONTROL: CONTROLLING HOSTESSES WITH CHARISMA

Publicly expressing desire for hostess companions is sometimes, but not universally, seen as appropriate and even mandated by the circumstances of the interaction. At other times, such expressions may be interpreted as a sign of weakness, excessive emotionality, and irrationality. Male customers perform their desire on the bodies of hostesses. I use the term *perform* to capture two meanings: first, men's "desirous" behavior is seen—indeed, is meant to be seen—by a range of audiences: his male confederates, his accompanying hostess, the other hostesses in attendance, and possibly himself. His desire thus becomes a semipublic spectacle: it is staged before a limited audience. Second, like a performance, the display of desire is ambiguously related to the man's subjective experience of his true self. The man as the actor may invest more or less "real" emotions through the performance. Thus to call such behavior a performance is not to suggest that it is "all a show," but that the social pressure to appear desirous at certain moments means that some displays will be experienced as more real than others.

Because of the differences between a gift economy and a market economy, in China, money relations are the weakest in dealing with emotional affect.[47] Money is the lowest in this scale because it is based on an impersonal exchange of currency for services. It is purely instrumental.[48] When money is devalued in the process of establishing relationships in society, men feel that the simple ability to buy a woman with money is not a strong demonstration of masculine potency. In the competition between men and hostesses, men's ability to dominate these jaded women with the force of their personalities and charm is seen as a demonstration of a man's prestige, power, and status.[49] In other words, if a man possesses the power and charm to control a commercial sex worker who is contemptuous of men without money, he is the man that is most admired in the circle of business partners. In this case, the hostess becomes an instrument for a businessman to demonstrate his power to his business partners through working on his skills and charm on the hostess.

As Client Peng said in an interview, "We love to show off our beautiful hostesses before our male friends. I always get carried away when my beautiful hostess compliments my singing and my looks. They said I was like a Hong Kong star singer. It really gives me a lot of face before the other guys. We want admiration from beautiful hostesses. It definitely satisfies our psychological needs before our peers. We don't go for sex at all." Client Shi, in his conversation with his hostess mistress, deliberately highlighted conversation segments to show off his charisma and in-control attitude before his partner and me. "Oh, you are missing me to death," Shi said, "You are missing me so much that you cannot stand the feeling anymore. . . . Oh, I will come to visit you sometime. . . . Oh, you have been waiting for me for a whole month. . . . Oh, I will surely come to visit you. . . . I miss you, too." After the conversation, Shi turned to me and said, "Tiantian, someday I will introduce you to a lot of my lovers." Shi bragged to his business partner that he played the hostesses without paying them. It was a flat lie because I knew that Shi's mistresses—my hostess friends—had gleaned a great deal of money from him.

Fantasizing that it is their "culture, egalitarian nature, and charm" instead of their wallet that attracts the hostesses, men comment that they admire those who can emotionally and physically control the hostesses. Client Ge was such a man. I was told that he had "the charisma and self-control" to play with the hostesses' emotions. After hostesses fall in love with him, he abandons them one after another. He was also admired for having "graceful and beautiful" hostesses. As client Zhao said, "If a man has a cultured hostess beside him, she will definitely add to his reputation before other men. You will lose face if your mistress is of low class or if you do not even have any mistresses." Client Ge was thus considered the most powerful man because he could play the beautiful hostesses without payment. Less powerful men, as I was told, are those who have a relationship with a large number of hostesses, but strictly through sex-for-money transactions. The weak men are those who lack charm or fall for hostesses. Client Xie was ridiculed because he "did not have the charm to attract hostesses." "But he looks fine," said other clients, gazing at Xie. "Just not the type to strike women. No one notices that he actually looks quite nice."

IN CONTROL VERSUS LOSS OF CONTROL
IN SEX CONSUMPTION

Patronizing hostesses challenged men to display their rationality and self-control by controlling hostesses as the tools for advancing their careers. Faced with such a challenge, men deliberately ordered hostesses around in front of their partners. One client I interviewed pretentiously claimed to his partners, "Hostesses are like toys, something to serve men and help them relax." Other similar expressions included, "For a real man, a woman is always secondary to his career."

Client Shi bragged about his self-control in sex consumption in the following ways. He described his relationship with his hostess mistress as that of "master and slave." He stated, "She is very obedient. She comes when summoned and leaves when dismissed." Shi also demonstrated his control by prioritizing career before women. He said, "She called me last night, saying she wanted to see me. I told her I was too busy to see her." Commenting that he had countless second wives, Shi continued, "I always forget their names. When they call me, I do not know which one it is." Finally, Shi accentuated his masculine self-control and charisma by boasting about his ability to "rein in at the brink of the precipice." "At the critical moment," he said, "I retreat and cut off our relationship."

Client Pei was despised for losing control in his relationship with host-esses. I was told that Pei fell in love with a hostess. He constantly went looking for her. Once in the bar, Pei found he was short of money to pay her. He explained the situation to her and promised that he would repay her the next day. Pei thought that since they were "deeply in love," it would not be a problem at all. To his utter shock, however, the hostess started cursing him. She insisted that he deposit his cellular phone with her until he paid her back. Broken-hearted, Pei returned home and eventually re-deemed his cell phone. His story was circulated by his male friends as a subject of ridicule. His image was completely ruined.

Such men are not only derided but also considered unqualified for part-nership in an alliance for three reasons. First, they are criticized for being irrational and weak. They are believed to easily betray their partners because of such character "defects." Second, they are ostracized for preferring the company of women to men *(zhongse qingyou)*. Putting male partners sec-ondary to women makes such men unreliable and untrustworthy. Third, their emotional entanglements are believed to lead to disaster for their partners' careers, as well as their own.

Official Zhang broke ties with entrepreneur Lin because Lin was too "indulgent in his relationships with hostesses." Lin was emotionally in-volved with countless hostesses as girlfriends. Zhang constantly com-plained to me that Lin, by being entangled with so many hostesses, could not "do big deeds" *(zuodashi)*. Zhang told me that once Lin, sidetracked by a hostess in his car on his business trip, hit a pedestrian, nearly killing him. Lin had to seek Zhang's help to bribe the policemen at the local police station. Although Zhang saved Lin from being imprisoned, Zhang later broke ties with him. Zhang commented that one day Lin's career would perish because of his "messy" relationship with the hostesses. According to Zhang, hostesses have a wide network.[50] It is impossible to know who are the high-profile men or gangsters behind them. Getting too close to them will invite trouble. Zhang commented that as a man, he should control the situation—to be able to get in and out without emotional entanglements. Lin's lack of rationality in sex consumption led Zhang to discard him as a business partner.

SEXUAL PROWESS IN SEX CONSUMPTION:
BASIS FOR SELECTION OF ALLIANCE MEMBERS

Ge, a nouveau riche, never had sexual encounters with hostesses for fear of contracting STDs. This strange behavior worried his friends and business partners. They continued to introduce young hostesses to him as "second-wife" candidates. Once I saw his friends bring him an eighteen-year-old rural woman, fresh from the countryside. Ge created an excuse— "She is too young"—to decline their "kind offer." All of Ge's friends had second wives, and it was a ritual for them to bring their second wives to banquets or sauna salons. Ge was the only one who did not fit in. After a while, he became everyone's laughingstock as his friends suspected his sexual potency. At meals, his friends would intentionally order dishes for him that supposedly remedied sexual impotence. When they talked about second wives, his friends would laugh and say to each other, "That's right. Ge is impotent. His thing doesn't work!" Under such tremendous peer pressure and the need to maintain male bonding by proving his sexual potency, Ge started demonstrating his "masculinity"—a representation of his social potency. Before his male friends, Ge aggressively pinched hostesses' breasts, insulted hostesses in karaoke bars, and had sex with them. Transformed into a different man, he started bragging before his friends about his sexual experiences (such as acts of fellatio) with hostesses.

In turn, sexual potency paralleled social power and business prowess. In sex consumption, sexual potency was an index of a man's business competence. Such an analogy is best illustrated by a common Chinese saying, which goes, "Men who return home after work are foolish men." But successful men, as the saying goes,

Never need to buy cigarettes,
Never need to buy wine,
Never need to touch the salary,
Never need to fondle wives.[51]

This common saying defines foolish men as those who copulate only with their wives. In contrast, successful and powerful men have sex with many women other than their wives. Client Gao vividly explained why he resorted to displaying sexual prowess to prove his social worth: "Men like me who do not have any education cannot impress others with degrees.

So we have to resort to money and sexual prowess to prove our ability and talent. Otherwise, I am really nothing in the society." Sex consumption becomes a crucial criterion to mark men's social status when men compete among themselves.

Client Liang, a bank clerk in his early thirties, commented:

> You just have to patronize hostesses. You've got to try it a few times. It's part of growing up and self-actualization. Otherwise, when other men are talking about it, you will look like a fool who never entered society in an experienced fashion. Nobody will respect you if you are like that. So you have to have this experience to gain others' recognition and respect. Meanwhile, you have to know when to stop and not get addicted to it.

As Liang's narrative maintains, sex consumption represents the rite of passage to manhood. This explanation is reminiscent of men in other countries undergoing certain rituals to be acknowledged as men.[52] For instance, men on Truk Island take risks in deep-sea fishing expeditions in tiny dugouts, spear fishing with foolhardy abandon in shark-infested waters, fighting, brawling, drinking to excess, and seeking sexual conquests. Men in Amhara demonstrate their aggressiveness, stamina, and sexual potency by waving before the assembled kinsman a bloody sheet after marital consummation as the proof of having deprived a bride of her virginity. Such demonstrations of "indomitable virility" not only earn these men respect and recognition, but also distinguish them from "effeminate counterfeits."[53] In China, as Liang stated, a lack of experience in sex consumption places men in the liminal zone as "effeminate counterfeits" who will not be respected by anyone. Thus, sex consumption is part of the necessary process for achieving "recognition and respect" from other men.

Entrepreneurs Li and Kun were business partners. Li admired Kun's sexual potency very much. Kun constantly boasted to Li about his sexual adventures. For instance, Kun had two second wives besides his own wife. Kun claimed to have had sexual relationships with thousands of women and to have spent thousands of *yuan* on his sexually transmitted diseases. Once Kun mentioned his experience of "double swallows"—having sex with two hostesses at one time. Kun also recounted his experience of spending 1,000 *yuan* dancing with a Russian hostess for an hour in a prestigious hotel in the city. Li was amused by the story that because of the language barrier the Russian hostess had to draw a circle with her finger to motion that an hour had passed. Li equated Kun's sexual potency to his business success and constantly commented to me that Kun was very successful and powerful in the business world as well.

The Maoist state suppressed sexuality allowing a small group of leaders to control the male population in China. In the post-Mao period, many men came to believe that they had been turned into eunuchs by the Maoist state. This feeling of castration explains why sexual promiscuity became an important expression of resistance against the state during this later period. The emasculation of men during the Maoist period was partially accomplished through the repression of female sexuality. I argue that the primary purpose of the repression of female sexuality and the masculinization of women was to allow the control of emasculated men; that by creating masculine women, Chinese men were robbed of the space in which they could demonstrate their unique masculinity. Thus the new image of Chinese women as sexualized beings in the post-Mao period is not primarily a liberation of women but, rather, provides a foil against which men can define themselves as so-called "real men."

Consumption of women in karaoke bars is only one model of Chinese masculinity, and not all men subscribe to it. As one might suspect, men find masculine identity through sports such as soccer, golf, and bowling, and through conspicuous consumption of clothing, automobiles, and elegant housing. In illustrating the kind of masculinity performed in the karaoke bars, I have argued that the underlying reason is far more complex than merely the recovery of male masculinity. On the one hand, the clients' engagement in sexual consumption becomes their weapon against the socialist morality and socialist state. It also demonstrates their masculinity through embracing global modernity. On the other hand, the consumption of sex is a criterion used to evaluate one another's deference, reliability, self-control, and sexual potency. Their moral qualities and business power will determine their chances of being accepted as a qualified member in an alliance. Thus, sex consumption becomes a business ritual for conducting the preselection of, and bonding with, potential partners to reach mutual trust in their alliance in the current Chinese system of state clientelism.

THE RETURN OF THE
PRODIGAL DAUGHTER

BEING THE ELDEST DAUGHTER IN HER FAMILY, hostess Hong took on all the responsibilities for her parents and three sisters. She gave money to her three sisters for their weddings; she bought a house and furnished it for her parents. She said, "Sometimes I feel really pressured and depressed with this heavy burden to support my whole family. I never think about myself. All my money goes to my parents." She said that when she was young, her parents always spoke ill of her because a fortune-teller had predicted that she would beat her parents in the future. She said:

> My father had four daughters because they were waiting for a son but never had the luck. My father almost killed me twice. When I was three, my father was upset *(xinfan)* one day and tried to crush my head with his foot. It scarred my eyes and made me temporarily almost blind. You can still see the scars around my eyes. The second time when I was six, my father quarreled with my mother and became furious. My father put his foot on my head and jammed my face into the soggy earth, nearly drowning me.

I asked her if she hated her father. She answered:

> I never minded it. All is past, so what's the sense of holding it against him? My mother would mention it sometimes, but I always stopped her. After all, they're my parents. They brought me up and they raised me. I don't mind it at all. I still hand washed my father's underwear and washed his feet when his feet were burnt and injured. My father cried and said no one had done this for him before. I said, "I'm your daughter—isn't it natural for me to do this for you?" Sometimes when I caught sight of him hiding his underwear under the bed, I would say, "What are you hiding?

Why are you hiding? I'm your daughter. When I was little, you didn't mind washing my dirty underwear. How can I mind now? It's the same thing. So don't do that anymore. I'll do all these things for you."

When I asked her why she was doing all this, she said, "I think my life in the future will definitely be a lot better than theirs. They lived through the Cultural Revolution and the bad times. They haven't eaten good things and have never experienced good things. I want them to see as much as they can and eat as much as they can when they are not too old [her father was fifty-three years old]. I have the responsibility to make their lives better in their remaining years."

Like Chinese women for thousands of years, hostess Hong has bought into the myth of patriarchy and used it to make sense of her difficult life. Despite her father's mistreatment and attempted murder of her, Hong still held fast to her moral role as a daughter, continuing the historical pattern of women taking an active role in embracing and perpetuating the patriarchal value of filiality.

Historically, Chinese values reflected the paradox that emphasized chastity among women but also called on them to sacrifice their chastity for a higher value—the value of filial responsibilities to the family.[1] Since early Chinese history, it has been the pattern that daughters and wives willingly sacrificed themselves in their dedication to their patriarchs. This resonates with the present situation in China where, as we will see, hostesses often still rationalize the sacrifice of their chastity for the benefit of the family.

This chapter will explore the background necessary to fully appreciate the challenges these young women have chosen to accept in the city of Dalian. The patriarchal family, the new market economy, and the state all seem to be working against them, and yet tough and resourceful, they keep their hopes alive. This study reveals the uniqueness of the situations and strategies of north China's migrant population compared to similar groups in South China, Japan, or Africa.[2] While all of these groups share similar problems of conflict between conservative traditional rural values and modernist urban practices, the specifics of north China make it a unique situation. While in the other studies, migrants tend to view returning home as a goal, whether in the end they achieve this goal or not, for the hostesses of Dalian home is seen only as a temporary refuge from their risky and dangerous lives in the city, or as a place to return for special festivals or holidays. As illustrated, not gender, marriage, or ideological conflict between generations constrains hostesses from living largely on their own terms in the countryside. The seeming contradiction between their desire for cosmopolitanism and their continuing practice of filiality only illustrates the depth of their conviction in the Confucian value of filiality, in spite of the New Culture movement, Republicanism, Maoism, and post-Mao consumerism. Filiality has survived. This is not surprising when one considers a similar contradiction between filiality and the cult of chastity during imperialist China. In fact, as we have seen, during hard times, this contradiction was often resolved by parents' asking daughters to engage in prostitution in order to fulfill their filial obligations to feed their parents. In the current conflict between cosmopolitanism and filiality, once again we see the triumph of the deep Confucian value of filiality.

While embracing filial responsibilities, they continue to challenge other conventions about dress, gender, and marriage. Their superior earning power and the relative absence of patriarchs from the countryside form the basis of their success in redefining themselves and their roles. This gives them the power to challenge and debate the entrenched rural ideology. Their ambivalent acceptance of elements of rural tradition while rejecting other aspects generates an ambivalent response from their kin in the villages. They are admired for their fulfillment of filial duty and, more superficially, are appreciated for their light city skin. (One of the distinguishing markers of peasants is their dark complexion, a result of their toiling in the field.) But they are the subject of condemnation and gossip because of their violation of gender traditions and conventions of dress. One might argue that the hostesses fail in their mission as ambassadors of modernity. It is their adherence to traditional filial values and their wealth that are recognized, not their message of modernity. However, I would argue that the filial values are a way of domesticating and controlling the modernity that they import with their wealth. In fact, the message of modernity is a very powerful one. That is why there are such strong countermeasures to control the hostesses by framing their position within filiality. While both the families and the hostesses are necessarily complicit in this process, it clearly represents a misrecognition on the part of the hostesses, whose efforts only contribute to their own victimization.[3]

Journey Home

The Hong Kong movie *Durian Durian,* directed by Chen Guo, tells the story of a migrant woman, Yanzi, who travels to Hong Kong to work in the sex trade for three months before returning to her hometown in north China. The movie portrays the dramatic differences between Yanzi's life as a sex worker in Hong Kong and her life as a filial daughter back in her hometown. The portrait of her journey back to north China captures the unresolved conflict between her image as an admired, affluent, and urbane woman from the glamorous city and the shame attending her profession. Accompanying my hostess informants as they journeyed back to their rural homes was like reliving the experience in the movie. My experiences in rural northeast China and my readings of anthropological studies of returning migrants in other parts of the world have taught me that returning to rural homes from urban lives is a complex and varied experience. Perhaps we can modify Thomas Wolfe's famous title to *You Can't Go Home Again Easily.* Traditional values do not flourish in large urban areas, and the return to the country seems to inevitably involve conflict and some modification of newly acquired urban habits.

While most of my fieldwork was in Dalian, I also spent several months traveling with hostesses to their homes in the countryside. This experience helped me understand more viscerally the forces propelling the mass migration in China. Facts explain a lot: the less-than-$300-per-capita income, the lack of infrastructure connecting many rural areas to markets, the small scale of much farming (making labor-saving equipment both unaffordable and inefficient) all tell a story. My day-to-day experiences on two separate trips deepened that story.

Fragrance and Dee, two of the hostesses I had become close to, were constantly complaining about the wretched living conditions in the countryside. Flies and mice infested their homes, and the toilet was just a small pit that overflowed with excrement. Their diets consisted largely of what could be grown locally and lacked variety and adequate nutrition. In Fragrance's mountainous home, they could grow little but potatoes and eggplant. Since the closest market was open only once a week and was an hour away by foot, even having money was little help.

I was thinking of this as we journeyed through the heavily forested countryside of Liaoning Province into the remote mountains that were

Fragrance's home. Beside me sat Fragrance, returning home to recover from a rape and abortion, a common hazard for hostesses. As the train clattered along the hundred-year-old, Russian-built railway, she told me of her past and her dreams for the future. She had worked for a year as a hostess in Japan, and it was her ambition to return there.[4] She had learned some Japanese and continued to study. Her plans did not include marriage.

We left the train in the dark, far from the lights of Dalian, and caught a waiting taxi. The driver knew her and seemed shyly eager to please her. As we bumped along the deeply rutted mountain road, he complained constantly about how much damage it was doing to his car. Fragrance, in turn, teased him mercilessly, making light of his complaints. At the end of the road he walked with us through the black forest. After a while, I could make out the village, sprawled along the valley floor, surrounded by steep hillsides, silent in the darkness. As we passed through a cherry grove, I could smell the stench of open-pit toilets. We descended into the valley to Fragrance's home, a clay-built, single-story house, one of several dozen scattered along the valley. Fragrance's mother greeted us but fell to arguing with Fragrance almost immediately about the cabdriver who continued to sulk around. She insisted that she tell him to leave for the sake of her reputation and the neighbor's gossiping. I was surprised at Fragrance's less-than-deferential response; she had become used to defending herself and was very strong-willed, something she would demonstrate many times in the weeks ahead.

Concern for reputation was paramount in the village, where gossip was a major pastime. Like village communities around the world, it was hard to keep a secret here, and gossip ruthlessly reinforced community values. Over the next weeks I watched as Fragrance's mother always called her in when she saw her talking to neighbors. The loose and heavily layered clothing, she feared, did not completely conceal the residual bulge of her pregnancy.

As I would again witness on a later trip into the countryside with Dee, the hostesses had constructed a worldview in which they had cast themselves as ambassadors of modernism to the countryside. While Fragrance accepted many of the traditional obligations to her family and considered herself a filial daughter, she also fabricated an identity for herself as a city sophisticate bringing superior habits to the country. This created a contentious relationship with the villagers. As cynical as the hostesses were in their relations with clients, it was clear that they were not bereft of values. To the contrary, they consistently defended their occupation as a means of meeting their filial obligations. About half of what they earned went to the support of their families. In this they were not breaking new ground, but continuing a tradition of subordinating sexual values to filial responsibilities that we have seen throughout Chinese history.

In the village the next day, I was struck by the absence of men. I saw only women and children. (As I would learn on a later trip, the number of men remaining had much to do with the productivity of the land. In this hard-to-farm mountainous environment most of the men were gone.) As in much of the developing world, those engaging in small-scale, labor-intensive farming were finding it difficult to compete with large-scale mechanized agriculture, particularly in marginal areas such as this. This also helped explain the high suicide rate of women left behind to endure this hardscrabble existence. The comfort of the city exacted a heavy price but in the minds of many women was worth the cost.

Following the decollectivization of agricultural production, individual rural households became responsible for their own economic well-being. To cope with these new pressures for survival, rural work has become just one of the many economic activities that rural households engage in. In Fragrance's village, the vast majority of men with labor capacity have migrated to Jinzhou, a nearby county-level city. They are concentrated in the construction industry where they work for 400 to 500 *yuan* a month. They return home only twice a year, once for the Spring Festival and once for the Mid-Autumn Festival. As with other villages whose men have left for wage labor, women villagers stay at home, take care of children and elderly parents, and tend the fields in the "feminization of rural labor."

The fact that these men worked in Dalian as migrant laborers reminded me of the migrants who visited the low-class karaoke bar that I was living in. They walked in to negotiate the price with the manager first; most times they successfully cut the price (which was already very low in the lowest-class bar) in half. At times the bar manager would not so easily concede when business was not that sluggish. You could easily tell their migrant identity from their appearance: worn slippers, smeared working outfits, and sweaty dark faces. Hostesses often joked to each other, "Our bar even accepts migrants *(mingong)* and garbage collectors. We should really change our name to Paradise of the Poor Trash *(qionggui daleyuan)*." It was a pastime to make fun of the migrants.

It is difficult for poor male migrants to replicate the adaptations of the hostesses from the countryside. This is illustrated by a scene I witnessed in this same bar. One night hostess Cheng waited on a migrant in a karaoke room. After a short while, she came out and the bar bouncer dashed into the room. In the backroom, Cheng filled us in: "I wasn't sitting there very long when the migrant spread his hands in imitation of gestures we have seen in Western films, and said, 'Shall we make love?' *[zanmen zuoai ba]*." As she was telling the story, she vividly mimicked his gesture, his tone, and his voice. Everyone laughed hysterically while teasing, "Hey Cheng, you should respond by spreading your hands like this, saying, 'Make love? OK, it's free! It's free to fuck once!' *[ganyixia buyaoqian]*." In the midst of everyone's mocking comments, Cheng continued the story:

> So I told him that no one in our bar goes out [engages in sex].
> Discouraged, he asked me to leave, and then he changed his mind and
> asked me to stay again. This situation repeated itself three times. The last
> time I stayed there for about fifteen minutes and drank some beer and tea.
> He gave me the tip of 50 *yuan* [the negotiated half price] upon my
> request. However, he refused to pay the bill of 60 *yuan*. He said to the
> waiter, "This hostess drank my beer and my tea, ask her for 50 *yuan*, don't
> ask me! Here is my 10 *yuan* for the difference."

Cheng's story was followed with fits of hysterical laughter, as the hostesses repeatedly mocked his words, "Hey Cheng, you drank my beer, you drank my tea. Why do you ask me for money? Why?" Everyone was bent over from laughing so hard. The end of the story was that the bar bouncer and waiters beat the migrant, threatening him that he could not leave the room unless he handed over the money. He said, "Okay, this room is a really good place. I'd like to live here and sleep here." The bar bouncer had to call the emergency number, and the police came over and arrested him.

As we see in this scene, the migrant laborers also wish to achieve an "imagined cosmopolitanism"[5] in the city just like the hostesses. However, their poor imitation of Western romantic style learned from foreign movies was not a match for the commodity possessed by the hostesses—their bodies. Thus the male migrants are seldom successful in making the

transition to urban status and often merely become the laughingstock of
the hostesses.

I was soon to experience the harsh environment from which both male
and female migrants were fleeing. Although it was summer, I noticed that
the only heat source available was contained in the Kang, the traditional
clay bed. It was warmed by a fire from leaves and twigs, which probably
made winter nights bearable but did little to alleviate the hard surfaces on
which we slept. At night lying on the unyielding surface, I listened to the
scurrying feet of mice and rats beneath me and brushed away hordes of
flies that settled on my face.

Part of the difficulty of living in the country is how labor-intensive
ordinary tasks become. Cooking, washing clothes, even bathing require
time and great effort. To bathe, Fragrance and I had to boil several pans
of water, pour them into a basin, and then scrub ourselves with a cloth.
The water had to be hand-pumped and carried inside. I could only imag-
ine how unpleasant this would be in the cold of winter.

Both Fragrance and Dee, as well as other hostesses from the country,
complained about the lack of adequate nutrition. This was especially true
in Fragrance's village where the nearest market was an hour walk away and
open only once a week. The thin mountain soil grew only eggplant and
potatoes, which could be supplemented by fresh cherries in season. The
family, the most affluent in the village, also owned a pig, and there were
a number of chickens running freely in the yard. A hand-pumped well
made water available, but it had to be carried into the house and heated
over a primitive wood stove if you wanted it hot.

Beyond the physical difficulties of village life there was the narrow social
order to negotiate. Gossip was vicious and focused on moral transgressions,
real or imagined, such as wife abuse or prostitution. Fragrance observed
that people in the countryside "know nothing but gossip." She referred to
them as "surveillants" *(jianshizhe)*, "spies," *(jianxi)*, and "treacherous court
officials" *(jianchen)*. Whenever Fragrance caught a glimpse of a neighbor
walking down the path to her house to visit, she would sound the alarm
to her family members: "The spies are coming again! They have come to
spy on me again!"

Clearly, Fragrance was the focus of village gossip. Once, Fragrance and
I joined a small gathering of seven or eight villagers for a little after-dinner

chatter. The designated spot for such powwows was a small hill between Fragrance's and a neighbor's house. Among the attendees was Jun, one of Fragrance's former middle school classmates. Jun was the only adult male who had not joined the exodus of able-bodied young men into the city. He was notorious for beating his wife, which he did apparently to the exclusion of any moneymaking activities. Seeing Fragrance with so much money had clearly injured Jun's ego, and he was set on bringing her down a notch or two. Jun called her a "rich woman" *(fupo)* and demanded to work with her so that he could earn some money as well. Fragrance just scoffed at his laziness and poverty. In response to her scorn, Jun replied, "If I were a woman, I would sell myself for money." Fragrance burst out with a loud laugh, "If you were a woman, you would sell yourself so much that you would not even be able to walk!" With these words, Fragrance spread her legs far apart and pretended to walk with great difficulty. "You would walk like this after being fucked so much," she said with another fit of laughter. Jun replied, "What does it matter as long as I can earn money?" Everybody followed his words with a loud laugh.

Surprisingly, Fragrance did not seem to realize that Jun's words indirectly conveyed the villagers' contempt for her. Instead, Fragrance took Jun's words to be a recognition of her profession. She even felt amused at Jun's inability to realize his dream of being a prostitute. She used his seemingly frustrated desires to reaffirm the value of her profession.

Fragrance and the other hostesses I studied have conflicting feelings about their homes and the city. On the one hand, they feel exhausted by their risky jobs in the city. On the other hand, their time at home reaffirms for them their decision to migrate. Experiencing once again the harshness of rural living allows them to rationalize their decision and encourages them to feel pride in their urban status and the wealth they have obtained. This is reinforced when they see their friends married to peasants and working all day in the fields. As hostess Dee says, "After seeing them and the country life, I do not complain about my life in Dalian anymore. They remind me that my life in Dalian is much better than theirs. Although my life in the city is full of tears, I am happy that at least I am not 'repairing the earth' [*xiuli diqiu,* tilling the soil] like them. At least my life is better than theirs."

Returning home reassures them that their decision to work as hostesses in the city, whatever its drawbacks, is at least better than stagnating in the countryside. Seeing women their own age suffer from tedious and heavy farm work, poverty, and the constraints of marriage, they surmise that no one is happy with their lives. At such times they are able to feel some contentment with their choice of the city.

A year later, as I sat talking with Dee at her home in the Jilin countryside, she confided her conflicted feelings about her home. On the one hand, she told me, having had enough of risky life in Dalian, where she had to evade the police and always worry about violent clients and disease, she longed to stay home forever. On the other hand she did not like her home anymore. Every time she came home, Dee felt a growing distance between herself and her home village. She no longer remembered her classmates' names or the location of her relative's houses. She felt that no one in her family cared for her any longer, that they were glad to take her money but only despised her in return. She felt that she no longer belonged to this place.

In spite of Dee's remarks that her family was willing to take her money but not accord her respect, it is important to remember that both Dee and Fragrance were the principal supporters of their families. Both their mothers confirmed that they were the main supporters of their families, and this support made their families among the richest in their respective villages. Dee's father ran into severe debt after his factory went bankrupt. Coming to the rescue, Dee helped pay off all of the family debts as well as her parents' hospital bills when they fell ill. Of the four breadwinners in Fragrance's family, Fragrance and her hostess sister made the most money and were the main supporters of the less prosperous family members. For example, they both contributed 10,000 *yuan* for their younger brother's wedding ceremony. Fragrance chipped in an additional 10,000 *yuan* as start up capital to open a vending stall in a Jinzhou shopping mall. Later, her brother and his wife sold commodities at the stall every day. Fragrance also hoped to buy a house for her mother and grandmother to live permanently in the city.

Although Fragrance and the other hostesses I interviewed and observed clearly had ambiguous feelings about family and home, they were, for the most part, filial daughters who, sometimes reluctantly, conformed to much of their village culture. Given their cynical attitude toward their clients in the city, how can we account for this? First, they earned enough to afford to take care of their families. They were, by the standards of the village, very wealthy. Second, they have learned, growing up in the countryside, to think of filiality as the basic virtue. Filiality also seemed to serve as a balance justifying their life in the city; it was a reason for what they do. Fear of village sanctions and personal guilt also played a part in their actions. Finally, the absence of state pensions and social service systems meant that if they don't care for their families, no one will.

Considering the ambiguous welcome given Fragrance in the countryside and the large amount of money she turns over to her family, including able-bodied people like her younger brother, the question is whether she and the other hostesses who meet their filial obligations are being exploited. Why should she sacrifice so that her brother can start a business or have a grand wedding? One can argue that these young women are being exploited by their families, as well as their male customers, the state, the system of patriarchy, and the market economy. Yet in spite of what seems an unfair system, they were almost unanimous in insisting on their filial responsibilities. It was also clear that they were getting something out of it. When they talked about how much they had helped their family members, their faces glowed and they proclaimed with pride, "I am a very successful woman." When I asked if they would stay in the city, most said they would return to the countryside to care for their parents. They felt it was their responsibility to support parents and siblings economically and emotionally. Their homes are also a place of refuge both physically and emotionally. It is a place that they can return to in old age or to marry, although I saw little interest in the latter.

In the case of Dee, whom I would spend the next summer with, she bent to the demands of her mother to agree to marry a boy from her village, a boy whom she detested. Clearly, this pushed the boundaries of what she would agree to; nevertheless she established a relationship that only ended when he abandoned her. Interestingly, her pride was hurt that he had left her, even though she disliked him. When he left, he disparaged her foul mouth and called her a shrew. In the end she got over it and asked me to introduce her to an American. She is the only hostess I know who returned to her village for marriage, and in the end she escaped that fate.

Although returning to the countryside for marriage was at best a last desperate option, the hostesses did not suffer a shortage of willing boyfriends, including some Japanese and Korean boys. Almost all had boyfriends, and as I observed on numerous occasions, the love between them seemed genuine. All seemed to respect them, and some seemed determined to marry them.

I was surprised that their professions did not seem an obstacle, but the boys seemed to respect their courage in having carved out a space for themselves and felt sympathy for the hard and bitter life they led. Their suffering seemed to enhance their sexual attraction, echoing the Maoist era when men fell deeply in love with reformed prostitutes.[6] Because these women cannot continue to practice their profession much beyond their late twenties, marriage to an urban boyfriend is an important option. However, my observations were that connections through boyfriends or important customers, which allowed them to establish themselves as small entrepreneurs, selling cosmetics, gifts, and so forth, provided a more viable option.

Although hostesses distinguish themselves as more sophisticated than their rural relatives, the rough environment of the karaoke bar engenders many crude habits in the hostesses. They curse, drink, and smoke. There is also a kind of rough sexual horseplay. I had to constantly protect myself from Fragrance and Dee as they playfully grabbed my breasts. In the village with Fragrance, much to my surprise, I saw this happen again and again: she grabbed her mother's breasts, her sister's, and even the breasts of other village women. She would hold them and say things such as "How small, you hardly have any breasts at all," or "You are lucky to have such wonderful breasts." This habit was so pervasive that her mother became used to it and simply laughed it off with embarrassment. Female villagers were more wary, learning to dodge and evade her grasp.

What they could not evade, however, was her foul mouth. For all of the hostesses, cursing had become a natural part of their speech, a deeply imbedded habit. This was inimical to village culture. Women were supposed to be subservient and decorous. There was no place for foul language in a proper woman's behavior. You may recall the language used by Fragrance in her conversation with Jun. As foul as the language was, it was at least used in the context of joking banter, but as often it was used as a weapon in serious arguments, and against people whom village culture required be respected. For instance, Fragrance challenged the authority of senior villagers by saying, "Fuck your mother!" Dee's hostess sister, Mong, told seniors in her village, "Why don't you die early *[lao bu si de]*? I hope you get sunstroke and die." Village gossip insisted that Mong would never find a husband with such a foul mouth.

I witnessed another example of the crude and unrestrained behavior learned in the karaoke bar and carried back to the village during the next summer when I accompanied Dee as she traveled back to her hometown. Dee's village in Jilin Province was bigger and more socially stratified than Fragrance's village. The village was on a flat plain, not too far from the county capital. Because it was more economically productive, it had not lost as many men. Dee's family was well connected, and she took me to visit an important relative in what, by country standards, was a pleasant and well-furnished house. As we sat on a sofa in her uncle's home, talking to her aunt in front of a large TV, she was reminded of rooms in the karaoke bars. She slumped back into the soft sofa, put her feet on the clean end table, and puffed on a cigarette. As her aunt watched speechless and in horror, she flicked the still smoldering cigarette into the corner. At this point her aunt bolted upright exclaiming, "What are you doing? How can you do this to my new end table and clean floor? The end table is completely new, and I just cleaned the floor! Get your feet off!" Embarrassed, Dee silently removed her feet.

Dee was a contrast to Fragrance. She was nearly a head shorter than Fragrance, with quick darting actions and a volatile intensity. Unlike Fragrance's mother, her mother is aware of her true profession in the city and wanted Dee to normalize her life. She had introduced her to a businessman from the city, hoping marriage would help her escape the dangers and violence of the karaoke bars, which she feared might lead to an untimely demise. In fact, at a time when there was no news of Dee for months, Dee's mother believed that Dee had been murdered in Dalian. Dee, however, preferred remaining single. She referred to herself as a "single aristocrat," an unmarried person who has the freedom to make life choices, including changing partners, uninhibited by a spouse. As she explained, "Seeing my classmates suffer from the constraints of marriage, I don't want to marry. I am still young and free to travel to America, Beijing, and Shanghai."

Although both Dee's and Fragrance's mothers had tried to arrange marriages for them, they were both content with their daughters living in the city. Both mothers depended heavily on their daughters for support and acquiesced in their decision not to marry. When I asked Fragrance's mother whether she was anxious to see Fragrance marry, she replied:

> Marriage? Why get married? Look around the village—nobody gets married at an early age. I'm for a late marriage for Fragrance. At first, I was not, but later on she convinced me. Being single allowed her to make her trip to Japan. If she married and had a child, her husband would never have let her go, and she would never have been able to do anything burdened with a child. So what's the good of getting married early? What's the use of marriage except to saddle you with a burden that only pulls you back?

While Dee's mother, knowing her daughter's profession, worried about her, she accepted the need for her to be in the city:

> Three of my daughters used to have partners in the village. I told them their future would be full of worries and anxieties if they stayed in a poor village like this. They have to find an urban partner to secure a better life. My three children have now found urban partners and are staying with their partners in the city. How can they stay at home! To starve to death?

Both mothers consider the country to be poor and backward and encourage their daughters to live and work in the city. This is also the parents' strategy for ensuring their own economic survival, which would be jeopardized if their daughters returned home.

Returning to the countryside reminded both girls of the uniqueness of their light skin. One of the distinguishing characteristics of the peasants was their dark, sun-baked complexions. Both Fragrance and Dee were proud of and anxious about their light skin, which was unequivocally admired by the villagers. One of the ways that they reinforced their own fragile identities was by looking down on and criticizing the dark skin and out-of-style fashions of their peasant kin. Fragrance was particularly cruel in haranguing her dark-skinned niece Lan for her ugly clothes, skin, and unfashionable hairstyle. Fragrance loudly berated the poor girl: "Look how ugly and dirty your clothes and hair are! If you wear such clothes and hairstyle, people will laugh at you as a country bumpkin!" Holding a club in her hand, Fragrance repeatedly screamed at Lan, "Do you know how ugly you are?" Lan opened her innocent and trusting eyes and said, "I don't know." Thereupon Fragrance bellowed at her, "You are so ugly! You are as ugly as death! You don't know? Look at your skin! So dark! As dark as a fucking donkey's!" Lan could only murmur, "I don't know." Fragrance's words exacerbated Lan's self-hatred of her dark skin and dirty hair. Lan would often tell me (I suspect because I am from urban Dalian), "Little auntie, look how white and slim you are! You are so pretty!" I tried to tell her that she was a beautiful girl (and she really was); however, by that time Lan had already internalized Fragrance's verbal assaults on her.

I believe the main reason Fragrance was so annoyed by Lan's dark skin was that Fragrance herself had made an excruciating effort to shed her dark skin as a signifier of her stigma of rural origins. This had led her to an extreme hatred of dark skin in general. Also, I believe that the prejudice she experienced in the city against her own dark skin had scarred her emotionally. By attacking Lan, she was able to release some of her own pent-up anger and frustration. In so doing, she was able to achieve a certain sense of satisfaction and a sense of superiority that she had been denied in the city.

On their first day back in their respective villages, both Fragrance and Dee were greeted with praise for their beautiful light skin. Fragrance responded by wearing low-cut clothing that revealed the whiteness around her breasts. Dee introduced a special cream to her female friends in the village that would help lighten their skin. Both took meticulous care of their skin and regarded it as a sign of their superior cosmopolitan status.

Hairstyle and clothing are also important markers distinguishing peasant girls from city sophisticates. On returning to their villages, Fragrance, Dee, and Dee's sister Mong all dyed their hair blonde to stand out from their country neighbors. At various times hostesses would streak their hair, or dye it red or chestnut. Dresses worn by the hostesses were often the object of gossip. Anticipating the controversy that their regular outfits would inevitably raise, they wore more conservative attire for the duration of the visit. By urban Dalian standards, these outfits could be classified as "cool," but not in the least remarkable. Even their purposefully toned-down look, however, left many villagers puzzled and outraged. The hostesses' clothes brought even more intense reactions from parents and relatives concerned about maintaining their families' reputation.

While both Dee and Fragrance did not dare wear the most provocative clothing they wore in their work, they were still criticized for immodesty and for flaunting what villagers regarded as garish bright colors. Dee brought her sister Mong a pair of white bell-bottom pants with outlandish flower designs. One evening as I accompanied Dee and her sister strolling along the village road, villagers stopped, speechless, and stared. Mong was wearing the white bell-bottoms, and Dee was dressed in an imitation of a Qing concubine costume. After a moment of silence, one villager uttered in amazement, "What kind of clothes are you wearing?!" *(ni chuan de zhe shi shen me yi shang a).*

Dee's mother, ever sensitive to village gossip, forbade her wearing them in the village. She expressed her disapproval by gathering up her daughter's clothes and setting them on fire. Dee responded with a campaign to educate her mother, combined with partial compliance. While lecturing her mother on the stylishness of urban dress, she resisted by putting on the accepted clothes outside and hiding the unacceptable clothes inside. When her mother was around, she wore the outside clothes; when her mother was away, she immediately took them off. Dee harangued her mother for clinging to old customs and not adapting to the new. Again, I observed Dee positioning herself as the bearer of new and superior culture to the countryside. Under her relentless lecturing, her mother finally relented saying, "I cannot judge my daughters according to the old cultural ways. It is the city way of living. The city is more modern than we are. We have to change our old thoughts and adapt to the new views. I am open-minded now. They can wear whatever they want, and I don't care anymore." So Dee, with the armor of modernism, won the battle of wills with her mother. For her part Fragrance had no opportunity to show off her gaudy clothes. Even in the heat of the summer, she had to wear the layers of loose clothing to cover her stomach and the trace of her recent abortion.

Fragrance's and Dee's deliberate attempts to distinguish themselves by their clothing were part of their campaign to identify themselves as harbingers of modernity. In their view, their superior economic power expressed as conspicuous consumption justified their lifestyle and distinguished them as culturally superior. Unfortunately, the villagers did not accept this representation uncritically. Their distinctive dress and hairstyles were met with gossip and disapproval. Only their light skin was met with uncritical admiration; however, it cannot be denied that there was some recognition even of their clothing, as exemplified by Dee's mother's grudging approval of her daughter's stylishness.

Part of the hostesses' presentation of themselves as sophisticates from the city involved an exaggerated pronunciation of their newly acquired Dalian dialect. Dee flaunted her Dalian dialect saying *bai pao le* (Don't tease me) instead of *bie pao le* (same meaning). The word *bai* (don't) came from Dalian. Her use of the word *dei* (right) instead of *dui* also reflected the Dalian dialect. She said *an jia* (my home) instead of *wo jia*. She appeared quite haughty when using this dialect. Dee's sisters responded to this affectation with shouts of "Shut up" or "Go back to Dalian and never return." Dee only laughed; she considered them lacking her cosmopolitan enjoyment of the dialect. Posing as a connoisseur, she insisted: "Other people comment that the Dalian dialect is not pleasant to the ears. But I don't think so. I think it's much more pleasant than Jilin dialect. People say that after you stay in the city for some time, you naturally learn their language. It's so true. See, now I don't even notice my Dalian dialect as it slips off my tongue unconsciously." Even though the dialect is vehemently rejected by the villagers as a betrayal of their hometown, hostesses cling to it as a sign of their distinctiveness.

Following this theme, Dee never lost a chance to make an invidious comparison between Dalian and her home village. On one occasion she told them, "Dalian is so clean. Unlike us, they plant trees, grass, and flowers along the streets and elsewhere in the city. The whole city is like a big garden. There is no dirt on the ground. Look at our area, so poor and dirty. Nobody has the consciousness to keep the environment clean." She went on lauding the courteousness of Dalianites, their good etiquette and manners. She praised them for cleaning their tables after meals and even for asking for doggie bags to avoid waste. She pointed out that in Dalian the waiters happily offered doggie bags, whereas in Jilin those with wealth flaunted it through unnecessary waste. Further, she proclaimed, "Dalianites do not litter as people do here, where they throw things out of the window or onto the ground as they wish."

One day I watched as Dee attempted to teach the villagers the Dalian way of playing cards. When the villagers rejected this style of play, Dee became almost nostalgic, describing the passion over cards in Dalian that even led to fights in the middle of games. She sighed with affection as she described the card-playing scene in detail.

Dee also tutored the villagers about the advanced acceptance of tattooing in Dalian. When the village girls responded to her praise of tattooing with disgust, she could only sigh and express her desire to get a rose imprinted on her breast. She finished by admonishing the women for their backwardness on this subject: "Dalianites get vibrant and colorful tattoos on various parts of their bodies—very pretty. Here people cannot accept it."

In many peasant societies around the world marriage happens early and is intended to produce lots of children. While the one child policy in China has significantly hampered fertility, this has not changed the cultural attitude in the rural areas. Many urban industrial societies produce very different attitudes toward marriage and fertility. Marriage often comes late and sometimes not at all. Cities do not need to produce children as a source of cheap labor, and many advanced industrial societies have substituted social security systems for care by children. Both attitudes reflect the pragmatism of their respective situations.

For Dee, however, the freedom of late marriage and the absence of children presented another sign of the superiority of urban life. Because of the villagers' acceptance of the importance of early marriage and childbearing, this was one of the things they quizzed Dee on. She would reply that her marriage was still four or five years off, and likely would be childless. Her freedom, as she insisted, was more important than having a husband. To the villagers these words must have felt like an atomic bomb exploding in their midst. Even her sisters were shocked, asking, "Isn't the purpose of life to bear kids?" Dee replied that many urbanites had no children. With pride, Dee proclaimed herself a liberated, single woman. Dee's characterization of rural life as backward, and her rejection of marriage and traditional gender roles invited criticism.

In spite of her boldness in challenging village convention, she was not prepared to admit her true profession in the city. When asked about her work, she claimed to work for a newspaper. When pressed further, she told them that she wrote and set type. Impressed, the villagers asked her where her newspaper was located. When she said Zhongshan Square in the center of the city, some said that they would look for her there when they were in Dalian. Backtracking, Dee said, "No, no, you can't find me there!" This aroused suspicion among some. Hearing that she worked at a newspaper office, Dee's cousin pursed her lips and said to me, "Look at her! She looks like a goblin [yaojing]. How can she be an editor? I cannot find a job anywhere. How can she, without any education, be an editor?" Clearly Dee's cousin did not believe anything that Dee told her. She suspected that Dee worked at an "indecent" profession in the city (what she was alluding to in her "goblin" comment). Even though Dee brought her cousin some clothes from the city, her cousin refused to talk to either her or her sisters. When we ran into her on the street, she passed us by without even saying hello.

Other villagers commented about how wonderful it was that Dee could make her way in the city. A male villager who had traveled to Dalian for work said to Dee, "You're such a pioneer. I've been to Dalian myself. I realized how difficult it is to live there. It's hard to live and work there all by yourself. That's so unusual that you're able to stay there. You're such an admirable woman." Villagers who made such comments were returned migrant workers. On the one hand, having worked in the city as migrant laborers made them acutely aware of the institutional constraints, cultural discrimination, economic exploitations, and possible physical abuse in the city.[7] Clearly, in their eyes, Dee was a heroine because she could make it in the city on her own, despite the harsh urban environment. On the other hand, having lived in the city as migrants themselves, they not only had witnessed the economic gap between the city and the countryside but also had experienced the pervading discourse on consumption in the city. The overwhelming signs and symbols of consumption in the city not only created a desire in them to achieve parity with the urban class but also conveyed a strong message that any means could be justified for the end—a cash income. Therefore, for them, the fact that Dee could obtain access to cash, consumption, and self-sufficiency in the city was a huge success. During our conversations, they would recall the labor of their female cousins who were married to peasants, working in the fields from morning until sunset. While they felt empathy for them, they felt relieved for Dee, who at least did not have to "repair the earth" and therefore escaped the fate of being a peasant.

In various other ways Dee invited the envy and gossip of the villagers. She flaunted her wealth, bragged about her city boyfriend, and flaunted her fake "decent" job before the villagers. She conspicuously offered the cabdriver 10 *yuan,* even though the fare was only 2. She often told others that in Dalian she always drank soft drinks such as Coke or Sprite or red iced teas rather than water. She boasted about throwing away food after tasting it, and that she never rode the bus in Dalian but only took taxis. Dee described with glee the exotic food available in Dalian—for instance, all kinds of live seafood, including fish, shrimp, oysters, and crabs—and she did not fail to mention how expensive the food was. She insisted, uncharacteristically, that she herself did not enjoy the raw seafood because, "I come from a rural area and cannot enjoy their food." She mentioned the names of the fancy restaurants where she had been served exotic seafood, such as the ornate Big Stage and various Korean barbeque restaurants. Once she told her audience that after tasting all of these exotic foods, she found only green onion and soy sauce to her liking. The villagers laughed heartily at this story.

Dee sought out every opportunity to establish her superiority as a consumer. Once, when we were bathing in a public bath near the village, she offered me her expensive bath lotion. Two peasant women enviously exclaimed, "We are too poor; we can only afford bars of soap."

Dee also bragged to the villagers about her city boyfriend, but when they inquired whether they lived together, she insisted that she did not live with him but lived in a dorm. She went on to describe him: "He's a local Dalianite. He works in an advertising company as a designer, earning 4,000 to 5,000 *yuan* a month. He treats me very nice. He looks just like Zheng Yijian [the Hong Kong movie star]. He and his parents have two big houses in the city." "Oh, how lucky you are!" exclaimed the villagers. She also boasted to the villagers that she and I were going to America next year. She repeated these stories like a mantra during our stay in the village. Her stories were met with general admiration, which she clearly craved.

As we have seen, the hostesses occupy a marginal world where their power and sense of identity are always threatened. The need for Dee to construct an alternative story of strength and secure identity seemed to be a direct reflection of her marginal power and identity status. In one area, however, the quest of the returning hostesses for control seems to have been successful. In the case of both Dee and Fragrance, they were able to achieve an uncharacteristically dominant role within the family. The exodus of males into the urban labor market means that hostesses' renegotiation of their power position within the rural family is an attempt to reclaim authority from the matriarch and elder sisters. Even though both Fragrance and Dee were second sisters, they both established their dominance within the family. Fragrance's dominance was largely unchallenged. Even when her mother successfully forbade her allowing the taxi driver to visit her, Fragrance screamed back, "Don't you have ears? Didn't you hear that I told him over the phone not to come here? He likes to come. What can I do?" Her mother could do nothing but sigh.

Fragrance maintained her edge through sheer force of will, constantly yelling at her mother, grandmother, and niece in a shrill voice. No one dared challenge her. Once, when her mother timidly urged her to eat more eggs and avoid spicy foods because of her postabortion condition, Fragrance continued to eat few eggs, preferring hot green onions, sour plums, and salty sauce. When her mother tried to stop her, she bellowed out, "Would you shut up already?" Her mother fell silent. When her mother tried to prevent her from showering on the eighth day after her abortion, Fragrance yelled at her, "I know my own business. What do you know?"

Fragrance used any occasion to intimidate her mother and maintain her dominance. She berated her mother for waking her up too early, and for visiting the neighbors all of the time. She made fun of her grandma's slight deafness and her nagging. Whenever her grandma spoke, Fragrance either laughed or screamed at her. "You don't understand a thing, so be silent! If you don't hear clearly or understand what others have said, be quiet! You are so annoying; you are annoying me to death! You always say stupid things and struggle for words when others are talking!" When her grandmother made a mistake, Fragrance yelled at her, "What are you good for? You are good for nothing [shenmo ye bushi]! Tell me what you can do! You annoy me to death."

Fragrance continued to dress down her niece Lan about controlling her body. She was more abusive than maternal toward Lan. Once when Lan spread her legs, Fragrance screamed at her, "How come you, a little girl, are not ashamed of revealing your lower parts? Who do you show it to? Do you think that it's so beautiful that you want to show it to others?

Fuck your mum, you whore *[biaozi]*! I will beat you to death!" At that she whipped Lan across her body with a switch. Fragrance always cursed Lan and frequently beat her. Lan responded with a terrified obedience.

In her family, Dee also assumed authority. When her third sister, Wu, had a fight at work and was fired, Dee's older sister tried to exercise her authority to support Wu. "Tell me who he is and I will have him beaten to death. I have networks," she said. Dee's elder sister did have a lot of male friends in the village who would, at her command, beat up anybody. However, Dee, reasserting her authority, cut in on the conversation, retorting, "How do you know that the other guy does not have a network that is much larger and more powerful?" Wu immediately agreed with Dee, saying that she knew that the boss did have superior force. Dee then turned on Wu, scolding her for fighting with her boss, and lecturing her on the need to be conscientious about her job instead of stirring up trouble.

Unlike Fragrance, however, Dee's newfound authority was not impervious to challenge. During periods of intense conflict, her sisters would trump Dee's economic power with hints at the "dirty" origins of her money. Most times, however, they acquiesced in her dominance, since all that they wore came from her. Still there was conflict over things like clothes. Dee lectured Wu on not wasting money on more clothes, insisting that she had bought her enough. She also criticized Wu's conservative tastes. Wu responded, "You are shameless and brazen *[buyaolian de]*. Do you think I am the same as you?" On this occasion I was surprised to see that Wu had gotten through her hard armor and had hurt her. Dee's countenance changed quickly, and she left the room.

Dee's older sister Lilly vied constantly to regain the authority she believed should be hers by virtue of being the eldest sister. Lilly used every opportunity to criticize Dee, but Dee was successful in warding off these forays by reminding Lilly of her failure, as older sister, to provide for the family. Dee shouted, "What have you done for the family? All you do all day is play mah-jongg and sleep." She urged her to take up her responsibilities and get a job. The conflict ended in a big fight that led to the end of our stay. When visiting relatives, Lilly wore a dress worth 800 *yuan* given her by Dee. When one relative we were visiting criticized Dee's dress, saying that Lilly's was much nicer, Dee angrily pointed at Lilly and said, "Ask her whose dress she is wearing and ask her how many of the dresses she wears are really hers! Whose dress do you think that really is? Ask her who bought it for her!" Challenged, Lilly shouted back, "You are shameless and brazen! Get lost as soon as possible! Leave here and don't ever let me see you again!"

Hearing these words, Dee began crying, tears streaming down her face. She grabbed my arms and asked me to leave with her immediately. She said she wanted to go as far as possible and never to return to this place again. When Dee was about to leave, everyone in her family was preoccupied. Her three sisters were playing mah-jongg next door. Her mother was sitting on the bed watching TV. I asked her mom why she said nothing to Dee. In response, her mother said:

> What can I say? This child seems to have no mum or dad—she always floats around, and her heart belongs nowhere. I really worry about her. Such an unmoored life leads nowhere. What brings her here is simply uncertainty. She cannot live like this all her life. She needs to settle somewhere to end this life of uncertainty, danger, and risk.

I turned to Dee and asked her to talk to her mother before departing. Raising her eyes from a popular novel, Dee replied that she just wanted to read. Later on, Dee said, "In fact, whatever my mum wants to tell me, I know already. There is no need for her to say it again." Walking away from Dee's home, I felt sad. Dee, however, dashed out happily in front of me, glad to have left her home far behind her. Without tears or regrets, Dee simply looked back and said, "I will not come back again unless I hear the news of my elder sister's marriage.[8] I want to go to Dalian so badly!"

While in the city, hostesses idealize their country home as a peaceful and restful place where they can nurse the wounds that their lives in the city have given them. Yet when they actually are in their hometown, they are pushed away by gossip, ostracism, and contempt. Each time, they vow never to come back again, yet they return nevertheless. Although over the years they have tried to forget and erase their feelings of home, attachment to home still pulls them back whenever they cannot endure the pains of life in the city.

Both Dee and Fragrance return home when they are hurt in the city. (Fragrance was raped and had an abortion; Dee's urban boyfriend hinted at a breakup.) Although they do not wish to linger home for long, home still offers them an escape from the place that scarred their hearts. However, when they do return home, they feel awkward and uneasy. They cannot avoid this tension between home and city, yet they must face and reconcile themselves to this dilemma.

Fragrance and Dee as second daughters successfully challenged the family hierarchy and assumed authority at home. Their authority derived from their contributions to their families' economic well-being as well as the skills at cursing and fighting developed as a matter of survival and self-defense during their time in Dalian's red-light district. This ability was primarily due to the economic power they wielded, which allowed them to defy and supplant traditional authority figures in the family. In spite of the acceptance of their authority by their mothers, their sisters continued to challenge them by denigrating their shameless and indecent work in the cities.

I had much to think about as I rode beside Dee on the long return journey from my second foray into the countryside. Here we were in the dark of night suspended between tradition and progress, rushing toward the bright lights of hope awaiting us in Dalian.

Unlike the migrants studied by other anthropologists, Dalian hostesses do not come home to stay. Rather, home is a temporary shelter and refuge from the risks and dangers of their lives in the city. They return to a countryside of grinding poverty, largely occupied by women and children. Unlike the women in south China in Cindy Fan's research,[9] the hostesses in my research did not bend to the pressures of early marriage or allow traditional attitudes toward gender to shape their actions. Unlike the subjects in John W. Traphagen's study of Japanese returnees,[10] the hostesses were not forced to stay at home to meet their filial obligations but were encouraged to reside in the city for the family's economic benefit. My conclusion about returnees' responses to the demands for cultural compliance is also in contrast to the findings of James Ferguson's African studies.[11] Ferguson describes an all-or-nothing requirement that forces returning migrants to accept the code of local culture. I found a much more complicated and nuanced negotiation of local culture among my subjects. While, as I have illustrated, the returning hostesses were loyal to their filial obligations, and were admired for their wealth and fair skin, they were criticized for their lifestyles, and even admiration sometimes was expressed as jealousy. The hostesses for their part were often harsh with relatives and contemptuous of the impoverished lifestyle in the countryside.

On the one hand, home is the place where they can nurse the wounds suffered in the city and exercise a certain degree of authority derived from their economic power. On the other hand, this authority is by no means impervious to challenge, especially with hints at the "dirty" origin of the money. Nonetheless, for the hostesses, experiencing once again the harshness of rural living reaffirms their decision to migrate and encourages them to feel pride in their urban status and the wealth they have obtained. Seeing women their own age suffer from tedious and heavy farm work, poverty, and the constraints of marriage, hostesses feel more contented with their choice of the city. Such an ambiguous attitude toward "home" was similarly found in other anthropologists' work on migrant women, notably Filipino domestic workers in Hong Kong, Chinese brides in the United States, Thai rural migrant workers in Bangkok, and Koreans in Japan.[12] These migrants all shared conflicting perceptions about "home." Home is no longer a peaceful and restful place as they had imagined, and they are reluctant to forgo the kind of personal autonomy, economic independence, freedom, professional identity, and economic progress gained in the host place. Their ambiguous perceptions toward the city and the rural home certainly add a touch of complexity to the question of whether migration can bring women social power.

Six

CLOTHES MAKE THE WOMAN

THIS CHAPTER SUGGESTS A TREMENDOUS IRONY: hostesses are important consumers and trendsetters in a fashion industry in which the clothes are manufactured in sweat shops manned by exploited women workers. Many hostesses started working in such factories before deciding hostessing was more lucrative. They are able to avoid factory work because they are supported by a sex industry serving men. Women literally get screwed by the sexist economy, both coming and going.

As a result of the historical trends of patriarchy and masculinity as the primary driving force behind the emergence of karaoke bars, a new and challenging entrepreneurial masculinity requires the hostesses to play an obedient and subservient role while in their personal lives trying to maintain a sense of personal dignity. The challenge to the hostesses is to achieve wealth through satisfying the consumption needs of the new entrepreneurial men while still claiming for themselves a cosmopolitan image.

How do hostesses enter hostessing? What are the attractive features of hostessing? How do the hostesses, through this kind of work, achieve a modern and cosmopolitan image in the post-Mao urban landscape? This chapter answers these questions by focusing on hostesses' appropriation of the cultural symbols of consumption to foreground a pioneering image. As migrants and sex workers, hostesses are subject to virulent institutional and social discrimination in the city. Hostesses are acutely aware of their status as marginalized second-class citizens and aim to achieve parity with their urban counterparts. Hostessing offers an effective venue to achieve equal social status with urbanites. These women struggle within a system of rural-urban apartheid to forge a new identity, but their freedom is sharply curtailed by the economic and political constraints under which they operate.

The characteristics exhibited by hostesses' consumption patterns defy analytical perspectives that treat consumption as individualistic expressive behavior. These patterns of consumption suggest that their consumption, rather than being the product of freely operating, individual imaginations, is directly curtailed by their social position as rural migrant women and sex workers. Their consumption practices aim at achieving an urban identity. Still, their body practices cannot be accurately described as an imitation of urban women. Imitation connotes a lack of originality and passivity. The imitator is limited to reproducing the master copy. In contrast, how hostesses refashion their bodies demonstrates a defiant and creative agency.

By remaking their bodies, hostesses not only seek to achieve social parity with urban women but to become their fashion superiors. Hostesses' body practices, taken as a totality, constitute a highly distinctive style. Hostesses form a prominent feature of the city's human landscape. Many of the accoutrements in the hostesses' wardrobes are rarely if ever used by other social groups. These include a variety of noticeably inconvenient shoe styles, stick-on tattoos, and fake eyelashes. These distinctive markings identify them as hostesses.

The public nature of hostesses' consumption points to a new way of treating consumption behavior as a form of claim. By *claim*, I mean a publicly addressed assertion directed toward the other members of society. In China's new commodity-oriented society, how one consumes expresses who one is. Thus the ability to consume well—in other words, to have taste—becomes a crucial aspect of identity. This cultural logic masks the economic inequality at the root of the rural-urban consumption gap by disguising it as a difference in cultural taste. Thus, the shabby appearance of peasants, rather than being a reflection of their poverty, becomes a symptom of their poverty in taste.

Indeed, this logic leaves open a certain amount of room for maneuver and contestation. Through their consumption and body fashioning, hostesses contest their image as country bumpkins who do not have the autonomous consciousness or cultural taste to consume well. Their consumption challenges and reinforces but, at the same time, expresses a parody of the stereotyped rural-urban bodies repeated in state and popular discourses, and, ultimately, calls them into question.

ANTHROPOLOGY OF CONSUMPTION

Recent developments in anthropological approaches to consumption make consumption practices easier to understand. Except for a few economic models on spheres of exchange and gifting, anthropologists remained silent on the question of consumption for an extended period of time (1950–1970).[1] As Daniel Miller explains, this lack of interest in consumption was due to anthropologists' view of the consumption of "Western goods" as a loss of culture and a threat to the anthropological object of study.[2] In recent years, however, studies have started to question the use-value of commodities in the Marxist paradigm and to reveal domination and manipulation hidden within consumption activities.[3]

During the past two decades, a new anthropology of consumption has arisen. This new literature can be divided into three main trends of thought. Anthropologists in the first trend lump consumption and production together in one integrated process and study the consequences of Western consumption for production in the developing world.[4] A surging interest has arisen around the Third World consumption of global forms of modernity as a form of resistance.[5] Rather than leading to cultural homogeneity, the appropriation of Western cultural products—variously called "localization," "domestication," and "glocalization"—has given rise to "alternative modernities," claim authors in this trend.[6] A second trend concentrates on the social dimensions of consumption. Marcel Mauss theorizes a dichotomy between gift and commodity exchange.[7] The gift economy in "traditional societies" is viewed as social, whereas the market economy that mediates commodity exchange in industrial societies is supposed to be divorced from social relationships and, therefore, rational and impersonal. Mauss's distinction has been challenged in recent works that question the existence of pure economic and market relations. These scholars employ a "social economy" approach that emphasizes social values and status.[8] Finally, a third trend links consumption with social relations and social hierarchy. Pierre Bourdieu provides the greatest example in this analytical inquiry.[9] Bourdieu employs a voluminous amount of empirical data to examine an array of consumption habits. He convincingly demonstrates how different consumption tastes in aesthetic and cultural products such as painting, music, attire, furniture, and food reflect and reproduce social distinctions in class, gender, and other social configurations.

Following this line of thought, Daniel Miller argues that social values and relations are created not prior to the cultural forms but during the processual formation of them.[10] He thus focuses on material culture in the process of its objectification. In his work, Miller argues that consumption constitutes the main arena in which individuals can struggle against social oppression. Miller not only celebrates the liberating nature of consumption but also argues against the anticonsumption position that labels consumption as a decadent form of self-indulgence. For Miller, commodities are toys/tools that consumers can integrate within their personal imaginative projects, thereby achieving greater levels of personal development.

Miller's approach to consumption marks a major advance, but my research findings suggest that his theoretical claims are incomplete. First, hostesses' consumption patterns are less about sheer liberation than they are about a cultural negotiation of power *through* and *within*—rather than outside of the enabling and constraining rural-urban apartheid system. In the course of such a struggle, they assert their claim. Miller's theory leaves out the power and politics embedded in the system that influences, if not determines, the forms of consumption. As illustrated in this research, hostesses' consumption choices enable them to struggle within their urban social surroundings, but they are also constrained by the economic and political forces at work in this setting. In addition, hostesses' consumption patterns raise questions about Miller's view that consumption is a form of individualistic expressive behavior. Rather, this chapter suggests that commodity consumption by bar hostesses possesses a distinctly public character.

Such an expanded view of consumption allows us to see the collective or communal dimension of hostesses' consumption of clothing. The use of clothing—that is, the wearing of clothes—is undeniably an individual affair: clothes in general can only be worn on one body at a time. Hostesses do not just wear their clothes, however; they also talk about what to wear. Thus, while clothing is worn by the individual, clothing fashion is still very much a matter for the group. Clothes talk provides the verbal environment within which hostesses and, to a lesser degree, other social groups interpret hostesses' clothing. This verbal dimension is often ignored in theoretical discussions of clothing semiotics that assume the wearer and viewer of clothing are disconnected or otherwise unable to communicate with each other. Grant David McCracken, for example, conducted experiments in which test subjects were shown slides of people in various forms of dress and asked to interpret their meaning.[11] The resulting incongruity and variety of responses were taken as evidence of clothing's "low semanticity," that is, the inability of clothing as a sign system to consistently deliver coherent messages or ideas. The participants in McCracken's study did not have an opportunity to talk with the people whose image they saw reproduced in the experiment. While this state of silence or noncommunication may be true of a majority of interpretive encounters (we do not always have the opportunity to discuss our clothes with everyone who happens to see us), there are also important exceptions. As this chapter explores, hostesses' clothing does not always have to "speak" for itself; hostesses often speak for their clothing and through their clothing.

The public character of hostesses' consumption practices can be discerned from the following two aspects. First, the physical dimension: hostesses' consumption takes the form of bodily alterations. Some of these alterations are permanent or semipermanent (for example, breast enlargement or double-eyelid operations). Thus, unlike typical commodity consumption, hostesses' consumption cannot be restricted to the private sphere of the home. Hostesses cannot "take off" their surgically altered body parts when they get off from work. In this sense, these body alterations are by nature directed toward an unspecified public audience. Second, the social dimension: hostesses as a distinct social group exhibit nearly identical consumption habits. This suggests that hostesses' consumption is directly related to their social position as rural migrant women and as sex workers rather than the product of freely operating, individual imaginations.

Entry into the Karaoke Bar Sex Industry

Hostessing was not necessarily the first job for the hostesses. Many started out in factories, restaurants, and hotels as workers or waitresses. Some entered hostessing because late receipt of their paychecks and severe deduction in wages put them in unbearable financial straits. Others went through the torture of abandonment and rape in the urban working environment. Most of them walked into the karaoke bars themselves, and some were introduced by relatives or family members. Being a karaoke bar hostess did not demand any educational background. As I learned from the hostesses, each of them had to go through a transitional period at the beginning of their work when they spent nights crying and then went to work with a smile. As Wu said to me, "During the first week, I could not sleep. I spent night after night in tears. I started writing daily journals. I wrote down all my bitter feelings. I asked myself, other people can do it [hostessing], why can't I? Is money not good? *[qian bu hao hua ma]*." Wu migrated to a nearby city to work in a plastic factory. She found herself working three months without being paid. At the end of the third month, she could not afford any food or drink. Later she fell seriously sick and was hospitalized. She said:

> Suffering from high fever, I was given a transfusion in the hospital. I was by myself in the hospital, lying in bed. Nobody from work came to see me. I was holding the transfusion bottle with my left hand, trying to hang it onto the hook above my head. But I could not reach it. I was trying and trying, but still could not reach it. How I wish someone were beside me— I did not ask for more. Just handing me a cup of water would have been more than enough! But there was nobody—only me. I was crying and crying. I was sick from work, yet nobody came to help me.

Wu was not paid a penny for three months. She was in debt as a result of her living expenses and hospital bills. She finally walked into a karaoke bar. She said, "I have no other way but to earn money from urban men." After working in the karaoke bar for one year, Wu not only helped pay back her family debt, but also sent more than 5,000 *yuan* for her mother's hospital bill. When I visited Wu's home in Jilin Province, Wu's mother told me, "Wu by herself has been sustaining our six-person family over these years." Wu knows that she would never have accomplished this if she had stayed in the factory that never paid her.

Rural women face limited employment opportunities in the city. First, in post-Mao China, there is a lack of private sector jobs.[12] Second, as migrants, they often lack the social connections essential for finding jobs in the already oversaturated urban labor market. Their ability to find work is further hindered by a discriminatory government policy that denies migrants equal status with urban residents.[13] Among the jobs that are available to rural women, most are in low-paid, labor-intensive industries. Under these circumstances, hostessing is a highly attractive employment option. The positive features of hostessing are many. I will illustrate how hostessing is their only venue to achieve equal social status with urbanites.

THE ECONOMICS OF BAR HOSTESSING

Hostessing held out the allure of high incomes in the least amount of time. Hostessing as a mode of sexual service was different from prostitution. Prostitutes engage in genital and oral sex with clients, but this was not necessarily true of hostesses. Hostesses' sexual services encompassed two forms: waiting on clients *(zuo tai)* and "going out" with clients *(chu tai)*. The former occurred within the karaoke private rooms. It included a range of behaviors from entertainment (singing, dancing, drinking) to non–genital-to-genital sexual contact (fondling). A *zuo tai* session typically lasts for one to two hours, for which hostesses earn an average tip of 200 to 400 *yuan*—the equivalent of, and often more than, other rural migrants' monthly wages, and almost half the average monthly wage of an urban worker. Hostesses could earn even higher incomes by "going out" with customers—that is, performing genital or oral sex with clients. The rate for such services could range anywhere from 300 to 5,000 *yuan*, depending on numerous factors such as the length of the service session (for instance, some customers contract hostesses for an entire evening) and other idiosyncratic bargaining conditions. Virgins commanded especially high prices: up to 10,000 *yuan*. Services were conducted either on the premises in specially designated, private rooms *(pao fang)* usually located on the bar's second floor, or at outside hotels.

Working as a hostess provided rural women access to a wide network of influential male figures in the city's business and political sectors and required a minimal upfront investment. Newly arrived hostesses typically borrowed money from other hostesses or friends to purchase the clothing and accessories worn while servicing clients. Because of the high profitability of hostessing, the borrower could typically settle her debt with the earnings from one or two sessions with clients. Thus, rural women who lacked economic resources could nonetheless enter the workforce as hostesses.

LEARNED URBAN CULTURAL STYLES

Karaoke bars, as flourishing new cultural spaces in the city, were the places where rural migrant women could achieve a certain degree of self-esteem by being accepted and desired by the urban men who chose them as companions for the night. The karaoke bar was also the place where these women could find secondary socialization by mingling with urban clients, where they felt "urban and cosmopolitan" both culturally and socially. Hostess Ying migrated to the city and worked in a factory during the mid-1990s. She was even selected as the model worker in the factory. Later on the factory went bankrupt and closed down. She was laid off without any financial resources. Her female friends took her to a dancing hall to accompany men. To make a living, she followed them:

> I thought nobody would dance with me because of my low quality [su zhi tai di] and rural origin. However, to my surprise, some urban men invited me. A man from the Labor Bureau even liked me a lot. Once I ran into him on the street and he asked me to have dinner with him in a restaurant. I refused his love but did go to the restaurant with him. I was such a foolish cunt [sha bi]—I was completely ignorant of a restaurant, let alone of all the eating or talking etiquettes. I was such a foolish cunt, so stupid, you mother fucker. I did not know how to eat or talk. I was a peasant. When had I ever seen a restaurant? You know at that time nobody in my village had ever been to a restaurant. Very few even heard about it. As a factory worker, I only earned 400 yuan a month. When on earth had I ever seen this amount of money and the atmosphere of the restaurant? After that event I was so shocked by my incongruity with the urban people. I started working as a dancing companion. Two months later I went back home with loads of money, several thousand yuan. At that time it was a lot of money. Nobody had ever seen so much money before. The money I earned meant a lot for everyone.

For Ying, living an urban lifestyle affirms an equal status with urbanites; chosen by urban clients in karaoke bars confirms her self-worth.

INDEPENDENCE

Hostesses' experience of rape and abandonment in the city taught them not to be duped by men's romantic words and to embrace independence through hostessing. Han worked as a hairdresser in the city. She lived with an urban man for three years in his house. During that time, she suffered

from all kinds of physical and verbal abuse from his aunt and mother. For
instance, they accused her of stealing their jewelry and associated her
"thieving habits" with her rural background. All these abuses were targeted
at her inferior rural background. Han exerted every effort to endure these
inhumane treatments. However, her urban boyfriend also worried that her
rural family would become a bottomless hole, draining all his money in
the future. He abruptly abandoned her, saying, "Our social statuses just
don't match." Devastated, she believed that she would never find happiness unless she became the social and economic equal of the urbanites.
She started working as a hostess. Within five years she had become very
successful. She possessed two household registrations, one urban and one
rural. She had purchased two houses, one in her hometown for her parents and one in Dalian for her siblings. She supported her two younger
sisters and a brother through school. She paid for the weddings of her four
older brothers and sisters and so on. She is now married to the financial
director of a prestigious hotel chain.

Likewise, another hostess, Hong, broke up with her client boyfriend who
failed to offer her the amount of money she expected. She commented:

> I myself can earn 100,000 *yuan* from hostessing in a month. To exchange
> for his several thousand *yuan*—so little money—I have to obey everything
> he says. Who will do that? He thinks I am fresh from the countryside, so I
> can easily be cheated. With so little money, he wants me to be his second
> wife and control me as his possession by tying my arms and legs. That's
> impossible. I want to earn money for myself and spend it happily at my
> will. There is no way for me to spend his little money at the price of
> abiding by whatever he has to say.

If rural origin and cultural inferiority were the root of the hierarchical relationship between rural migrant women and urban men, then hostessing
offered an opportunity to escape subordination. As paid work, hostessing
represented an act of defiance against the misogynist urban men who
freely exploited their bodies and emotions. At the bar, men had to pay a
high price to hostesses in exchange for even approaching them. It transformed the situation where migrant women were enjoyed like a free dinner, available at the men's whim.

Hostessing allowed them to achieve economic profit and hence independence from men. In the monetary transaction, hostesses attained a kind of

equality with urban men by taking advantage of their resources. Having financial resources at their disposal brought them power and confidence. Many hostesses who were either married or kept as second wives sneaked out of home to work. Setting up their own separate accounts allowed them to spend their own money at will and secretly support their natal families. The economic power brought by hostessing earned Han and Hong a great degree of independence and equality in social and gender status in familial and spousal relationships with urban partners.

Body Practices of the Hostesses
resocialization in karaoke bars

In the context of this highly charged rural-urban divide, bars served as crucial sites for hostesses' resocialization from a rural orientation to an urban-based, hostess culture. Newly arrived hostesses' interaction with male customers and more experienced hostesses introduced these rural women to new aesthetic standards and body culture. In the bars, hostesses were also exposed to a myriad of media products that helped shape their aesthetic sensibilities. For some hostesses, this might be their first, prolonged exposure to these cultural forms. For others, it might be a continuation of previous encounters. Whatever these individual variations, however, all newly arrived hostesses went through a period of adjustment in which they abandoned certain aesthetic values and practices and picked up others.

These processes of resocialization involved learning about new cultural products, and getting feedback from male customers and from interhostess exchanges that involved both imitation and explicit teaching. Hostesses were avid students of television advertisements and fashion magazines. While waiting for customers, they passed the time by viewing Hong Kong and Taiwanese films and pornographic videos (both Western and Asian in origin). These different products were all potential sources of new ideas for body practices. Male customers' responses to hostesses' appearance also helped shape hostess body culture. On the one hand, customers communicated their preferences by making direct verbal comments on hostesses' appearance. On the other hand, customer preferences were indirectly communicated through their selection of some hostesses rather than others when they visited bars.

Customer feedback had a powerful influence over this body culture. No hostess body practice could persist if it violated customer preferences. By rewarding or punishing certain practices, customer opinion was perhaps the single most important influence. At the same time, however, the impact of customer feedback should not be exaggerated. There were several factors that mitigated the influence of customer feedback on hostess body practice. Customer feedback in most cases was highly ambiguous. For example, there was no way for a hostess to know whether she had been selected for her skirt or her hairstyle or some combination thereof. The same uncertainty plagued hostesses when they were rejected. Even direct feedback was of limited use in affecting hostess body practice. This was because the form of customer comments was usually an absolute statement: "I like this" or "I don't like that." Ambiguity increased because customers did not necessarily have fixed or clear preferences, and because different customers had different preferences.

Thus, the formation of hostess body culture was neither a male-dictated process nor a simple externalization of male customers' preferences. Rather, customer preference set the basic parameters within which hostesses created their own body culture. Indeed, body practice was a favorite topic among hostesses. During downtime, waiting for customers in the lobby, they swapped techniques and discussed the pros and cons of different products and brands. As a result, hostesses' standards for evaluating new fashions were only tangentially related to customer preference. The following scene illustrates the influence of interhostess commentary on fashion choices. One day, hostess Li came into work wearing a red dress similar in style to the frilly gowns commonly used at wedding photograph parlors. The dress was universally greeted by other hostesses with outright revulsion ("How can you wear that thing?"). At first, Li was defiant and persisted in wearing the dress despite the other hostesses' incessant remarks. To the surprise of everyone, this hostess was still chosen by customers to wait on them. Her success in attracting business, however, did not lead to a revision of the majority opinion. Hostesses continued their stream of derogatory comments. Eventually, Li abandoned wearing the dress.

This case demonstrates an important point about fashion commentary between hostesses: hostess evaluation of fashion was not fully constrained by customer preference. Hostesses maintained their disapproval of the dress even in the face of apparently contradictory customer appraisal. Hostesses found it perplexing and even a little vexing that customer opinion seemed to be contradicting their evaluation of the dress. They complained: "What are these customers thinking? How is it that they choose her?" Moreover, faced with contradictory feedback from customers and hostesses, Li eventually chose to heed the admonitions of her fellow hostesses. Hostesses were more direct and articulate about their likes and dislikes than customers. They were very outspoken in their opinions of one another's appearance. Such reciprocal commentary made up a large portion of hostesses' everyday conversation. It reflected the importance that hostesses attached to their appearance, and at the same time it offered a kind of light conversation that was good for killing time during the long stretches of downtime between service sessions.

BODY CULTURE OF HOSTESSES

Hostesses often jokingly asked each other to cut off their breasts and legs to be weighed so that they could compare these body parts with each other. They subjectively viewed their body as a collection of segmented parts. Hostesses invented a drinking game in which different parts of the body represented Hong Kong movie stars. In the game, the buttocks were defined as Feifei (literally, "fatty"), a Hong Kong movie star famous for her full figure; the head as Chow Yun Fat (a Hong Kong movie star who appears in an advertisement for a popular brand of shampoo); the breasts as Ye Limei (a Hong Kong movie star with large breasts); and the eyes as Lin Yilian (a Hong Kong singer with attractive eyes). A player said the name of one of these Hong Kong stars, and the other player had to correctly point to the part of her body associated with that celebrity. When performed in rapid succession and after a few drinks, matching the celebrity to the correct body part became quite difficult.

The hostesses' subjective view of their bodies was grounded in the unique economics of hostessing. Hostesses, unlike prostitutes, did not necessarily engage in sexual intercourse with customers. Sexual contact between hostesses and customers was often limited to fondling performed during the course of other, social-oriented services (like singing and dancing). This kind of sexual service led to a highly differentiated system of pricing. Hostesses attached a price tag to different body parts and levied cash from customers according to the parts that they had touched. From lowest to highest value, these parts included legs, breasts, and vagina. Once hostess Song found that she was 1 *yuan* short for the taxi fee of 6 *yuan*. Song said to the others, "I am going to tell the driver, 'You can touch my breasts once. Then I do not owe you anything.'" The other hostesses immediately responded, "No, that's too cheap for them. Go tell the driver, 'My ride is 6 *yuan*. One touch of my breasts is worth 50 *yuan*. So you should give me back the change of 44 *yuan!*' Remember, our bodies are our capital *[ben qian]!*"

This conversation reveals how hostesses viewed their bodies as resources to be capitalized upon. Any man, no matter their boyfriend or their client, had to offer gifts or monetary rewards for the parts they had touched and for the sexual services they had engaged. (As I will discuss in the next chapter, the hostesses insisted that no one could freely use their bodies on the basis of pure love and romance.) This form of body commoditization led to profound psychic consequences that extended far beyond the sphere of work into hostesses' personal and imaginative lives. Reflecting this elaborate pricing scheme, hostesses viewed their own and other hostesses' bodies as an assembly of fragmented parts. In my fieldwork, I encountered many different behaviors that manifested this view.

Hostesses' body practices exist on two separate levels. On the one hand, body refashioning is a form of market behavior. Its underlying impetus is the maximization of economic gains. On the other hand, ornamentation is a form of symbolic behavior. Its underlying cause is thus more complex and less easily discerned by the social analyst.

An economic-reductionist approach would attempt to explain hostesses' beautification entirely in terms of its economic dimension: sex workers beautify themselves to attract customers for sexual transactions. This is only part of the picture. First, hostesses are not merely sex workers, but also rural migrant women. The economic-reductionist approach considers only the work identity of the hostesses—as if migrant women shed their rural backgrounds after entering the sex industry. Second, economic-reductionism can explain only a portion of the beautification practices of the hostesses, leaving some behavior unaccounted for. Hostesses dress up in their free time—when they go out shopping, dating, sightseeing, and dining—when there is no obvious economic incentive for them to do so. Although work-time and free-time wardrobes are not entirely the same, this difference is only in degree, not quality. For example, hostesses wear more makeup during work time than off time. Likewise, the work outfits of hostesses tend to be more provocative than their off-time clothing. Some of these differences, however, simply reflect pragmatic considerations. For example, hostesses wear heavier makeup while working because the private rooms in the karaoke bars are dimly lit to create an intimate effect.

The argument could be made that the hostesses are looking for business even in their free time. Although it is not unheard of for hostesses to pick up new male "friends" in their free time, it is nonetheless far too uncommon for this to be the prime motivation behind free-time dressing up. Rather, there are noneconomic motives for dressing up.

The hostesses' own accounts of their beautification stress noneconomic motives. Hostesses dress up not only to appear beautiful for their clients but also to surpass their urban counterparts by appearing more modern and fashionable. They often negatively comment on the wardrobes of urbanites, using terms such as *tuqi* ("provincial," literally, "hick"), usually used by urbanites to deride peasants. Dressing up is also seen as a way of effacing their rural origins. One hostess often bragged that her boyfriend, a native of the city, said that she did not look like a person from the countryside at all. Other hostesses also made similar statements that their modern dress style made them indistinguishable from real urbanites.

To appear more attractive to male clients and to efface their rural background, hostesses pursued techniques of body refashioning and ornamentation. This entailed consuming various forms of body-altering products and surgical services, which included both permanent alterations (plastic surgery) and non- to semipermanent bodily modifications (whitening creams, fake double-eyelids, permanent hair waves).

WEIGHT

While escorting customers, hostesses consumed large quantities of alcoholic beverages, mostly bottled beer. Over time this resulted in protruding pot or beer bellies. To counteract this effect, hostesses used various diet formulas to achieve and maintain a slender figure. Many of these diet products were extremely harmful to their health. One of the most popular products, a diet pill called Gudao, induced extreme nausea, frequent diarrhea, and a disgust for food. Despite the obvious physical harm caused by these drugs, a majority of hostesses still used them on a regular basis.

BREASTS

Hostesses' change in attitude toward breast size reflected the gap between rural and urban body cultures. According to hostesses, in the countryside large breasts were interpreted as a sign of female licentiousness. It was typical for rural women to bind their breasts with a cloth band to restrict growth. This breast-binding practice, however, was rapidly abandoned after migration to the city, where hostesses' access to television and print media exposed them to a myriad of advertisements and messages that overtly and covertly promoted large breasts as beautiful. Also, male customers' preference for large-breasted hostesses created a powerful economic incentive for hostesses to increase their breast size. Full-breasted hostesses possessed a clear advantage over small-breasted hostesses in the competition to attract customers. Customers markedly discriminated against small-breasted hostesses in their selection of escorts, and they often compared the breast size of their female escorts. During service sessions, customers continuously fondled hostesses' breasts. As a result, hostesses with large breasts were said to "have it made" and were the subject of other hostesses' envy. Thus, hostesses were intensely preoccupied with breasts and breast size, and they regularly swapped tips on the most effective breast enlargement techniques, including breast-enhancing undergarments, creams, electric devices, herbal pills, and soaps. In addition to these over-the-counter products, some hostesses underwent breast augmentation surgery. However, the high cost of the operation—Dalian's most upscale plastic surgery clinic, a Chinese-Japanese joint venture, charges 10,600 *yuan* (roughly equivalent to $1,325)—was prohibitive for most hostesses.

SKIN

Skin tone is one of the physical indicators commonly used to distinguish rural migrants from urbanites: light skin indicates an urban background, dark skin, a rural background. This classification method is rooted in China's spatial division of labor: urban laborers work in the indoor settings of factories and offices; rural laborers work in the outdoor setting of the farm field. As a result, dark skin has become a working-class signifier associated with agricultural toil.[14]

Hostesses almost universally believed that their skin was too dark and took great efforts to lighten their complexions. Hostesses commonly employed two means to create whiter skin: one was the use of whitening cosmetics and creams. A popular brand of "herbal" facial cream called Luhui burned off the outer layer of facial skin to allow a new layer of whiter skin to grow. I was amazed to see these women, as young as seventeen years of age, peel off a layer of their facial skin after applying the transparent, glue-like cream to their face for ten minutes. The other means was to decorate their bodies with brightly colored body ornaments such as red rings and multicolored bracelets. The purpose was to create color contrast between the ornaments and skin so that the latter appeared to take on a lighter tone.

HAIR

Hairstyle functions as a diacritical marker distinguishing rural and urban women. This is reflected in many mass media works. A television advertisement for Ai Li Si shampoo differentiates rural women from city women according to their hairstyle and hair quality. In the advertisement, three countryside women have just arrived in the city. Their hair is braided into two braids. As they are marveling at the tall buildings, they catch a glimpse of a city woman as she enters into a beauty parlor. The city woman's hair is treated with the advertised shampoo. When she emerges, her shiny, straight hair sweeps freely along her shoulders. The three countryside women are taken in by her beauty and enter the hair salon to apply the shampoo. When they emerge, their twin braids have been replaced by the city woman's hairstyle.

This advertisement follows a familiar cultural script of personal metamorphosis: the advertisement promises to transform rural woman (Cinderella) into a modern urban woman (the Princess) through the use of the advertised product. The advertisement puts forward the city woman's hairstyle as the desirable aesthetic standard. This imposed standard incites peasant women's dissatisfaction with their appearance and tantalizes them to imitate the urban women. By consuming the shampoo, rural women can produce an improved alternative to what they are by copying the image of a modern urban woman.

Hostesses expended large amounts of time and money on hair products and hair styling. They were very adventurous in their choice of hairstyle and color, changing their look almost on a daily basis. They had their hair dyed in different colors or in stripes and styled into a variety of fashionable shapes. Some of them dyed their hair a red so bright that it hurt your eyes. In part, this was due to the demands of the hostessing profession: hostesses needed to constantly change their appearance in order to prevent returning customers from becoming bored. At the same time, hairstyle was also a way of dissociating themselves from their rural backgrounds. According to the hostesses, dirty or unfashionable hair revealed your rural background. They often critically commented on each other's hair, saying, "That is so hick *[tuqi]*!"

Hostesses used these techniques to achieve two separate but interrelated goals. First, hostesses hoped to make themselves more attractive to male clients, thereby increasing their earning power. Second, hostesses attempted to efface their rural background and construct a new urban persona as demonstrated in the media images.

Consumption Practices as Forms of Public Struggle

My research findings demonstrate that hostesses tried every means to avoid being victimized by this overarching antagonistic system. Among their widespread forms of "everyday resistance," consumption practices constituted a crucial weapon hostesses used to wrestle with the surrounding society. Their routine consumption habits could be seen as attempts to undermine while conforming to a system in which they found themselves exploited.

As we have seen, the hostessing profession allowed resource-poor rural women to realize rapid economic gains. This increase in economic power opened up a myriad of previously inaccessible consumption options. Working and living closely with the hostesses helped me understand their spending patterns. I accompanied the hostesses as they shopped and visited hair salons, while recording in minute detail their expenses in every category: clothing, cosmetics, education, remittance, and room and board. At the low-class bar, the average monthly wage was 6,000 *yuan,* when business was sluggish. This amount was strictly limited to sitting on the stage—accompanying clients singing, dancing, and drinking. It did not include the extra money that they regularly or irregularly snatched from clients; some may earn an extra 5,000 *yuan* for a single sale of sexual services. Mobile phones, phone bills, rent (only three hostesses chose to rent an apartment together instead of living in the karaoke bar), and much of the clothing, food, and education fees were covered by their client friends.

If we take 6,000 *yuan* as the average monthly wage at the low-class bar, aside from remittances (50 percent, or 3,000 *yuan*), clothing and cosmetics (30 percent, or 1,800 *yuan*) constituted the largest portion of hostesses' economic resources. Other expenses such as education and room and board only consisted of 10 percent each (600 *yuan*, or 1,200 *yuan* in total).

Thus, hostesses used various forms of conspicuous consumption to erase their rural origins and lay claim to a new urban identity. The example of hostess Hong from a low-ranking karaoke bar will help to explain these data. Her average monthly income was 6,000 *yuan*. Like all other hostesses, she paid 50 *yuan* a month to live at the karaoke bar and ordered three meals from the several restaurants on the street opposite to the bar. These restaurants were specifically targeted at the hostesses. The meals were very cheap, about 5 *yuan* a dish. Hong always ordered her meals with other hostesses and shared the meals and the cost. In addition, Hong spent about 600 *yuan* to study computer science in an adult college. Computer science, Japanese language, cooking, and tailoring were the major programs pursued by the hostesses. These expenses on average were small compared with the money she sent home. To help her family withdraw her money, Hong opened a checking account in a local bank and applied for a bankcard. She sent the bankcard home to her parents and other family members so that they could withdraw money from the card whenever there was a need. On average, as much as 50 percent of her monthly income was withdrawn by or sent to her family. At times of exigency, additional money was required. For instance, once her mother was hospitalized for several months and the money on her card was not enough to cover the hospitalization fee; she called her previous client of great wealth to prostitute herself and afterwards immediately sent the 5,000 *yuan* she had earned home. Later when I interviewed her mother, I realized that her mother helped her save some money because she said she would cover Hong's wedding when the time came because she owed so much to her.

Clothing and cosmetics were another major area where Hong spent her wages. There were several specific markets where all hostesses shopped because the kinky style, mostly Korean or Japanese, was directly targeted at the hostesses with lower prices and of mediocre quality. I interviewed some of the vendors in these shopping markets, and they told me that hostesses were the ones who knew how to bargain and always succeeded in paying the least for the better-quality clothes. Buying cosmetics and doing hair were also important elements in their lives. They had great tactics to bargain for these products and services.

The consumption patterns of hostesses are more complex than the traditional economic conception of upward mobility. From an economic perspective, upward mobility is the natural consequence of improved economic conditions that are mainly measured by an increase in income. From a sociocultural point of view, however, upward mobility entails a transition in social identity from a lower or less desirable status to a higher or more desirable one. An increase in income by itself does not necessarily index or result in an increase in sociocultural standing. On the contrary, any upward movement is likely to be contested by the climber's social superiors who fear that the climber will oust them from their position. Social climbers, for their part, are likely to strengthen their bid for higher social status by re-creating their social image, including masking or erasing their former social identities.

AWARENESS OF THE URBAN-RURAL DICHOTOMY

To unravel the multilayered significance of hostesses' consumption practices requires placing their behavior within the larger social context of China's rural-urban gap. In the bar Romance Dream, I showed a magazine article titled "City Women" to hostess Hong. She was quite excited to read it aloud to the others, as if she herself were one of these "city women." As she read, I said, "Yes, you are one of them." She agreed in silence without any denial. However, later I confronted her specifically, "Do you think you are a city woman?" Immediately turning sullen and grim, she stood up and left, blurting out with contempt, "No, I am a rural woman!"

Hong's conflicted reaction to my question revealed her awareness of the rural-urban difference and the discrepancy between her rural identity and her admiration of, and aspiration to be, one of the "city women." To hostesses, being an urbanite signified power and status in the city. As hostess Dee said:

> My experience in the city made me really grow up. How I miss the time
> when, in my hometown, my friends always helped me out when I was in
> trouble. Here in the city, I do not have anyone to protect me, and I am
> easily bullied by urbanites. I do not have any power in the city. Nobody
> needs to be afraid of me, and nobody cares about me. After all, I am an
> outsider *[waidiren]*; they are Dalianites *[ren jia shi dalian ren]*. I dare not
> confront them.

Dee's words revealed her consciousness of her powerlessness and vulnerability as an outsider and rural native in the city. Hostesses often actively discussed this issue in the bar. Hostess Song came from a rural area of Dalian; however, she still considered herself to be a Dalianite in front of other hostesses. Once in the bar, she contemptuously confronted the other hostesses, "What do you eat in the rural areas?[15] What do we eat here in Dalian? I know what you eat there. How can you compare yourselves with us?" Immediately, hostess Liang, from a rural area of Jiangsu, retorted, "You yourself are from Lushun, not from Dalian. It's the countryside, not the city!"

Confronted by Liang's open challenge, Song reasserted her "urban identity," "What a joke! I bought a house there in Lushun and two houses in Dalian." Her claim to urban membership was based on her economic capital—her properties in the city of Dalian rather than a permanent residential permit. Song's words had some effect because nobody questioned the authenticity of her urban membership anymore. Hostess Hong, a rural woman from Heilongjiang, agreed with Song's denigration of the countryside: "Who wants to live in the countryside? I remember the difficulties of country life. Even if you have money, you cannot buy anything. It's dirty, too. There is just soil on the ground and no road."

Hostess Wen answered back, "However, the air, earth, and sky are all cleaner than in the city. If you have money, living in the countryside is better than in the city. Too much pollution in the city." Wen was trying to counteract this talk of urban power by highlighting the unpolluted and natural countryside environment. However, Song sneered at her words. Song challenged her migration: "Okay, if the countryside is so good, why have you come to the city?" Wen replied, "For money, of course." Then

Hong said, "What do we live for? Isn't it for money? Money is everything. If we have money, it does not matter where we live." Hong brought up the topic of money, about which everyone agreed. Each of them realized that money was the only avenue for attaining legitimacy, respect, and power— no matter where they chose to live. Such a lack of choice has been the result of the rural-urban divide over the decades.

Song challenged them again: "How many college students do the rural areas produce? So few! How about the city? A lot!" Wen said, "But how much is the tuition? Students have to pay a lot of money. Children from the countryside cannot afford it." Song said, "Okay. Are you going back to the countryside or staying in Dalian?" Wen said, "Of course, I'll return to my hometown." Hong said, "I will stay in Dalian. I cannot tolerate the countryside. I am not used to that life anymore." Song disdainfully retorted, "Okay, find a Dalian guy and marry him." Hong said, "Who wants to leave the city? The city has interesting sites. It is the ideal life. Dreams are in the city, not in the countryside." Song continued, "Children in the city have much wider vistas than those in the countryside." Wen agreed but said,

> That's only one side of the city. Look at the laid-off urban workers. Their life is more wretched than the life of rural people. They even commit suicide. Peasants are living much better lives than these workers. At least they do not need to be depressed by comparing themselves with other people. I hate when clients, including hostess Hong, always comment that countryside people are stupid *[ha le]*, with "peasant consciousness" *[nongmin yishi]* or "small peasant psyche" *[xiao nongmin xinli]. Peasant* seems to be the only word to describe stupid and foolish kinds of words and people. Everyone looks down on rural people. However, we cannot, because we ourselves come from the countryside. We are from the countryside. How can we speak ill of our own hometown? We cannot. We have to remember our roots *[ben]*. It's immoral to forget them.

Wen bravely identified herself as a rural woman who had pride and contempt for urbanites, protested against social injustice, and fought against social prejudice. She challenged Song's characterization of "stupid peasants" and stated that rural children were not innately stupid but simply "unable to afford education." This was once again an issue of economic opportunities, money, rather than something intrinsically defective about rural people. At the same time, Wen stated that the city was not as wonderful and the countryside was not as awful as others believed. She confronted Song, reminding her that she had a moral obligation not to forget her rural roots.

At Wen's words, Song answered back, "But the urbanites live a much better life than country folk." To this, Liang retorted, "The city cannot exist without the countryside." "The countryside cannot exist without the city," Song exclaimed. Liang answered back, "No. The rural areas can definitely live without the city. My hometown has changed so quickly. Before I left home, it was so poor. Now when I return, there are new houses and every household has a color TV and a telephone. Life has completely changed." Song insisted, "I don't believe it. Only the countryside in Dalian is better, not other places."

In this discussion, on the one hand, Song and Hong denied their rural roots because of rural "poverty and dirtiness." On the other hand, Wen and Liang praised the "self-reliant" countryside with its "pure" environment and made the point about the city's dependence on the countryside. This argument is the reverse of the dominant discourse about the countryside as the "Other" and the city as the "I." This discussion manifests the hostesses' struggle with their rural past and contestation of the dominant discourse. This tension eventually culminates in one point of agreement: "As long as you have money, it does not matter where you live." In other words, money is regarded as the only instrument that can erase the rural-urban dichotomy and help these women achieve respect and power in the city. This reflection is derived both from their inferior feelings about their "second-class" citizenship and their staged arrogance to compensate for their suppressed feelings of inadequacy. They carry the historical baggage of the rural-urban divide to the city and respond to it in an ambiguous and contradictory manner. Their debate reveals how the rural-urban dichotomy was a tangible daily reality with which the hostesses constantly wrestled, both between and within themselves.

CONSPICUOUS CONSUMPTION

Hostesses engaged in conspicuous commodity consumption. The paraphernalia of hostesses typically included the latest models in mobile phones and pagers. More successful hostesses frequented the city's most upscale discos and luxurious restaurants. The birthday dinner of one of my hostess friends was held in Dalian's finest all-seafood restaurant for a total amount of 1,000 *yuan*. Hostesses frequented "modern" sites, such as global supermarkets and American fast-food restaurants, such as McDonald's, Kentucky Fried Chicken, Popeye's, and Pizza Hut. They consumed "modern technologies" in Internet bars, disco bars, saunas, beauty salons, and other new recreational places that have cropped up during the post-Mao era. They took taxis wherever they went regardless of distance and never waited for a bus. They traveled to big cities such as Beijing and Shanghai with clients or hostess friends.

This form of consumption conforms to the traditional concept of conspicuous consumption. *Conspicuous consumption* refers to two scenarios: either the consumer purchases commodities in excess of her actual needs, or the object of consumption itself does not fulfill any practical life need. Because of its extravagance and showiness, the commodity refutes any use-value and becomes a pure public symbol of the consumer's economic power.[16]

FASHION

In many cultural settings, clothing and other forms of body decoration encode information about the wearer's social position and ranking. During the Maoist period, clothing was standardized to reflect the Communist revolution's leveling of class distinction. Since the relaxation of sumptuary controls, however, China's consumers are able to choose from a plethora of ready-to-wear clothing and fashion accessories. As a result, fashion has reemerged as a signifier of social difference.

Derogatory images of rural women abound in China's mass media. The figure of the rural woman frequently serves as a foil to accentuate urban women's modern and fashionable qualities. In fact, the very concepts of modern and fashion depend on their opposites, notions of backward and outmoded as embodied in the peasant woman's image. Articles on fashion technique commonly use rural women as negative examples to avoid: "The fair lady is never a countryside bumpkin, but a refined city woman."[17]

The oppositional construction of rural and urban women's public images is also found in the state's language on modernity. This discourse links the figure of the urban woman to modernity in the following ways: first, urban women's consumption of luxury goods is taken as indirect proof of the success of economic reforms to deliver material prosperity. Second, urban women's connection to the city as the center of economic growth and commerce makes them an ideal symbol of China's modernization.

An article in the *Shenzhen Weekly* compares rural migrant hostesses to South Korea:

> To use a not-entirely-apt metaphor, South Korea almost seems like a young country girl who suddenly arrives in the city. She sees all kinds of strange and novel things and doesn't wait a second to try them out on herself. The result is an odd-looking mess of colors. It seems to be ultraextravagant *[chaoxuan]* and ultramodern *[chaoxiandai]*, but in fact it cannot cover up her country air *[xiangqi]*. Country air goes hand in hand with South Korea's astonishing rise to wealth *[baofu]*. We can see the same sort of cultural mentality reflected in those Chinese youth who hold the Korean Wave [the popularity of Korean popular culture in China] in highest esteem.[18]

The comparison is not merely fortuitous. Most Chinese readers would instantly recognize the "young country girl" of this quote to be a hostess. First, the vast majority of hostesses come from rural areas. Second, they are among China's most conspicuous consumers of Korean-made clothing and fashion accessories. Third, sex work has made some of these young women very wealthy, very suddenly. Indeed, the author may have questioned the aptness of his "metaphor" precisely because of the audacity involved in comparing South Korea to a Chinese prostitute (as hostesses are commonly regarded).

This is important not for what it has to say about urban women but, rather, for what it says about China's country girls/hostesses. On the one hand, it is yet another example of the sort of put-downs that urban folk have always used to denigrate country folk. On the other hand, it reflects the changes wrought on the rural-urban apartheid system by the past twenty years of massive interregional migration. The young peasants of today are not the same as their parents' generation. These changes can be fruitfully examined through a key concept in antipeasant discrimination: *tuqi*.[19]

The semantics of *tuqi* has undergone subtle but significant reworking over the past twenty years. The derogatory thrust of *tuqi* has shifted from an emphasis on the body to an emphasis on clothing. The symbolic logic of *tuqi* is an application of the Chinese metaphysical concept, *qi*. An essence or energy, *qi* both permeates and radiates from the individual's body. Thus, *tuqi* reifies antipeasant sentiment by turning it into a semi-physical, semispiritual property of the body. Indeed, the common use of *tuqi* in everyday rhetoric centers on the peasant's body and extensions of the body: clothes. Urban folk commonly claim to possess a kind of "peas-ant radar" (my term) that allows them to detect individuals with rural backgrounds. Such discernments, it is said, are based on a combination of bodily and sartorial clues.

This latter element, clothing, has grown more salient with the rise of nonagricultural rural industry, the fact that China has become a key producer of clothing for the world market,[20] and peasant migration to the city. A small but growing number of rural youth have never or only peripherally engaged in agricultural work. Their bodies, therefore, do not bear the imprint of outdoor, field labor that marks the older generations of rural residents. If the contrast between the bodily appearance of rural and urban youth has grown smaller, and in this case, it definitely has, clothing has replaced dark and coarse skin as the primary signs of rural origin. Not surprisingly, then, rural migrants to the city are quick to shed their old garments in favor of a new, fashionable wardrobe.

For instance, hostesses in my study are highly conscious of the fashion differences between rural and urban areas. According to popular concep-tion, only urbanites possess the cultural taste and refinement to dress well. In contrast, peasants' low cultural level manifests itself in their low-taste and outdated clothes.[21] This view was reflected in my conversations with hostesses. Hostesses commented that the homemade green and red clothes they used to wear in the countryside made teenagers look like middle-aged women. In order to correct this fashion deficiency, they purchased luxuri-ous fashions, changed, exchanged, and eventually abandoned for new items at an alarmingly rapid rate.

Urban folk, for their part, insist that they cannot be fooled. The peas-ant's new clothes take on a double significance: one, they are considered to be a false cover that fails to contain or disguise the peasant's *tuqi*. As in the example above, the *tuqi* of the peasant girl almost seems to seep through the fabric of her ultraflashy and ultramodern clothing to betray her true identity as a peasant. Two, the peasant's clothing itself is an expression or manifestation of *tuqi*. The *tuqi* of the country girl, it is suggested, prevents her from fully comprehending the modern and urban fashions. Her clumsy foray into the world of fashion results in a garish display of colors that reveals rather than conceals her rural identity.

Both Sandra Niessen and Arjun Appadurai pay special heed to dress as a class signifier.[22] Niessen observes that Western elites are considered to have fashion whereas the others have little or no fashion at all. In China, the country girl's fashion ineptitude serves as the foil for the city woman's mastery over fashion. Dalian in particular has raised the figure of the city woman to the status of a fashion goddess as part of the local government's promotion of the city as an international fashion capital. The images of Chinese "city women" (in fact, professional models) are juxtaposed with those of fashionably dressed White women (also models).[23] For instance, since 1999, the Dalian city government has staged the City Woman Fashion Contest every two years. Along with the Dalian Beer Festival, it is one of the major regular events organized by the municipal government to enhance Dalian's domestic and international prestige. The advertisement for the 2001 session reads: "Youthful and beautiful city women, this is your chance to beautify the city with your special fashion. . . . The city of Dalian needs you beautiful angels as the spokeswomen for its image *[xing-xiang dashi]*. You will represent and display the city's beautiful fashion, culture, landscape, and Oriental women's charm."[24] This advertisement turns the "city woman" into a symbol of all that is good about the city. She is positioned as the bearer of a solemn mission to represent the city. It is as if the city itself calls out to her ("The city of Dalian needs you . . ."). Rural women, on the other hand, have been completely left out of the picture. The fashion incompetence that urbanites attribute to peasants is not just a slander on peasants' aesthetic sensibilities. Much more gravely, it denies them membership in the transnational community that crucially depends on fashion as an imaginative tool. *Tuqi*'s seat in the body means that peasants' resistance against their stigmatization by urbanites and an urban-controlled media is also situated and centered on the body.

Clothing has always been at the center of my perception of hostesses. Like many Chinese people, I first came to notice hostesses through their appearance. These women are a conspicuous component of Dalian's human landscape. Their wardrobes buck conventional Chinese sartorial practices on a number of different fronts by combining loud colors, unfamiliar cuts and styles, and, most important, the exposure of large portions of the female body. In fact, a huge proportion, if not the entirety, of hostesses' "look" is constructed out of foreign or foreign-inspired fashion products. Hostesses are covered from head to toe in Japanese but mostly Korean fashion. A very partial list of these products would include (from top to bottom): a variety of plastic hair trinkets, fake second eyelids, fake eyelashes, cosmetics in general, bracelets, clothes, and shoes. Several of the hostesses' staple fashions and signatory items of wardrobe are also of Japanese or Korean origin: nearly every hostesses' feet are sheathed in pointy-toed, high-heeled shoes, first introduced from South Korea and later manufactured locally; black and other dark shades of lipstick are both manufactured in South Korea and inspired by the style of female South Korean film and music idols; and pink, transparent plastic baubles bearing the Japanese Hello Kitty logo adorn hostesses' cell phones and flash blinking lights whenever hostesses receive a call.

Hostesses' sartorial practice manifests some of the attributes generally associated with the antifashion style of punk, hippie, and other subcultures. These similarities, however, are more cosmetic than substantive. Like antifashionists, hostesses make a conscious effort to distinguish themselves from other social groups by wearing highly distinctive clothing. This trait makes the style of both antifashion and hostess fashion alluring targets for "raiding" by mainstream fashion designers and wearers in search of new material—establishing the often-noted "parasitic" relationship of mainstream culture to the subculture of marginal groups.[25]

In contrast with antifashion, however, hostesses do not attempt to express a broad-based critique of mainstream society through the mechanism of a "fashion statement." Nor do hostesses embrace those attributes that the dominant society stigmatizes and devalues, as with the 1960s and 1970s African American liberation movement's affirmation of black skin and the Afro.[26]

Despite these surface similarities, the aim and angle of attack of these two fashion modes are nonetheless quite different. Hostesses' sartorial strategy is best described as ultrafashion. Here, emphasis is not placed on rebellion against a fashion mainstream but, rather, on pushing beyond the boundaries and limits of current fashion. Where antifashion supports and cultivates a subject-position of the rebellious outsider, ultrafashion substitutes the figure of the hip insider. The goal, far from bucking fashion, is to be more fashionable than anyone else.

Hostesses' fashion strategy can be summarized as follows: avoid *tuqi,* strive for *yangqi. Yang* literally means sea or ocean and has served as a general signifier for the extra-China, foreign world at least since late imperial times. As with *tuqi,* the addition of the *qi* character turns the concept of *yang* into a quality or property that can be attributed to some thing or person. Thus *yangqi* refers to a foreign "flavor" or "style." In its current usage, *yangqi* carries a strong positive connotation and is often used synonymously with other terms such as "stylish" *(shimao, shishang)* and possibly "cool" *(ku).* Hostesses, however, prefer *yangqi* to these alternative terms, reflecting the greater and more explicit emphasis that hostesses place on foreignness as a basis for making their own fashion choices and judging those of others.

Hostesses' fashion Other is the city woman. Hostesses deride city women for their inferior fashion sense. Yet hostesses have little actual contact with city women while they are still working at the bar. The problem of how to get along with city women comes to the fore once hostesses take the inevitable step out of the karaoke bar and into other, more conventional lines of business. The high rate of business failure characteristic of many small enterprises in the city, however, often pushes hostesses back into their old profession and social environment. This process of moving in and out of the karaoke bar may repeat itself several times throughout the career of a hostess, intermittently exposing them to the wider urban society before their final retirement from hostessing.

I helped out during the days at a small clothing boutique run by a former hostess, Zhang. At the time we were introduced, Zhang had been retired from hostessing for a few months. Her ability to open the store and keep it afloat, however, crucially depended on the financial backing of her lover, whom she had met while still working at the karaoke bar. Money from her lover also made it possible for her to maintain her former fashion habits. Clothing remained a central preoccupation for Zhang, even though she was no longer subject to the occupational demands of hostessing. Her particular clothing practices, however, had been altered to fit in with her new environment. Zhang was now surrounded not by other hostesses but by city women who worked in the surrounding stores of the same shopping plaza. Her old wardrobe from her days at the bar would have scandalized these women and instantly revealed her former identity as a sex worker, exposing Zhang to discrimination, harassment, and most likely eviction. The threat of exposure was intensified by the talk of other vendors who claimed to be able to detect hostesses by their unseemly garb.

By looking for those elements that remain constant across these changes, we can tell which aspects of hostesses' clothing are nonnegotiable and therefore most likely tied up with their sense of identity and self. Zhang toned down her look but tellingly without discarding hostesses' characteristic emphasis on foreign fashion. In particular, Zhang switched from the sexy fashions of Korean clothes to the cute Japanese fashions. Zhang would sometimes take advantage of my presence at her boutique to slip out during lulls in business and do some shopping of her own. After one such shopping excursion, Zhang returned dressed head to toe in a new Japanese outfit. The centerpiece was a form-fitting, pink T-shirt with the Hello Kitty cartoon emblazoned across the chest. Zhang introduced the outfit to the other vendors, emphasizing above all that she was wearing genuine imported Japanese clothes. Her strategy worked. Zhang was awash with accolades from the other vendors. "It's so cute *[zhen keai!]*!" they chorused.

This pursuit of *yangqi* leads hostesses to engage in bold fashion experiments that consistently push the envelope of China's fashion norm. On the one hand, hostesses act as engines for sartorial change in urban Dalian. Fashions that are initially considered by the general public of city women as too risqué or simply unfamiliar become incorporated into "everyday visual parlance"[27] by first being seen worn on the bodies of hostesses. The pointed-toe, high-heel shoe in this manner went from an exclusive hostess fashion to the "latest" footwear for fashionable young city women.

On the other hand, hostesses receive no credit for the fashion innovations they help to introduce. Quite the opposite, the visual radicalness of hostesses' wardrobe leaves them vulnerable to a variety of attacks. The fashion style of hostesses is open to charges of excessiveness or exaggeration. While hostesses may act as fashion innovators, city women are the final arbiters of which sartorial practices become recognized as fashion. Before such judgment is passed, hostesses' clothes remain of questionable taste. Indeed, some aspects of hostesses' dress—particularly those that reveal large portions of the female body—may never become a part of wider city fashion or only become accepted after undergoing modification to tone down its offending features.

Relative to hostesses, city women are slow to adopt the more unconventional offerings of the foreign fashion world. Their more conservative sartorial tendencies result from their roles in urban society as daughters, wives, mothers, employees, and occasionally "women bosses" *(laoban niang)*—all of which require them to maintain a gendered image of female respectability and propriety. Hostesses in contrast are free from such constraints by virtue of their marginal status in the city. As migrants and unmarried women, the absence of familial authority figures or concerned husbands permits hostesses to experiment in foreign fashions that are generally off limits to other female social groups. As sex workers, too, the implicit or explicit dress codes enforced at most business establishments do not restrict hostesses' dress. Indeed, the difference between their at- and off-work apparel exists as a matter of degree; for example, hostesses wear more makeup under the dim lights of karaoke bar suites than they wear under the natural sunlight and bright neon glow of Dalian's day- and nighttime streets, respectively.

It is interesting to note, however, that city women have very little to say about hostesses' clothing. Rather, most comments emphasize how hostesses' clothing exposes their identity as sex workers—in the words of city women, hags *(ji pozi)*. Indeed, hostesses' distinctive appearance invites a variety of undesirable attention, from police harassment and sex crimes to sidelong glances and hurtful comments whispered under the breath. The reason that city women remain relatively silent on the subject of hostesses' clothing may indicate their semiconscious recognition of this dynamic—in other words, that the clothes of hostesses today may become their fashion tomorrow.

FASHION CONSUMPTION: CLOTHES TALK

Below I will examine hostesses' pursuit of *yangqi* through two examples of hostesses' clothing-related practices: one, where they shop and how they talk about clothes; two, how they present their clothes to a nonhostess, outside audience.

Clothes talk ran throughout the consumption process, from prepurchase fashion advice to postpurchase fashion commentary. Shopping was often and ideally done together in a group with other hostesses, although it was not unheard of for a hostess to shop individually or with nonhostess companions, like boyfriends. Hostesses preferred shopping with other hostesses because it allowed them to have immediate access to the feedback of their cohorts. Hostesses gave and received fashion advice throughout the course of shopping. They modified their purchase decisions to accommodate the views of the group. A hostess might be dissuaded from making a purchase by the group's negative reaction or encouraged by its positive appraisal. This prepurchase fashion counseling not only guided hostesses' fashion selection but also helped them avoid committing fashion faux pas that in the postpurchase stage could only be corrected through the difficult and usually impossible act of returning the offending item of clothing.

Clothes talk continued on into the postpurchase phase of consumption. Hostesses made elaborate comments on the clothes of their cohorts. Commenting constituted a second round of fashion input from other hostesses. There was no guarantee that clothes that received the approval of companion hostesses during the shopping process would win favor with the wider group of hostesses at the karaoke bar. In fact, many clothes were eliminated. Over months and years of clothes buying, every hostess accumulates several boxes worth of rejected clothes. Hostesses sometimes tried to pawn these rejects off on other hostesses but never with success. The usual fate of such castoffs was as hand-me-downs to relatives and close friends back in the countryside (more on this below).

As we saw earlier when hostess Li was heavily criticized by other hostesses for her red dress, fashion comments are often brutally honest but usually made in a spirit of genuine concern. Indeed, providing fashion advice and comments was one of the basic ways in which hostesses expressed concern for the well-being of their cohorts and thus served as a basis for solidarity-building. Many friendships between hostesses had been cemented through the giving and receiving of fashion advice. By the same token, the sentiment of sorority expressed in such advice giving played an important role in interfactional contests within the karaoke bar. Experienced hostesses would often attempt to recruit newly arrived hostesses into their personal networks by offering their fashion expertise as a gesture of friend-ship. Neophytes for their part critically relied on this kind of personalized image counseling to reshape their appearance—a very serious and practical issue for young women who depended on their looks to make a living.

Without the counseling of an experienced hostess, greenhorns would face great difficulty acclimating to hostesses' sartorial culture. The instructor provided two types of resources: money and knowledge. The experienced one might make a loan of a couple hundred *yuan,* which the greenhorn would pay off from the tips she earned in the first few sessions with customers. The second resource, knowledge, included the answers to the two basic questions of shopping: where to buy and how to choose. Although Japanese and Korean fashions could be found intermingled with locally produced and other foreign clothes, the attention-grabbing clothes that were the hallmark of hostess fashion could only be found in specialty stores that sold nothing but Wave fashion.[28] Several malls and underground plazas specialized in the sale of Korean fashion, which they announced through names like Korean Clothing City. Hostesses were among these establishment's most loyal customers, if not their primary client base. Even some vendors were themselves ex-hostesses. Thus Korean clothing shopping centers came close to being all-hostess environments.

Korean fashion products could be found almost wherever hostesses could be found. Small stores that catered to hostesses' fashion needs cropped up around those areas where the women were most concentrated. They provided hostesses with a convenient way of replenishing many of the disposable, less expensive items of their wardrobe. When hostesses in Dalian's red-light district ran out of Korean-made fake double eyelids and other accessories, they needed only take a few steps out the door of the karaoke bar to any of the several small stores that stocked their favorite brands.

Assuming that an uninitiated greenhorn had the wherewithal to locate these stores, she would still face the formidable challenge of selecting the appropriate clothes. Even hostesses with some experience under their belt often failed to correctly gauge the nuanced responses of their hostess peers. Thus, hostesses regularly served as fashion consultants for other hostesses through the nonstop, mutual exchange of advice and comments. Clothes talk helped hostesses stay abreast of the fast-paced changes of fashion by pooling the information gathered by individual hostesses into a collective reservoir of fashion knowledge. These benefits accrued to greenhorns and more experienced hostesses alike.

Examining how hostesses present their clothes to those uninitiated in hostess clothing culture provides important clues into hostesses' perception of their clothing and the way that they integrate clothing within an over-all strategy of self-presentation to the outside world. Earlier we saw how Zhang presented her Japanese fashion to the urban women who owned small businesses. Now we will see how in a similar fashion, Dee presented her unwanted clothing to relatives and friends in her hometown.

A common practice among hostesses in presenting their clothing to an outside audience was to give unwanted clothing to nonhostess relatives and friends. As I mentioned in the last chapter, I accompanied Dee back to her home village in Jilin Province. It had become established practice that on each trip home she would bring gifts for her family members. Almost half a year had gone by since her last visit, so everyone would be expect-ing something from their "family in the city." For her elder and younger sisters, these gifts were clothing. On the train ride over, Dee told me of her gift-giving plans: she had several articles of unwanted clothes that had scarcely been worn. She intended to pass the garments off as new, since giving used clothing might offend her sisters, not to mention detract from the accolades of generosity that she eagerly expected for this act of famil-ial duty. I of course was expected to play along.

Every article of clothing was presented with an oral description by Dee. In order, this included location of manufacture, price, and quality. On the one hand, such a description was simply informative: many clothes do not come with inside labels to provide manufacturer's origin, and even truly new clothes rarely if ever have a price tag directly attached. On the other hand, it reveals how Dee wanted to shape her sisters' reaction to the gifts and by extension reflects what Dee herself believes are the most salient, value-laden aspects of hostess fashion. The arrangement of the three ele-ments of information into this particular order also conforms to a certain logic. Placing the origin of the clothing at the beginning of her descrip-tion indicates that Dee found it to be the most important feature. It also logically leads into the other two elements: the clothing's origin in South Korea implies a high price; both foreign origin and high price are seen as equivalent to a guarantee of high quality. Dee and her sisters followed the moment of gift giving by promenading through the village streets in their new clothing. (Her sisters were either truly taken in by Dee's deceit or else flawlessly disguised their awareness.) I tagged along. They were quite a sight: three young women dressed in the latest Korean fashion, traipsing along the unpaved village road as if it were a model's runway in Paris (or, perhaps it would be more apt to say Seoul). Along their route, Dee repeated her description of the clothes in more or less identical form to whomever they happened to run into, which turned out to be a lot of people, due to the minor sensation that their performance stirred up.

As we saw earlier, villagers' response to Dee and her sisters' fashion parade was by no means uniform or entirely positive. Older villagers tended to be more impressed by the wealth and worldliness displayed by Dee's clothing than younger people, who raised pointed questions about the source of Dee's wealth in the city. This difference in reaction seems to be a product of a greater propensity toward invidious comparison among younger villagers, who compete with each other to grasp the fleeting opportunities that market reforms have opened up. Like the hostesses themselves, these village youth find themselves the victims of an identity crisis created by the superior display of wealth of the hostesses. It is not surprising that they attempted to regain their lost sense of equality through questioning the origin of this wealth.

While aware of the ambivalence inherent in her fellow villagers' reactions, Dee nonetheless felt confident that this ostentatious display of her gifts had won her a good deal of face—deriving not only from the demonstration of her "pecuniary abilities" (à la Veblen's theory of conspicuous consumption) but, more important, from the image of worldliness that the foreign origin of the clothing helped her cultivate. Dee strengthened her connection with the foreign, outside world by speaking openly and freely about her plans to go abroad. In her imaginary itinerary, Dee jetted across global space from Japan and Korea to the United States and Europe. In this way, the clothing that Dee had brought and displayed on her body and the bodies of her sisters had turned her into something of an international figure—in the eyes of her family, other villagers, and herself. This parallels the practice of *les sapeurs* among the Congolese who also distinguish themselves by appropriating the style of outsiders.[29] Jonathan Friedman points out that the identity of the Congolese is outside of the body, and appearance equals being: you are what you wear.[30] The valorization of *les sapeurs*—the art of dressing elegantly—is manifested in the clothing of the Congolese, who "consume modernity" and accumulate signs of status through their outward appearance. In both cases, fashion becomes an externalization of one's identity.

In her work on the Zambian market in Western second-hand clothing, Karen Hansen argues that such clothing is symbolically re-created as "new" clothes divested of any Western imprint.[31] Thus, while the clothing may be of Western origin, its meaning is 100 percent Zambian-made. Hostesses, in contrast, accentuate the foreign origins of their clothes. Indeed, the fact that these clothes come from Japan and South Korea constitutes one of the major attractions to consume them. In so doing, they assert their membership in the transnational community denied to them by the urban society. Like the Congolese, Chinese hostesses are not just aware of where their clothes come from. This is not to deny that other "objective" features of such clothing help make them an easy sell with hostesses. The foreign style that characterizes much Japanese and Korean fashion appeals to hostesses' ultrafashion sensibilities for display.

Whereas Hansen's Zambians find ways to downplay the association with the West, the practices of hostesses serve to emphasize and even cultivate their clothing's foreign associations. Most talk about the origins of clothing occurs between hostesses and nonhostesses. Hostesses' choice of *yangqi* or foreign-style clothing is a more or less conscious response to urban society's stigmatization of the peasant's body. In particular, their sartorial practice contests the notion that peasants' fashion incompetence prevents them from participating in the transnational world of fashion. Hostesses have not only plunged into the transnational fashion currents represented by the Wave but also have taken the lead in Dalian's fashion change. The visual radicalness of hostesses' wardrobes leaves them vulnerable to a variety of attacks, including charges of fashion excessiveness as well as police harassment and sex crimes. The logic of hostesses' fashion rebellion, however, demands that they expose themselves to these risks by always staying one step (often many steps) ahead of city women's fashion. As their sartorial practices are co-opted by city women, hostesses search for new fashions to visually distinguish themselves, both spurring on urban fashion change and opening themselves up to fresh attacks.

THE COSTS OF CONSUMPTION

Hostesses are neither totally free to fashion an individual identity nor totally determined by economic or political forces. Contemporary conditions in China afford them a little room to maneuver in which they can struggle to forge a new identity, though their degrees of freedom are constrained. In the course of this struggle to resist a system that sets limits, hostesses assert their claims for social recognition. An overview of the hostesses' consumption behavior can only reach an ambivalent conclusion. On the one hand, hostesses' use of economic resources to construct a new urban persona in defiance of cultural stereotypes of peasants exhibits a creative agency. On the other hand, hostesses' consumption is fraught with hidden dangers and costs.

HEALTH COSTS

Hostesses are heavy consumers of body-altering drugs and surgical services that in some cases result in deleterious health effects. This is due in large part to the coercive power termed by feminist scholars as the "male gaze." This takes two forms, direct and indirect. First, male customers as the distributors of scarce economic and social resources directly influence hostesses' aesthetic choices. Through their selection of escorts, customers reward or punish hostesses according to the degree to which they fulfill their expectations. Customers also make direct verbal comments on the appearance of hostesses' bodies. To gain access to male-controlled resources, hostesses must modify their bodies to meet male customers' demands.

Second, the cultural productions in the mass media that form the basis of hostesses' aesthetic taste are themselves a manifestation of the male gaze. As feminist critics of the media point out, the media often project an unattainable female image that once internalized by the female subject can lead to self-destructive, harmful behavior.

The combined effect of these factors leads hostesses to engage in physically harmful behavior. To please clients, almost every hostess I know in the bars has gone through either minor or major plastic surgeries: eyelid operations, breast augmentation, nose adjustments, change of face shape, eyebrow and eyeliner tattoos, and so on. They also expend large amounts of economic resources to purchase various beauty products, such as breast-augmentation pills, soaps, and electronic gadgets.

SOCIAL COSTS

Hostesses' body refashioning betrays their identity as migrant sex workers, leaving them vulnerable to social discrimination perhaps more virulent than that faced by other migrant groups. I have sketched a dual-level model of upward class mobility, divided into economic and sociocultural dimensions. It is clear that hostessing helps rural women to realize substantial economic advantages. From a sociocultural angle, however, the conclusion must be more mixed. As we have seen, hostesses attempt to transform economic capital into social respect by creating a modern and fashionable body image. Their success in realizing this goal should be separately evaluated according to rural and urban contexts.

In the city, their effort is largely thwarted by urbanites' ingrained anti-peasant prejudice and by the moral stigma and legal sanctions against sex work. In this context, the distinctive body culture of the hostesses becomes a mark of their rural background and illicit profession. Their distinctive style, rather than earning society's respect, allows them to be singled out as targets of virulent social discrimination. Hostesses found it difficult to admit that their appearance gave their identity away. As one hostess proudly boasted to me, "My boyfriend always says that I do not look like a rural woman at all. When I walk on the street, police cannot tell that I am from the countryside so they don't ask me for my temporary residence card." In reality, hostesses are not only subject to arbitrary police searches but also are targeted by muggers and other criminals and daily face the whispers and side-glances of urbanites.

In the countryside, however, the story is somewhat different. In comparison to urban areas, China's countryside faces economically depressed conditions. Thus, hostesses' ostentatious displays of wealth are more readily translated into social respect than in the city. Their earnings are often the main source of family income, used to refurnish or purchase new homes, pay for siblings' education, repay family debts, and cover other miscellaneous expenditures. As the providers of these substantial economic benefits, returning hostesses are granted a certain degree of social respect.

However, their body decoration quickly becomes a source of controversy. Hostesses keep the true nature of their work in the city a secret from the village community. As in the city, rural residents frown on hostessing and sex work. At home hostesses' outlandish and revealing wardrobes become the basis of rumors and guessing about their true profession in the city. The result is often strained relations between hostesses and their rural communities and families.

ECONOMIC COSTS

Hostesses' attempts to gain social respect through conspicuous consumption (especially fashion and cosmetics) impose a heavy financial burden on them and wastes resources that could otherwise be channeled into more productive pursuits such as business investment and education. These costs, however, are somewhat defrayed by client's direct gift giving, including mobile phones, clothing and fashion accessories, and so on.

Performing Love:
The Commodification of
Intimacy and Romance

People will laugh at your poverty, but not your prostitution *[xiao pin bu xiao chang]*.

>—Common saying among bar hostesses

Outside of this bar, whether in the city or in my rural hometown, nobody knows where my money comes from. . . . With your wealth, everybody will respect you. They will think of you as a very capable person. It's no use being a pure and chaste rural girl—nobody cares about that. As long as you show them your wealth, they will afterward treat you differently.

>—Bar hostess from Heilongjiang, age twenty

Why doesn't society treat us as human beings? Why does society only allow men to play around and flirt with women, and not allow women to play around? Who is better in this society? Those urban clients and women are no better than we are. Who is better? Let's see who can earn more money and be more modern! Look at those urban laid-off workers, so pathetic and poor. We are much better than they are. Remember, any means is justified as long as you can earn money.

>—Bar hostess from Jilin, age twenty-two

As hostesses manipulate and perform different characters, there is a tension between feelings and money as sources of power. Hostesses deliberately trump feelings and seek money and rational control. This reminds us of the earlier discussion of "paying the grain tax." Money for the hostesses and "misappropriation of grain/semen" for the clients are metaphors for different forms of power. For the clients, misappropriating grain/semen stands as their source of power to resist the authority of the government/wife. For the hostesses, money represents their source of power to defy the authority of the clients who may abandon and deceive them. Hostesses' performance of different characters is ultimately about power or, more specifically, about how they need to feel empowered, about how they find ways to feel empowered, even while in an objective position of disempowerment.

Wendy Chapkis argues that the construction of "multiple identities" is a general characteristic of all sex workers (prostitutes).[1] This behavior is rooted in the nature of sex work itself—indeed, Chapkis sees it as a form of labor in its own right (what she calls "emotional labor"). As she writes, sex workers change between identities to "manage" their emotions in the process of sexual labor. Identity switching allows sex workers to both summon and contain emotions at will. In other words, sex workers' multiple identities function as a defense mechanism to protect themselves from the harmful psychological ramifications of their work. Sex workers' chameleon-like capacity renders attempts at pinpointing a unitary, "true" identity fruitless or irrelevant. This defense tactic, however, entails its own risks, namely, that the sex worker will begin to identify too closely with a single identity, thus losing the necessary plasticity to survive.

The hostesses' sexual labor bears significant similarities to Chapkis's analysis. Hostesses act out different characters in the course of serving clients. Likewise, character shifting is part of a conscious strategy that is linked to the performance of their labor. As my language indicates, however, the hostesses remain emotionally distant from these various personas. Unlike the diffuse and indeterminate psychology of the sex workers described in Chapkis's account, the hostesses maintain a stable, unified identity as against their multiple work roles. Thus I argue against Chapkis's depiction of the identity of prostitutes as fragmented.

Hostesses alternate between different characters depending on the social profile of the client that they are serving. On a busy night, a hostess might accompany as many as seven different clients, each client requiring different character performances. The high frequency of character switching impedes the process of character identification theorized by Chapkis. Hostesses also reduce characters to a repertoire of acting techniques that are then studied with conscious mental effort. Getting the part down does not mean becoming one with the character but, rather, is a matter of technical skill. This requires patience and, above all, lots of practice.

Hostesses hone their acting skills offstage. Certain techniques become established tools of the trade that are handed down from veteran to novice hostesses. Winking techniques *(feiyan)* are one such example. Hostesses summarized this technique as follows: "Slightly closing your left eye seduces a man's soul. Slightly closing your right eye conveys your devotion. Slightly closing your two eyes means you agree to have sex with him." Hostesses view characters not as fully fleshed-out "identities," as in Chapkis's analysis, but as a collection of separate techniques to be studied and applied in their work.

As illustrated in chapter 5, the identities of the hostesses do have a central, unifying axis: the persona of the filial daughter. The distinction between the Chinese hostesses and Western sex workers could also explain the surprising marriageability of Chinese sex workers. In China, the notion of chastity is fluid, and female virtue is defined first and foremost by filiality.[2] As long as the hostesses subordinate their sex lives to their filial obligations, this mitigates social criticism. Given the importance of filiality, they have in some sense proven themselves to be worthy and virtuous women. Filiality gives them a modicum of power in Chinese society. Thus, women use filiality, an ideology that essentially oppresses them (from a social science perspective) to endow themselves with a degree of power (from the perspective of their individual life histories). But in so doing they reinforce the structure that oppresses them.[3]

Below I avoid Chapkis's psychology-based terminology *(identity)* in favor of a language of performance *(character)* to make this distinction. Chapkis's claims about the particular psychology of sex workers need to be contextualized according to the particular circumstances of their labor and their wider social environment. Following this research agenda, the last section of this chapter analyzes the hostesses' relationship to their work roles in the specific context of the karaoke bar's sex labor regime.

MANIPULATION OF THE RURAL-URBAN HIERARCHY

The job of the bar hostess was to serve her clients. In exchange, the client compensated the hostess with a certain amount of money. Within this seemingly simple exchange relationship, however, hostesses were in constant negotiation with male customers. Hostesses attempted to extract from their clients additional benefits that went beyond the basic, flat rate fee for their services. These perquisites included tips and gifts and, most important, access to the customers' social networks.

One of my informants, a twenty-year-old rural woman from Hunan, explained to me that the key to being a successful hostess was the ability to establish a stable relationship with the customer and then to exploit him. To reach this goal, as she and many other hostesses emphasized, the hostess needed to play on the customer's expectations and the stereotypes of how a hostess should act.

The hostesses' repertoire included three characters: the docile virgin, the rapacious prostitute, and Cinderella. Hostesses chose to act out different characters based on their clients' social profiles. In general, hostesses classified clients according to age ("old" for clients older than thirty-five; "young" for those aged twenty to thirty-five) and residence (local or non-local). According to hostesses, clients from the outside were the easiest to manipulate and cheat. Old clients were described as preferring lewd and seductive hostesses. Young clients, in contrast, favored more pure and innocent-looking hostesses.

ONSTAGE PERFORMANCES

A key feature of the hostesses' work lives was the distinction between on-stage *(zuotai)* and offstage *(chutai)*. These two categories referred to opposing states or conditions rather than concrete locations. Thus, onstage was the state of servicing clients, whereas offstage indicated the absence of clients. The hostesses' on- and offstage lives were characterized by radically different behavior patterns. Whereas their onstage lives were preoccupied with serving clients who channeled and controlled their behavior, hostesses enjoyed a greater level of expressive freedom in their offstage time that allowed them to contest their marginalization. This section explores the hostesses' onstage performance of their stereotyped images in state and media representations.

THE UNRULY WHORE

Here is a scene in a karaoke room that I witnessed during my fieldwork. Around twenty women, sent in by *Mami* (madam), lined up before several male clients in a KTV suite. The male customers, casually sitting on a sofa, inspected the women from left to right, with critical expressions on their faces. Eager to be chosen, the women struck provocative poses to gain the men's attention. They played with their hair and winked at the clients. In the middle of this examination process, *Mami* pulled one hostess over to the front and said, "What about this one? She's got big eyes!" A customer pointed at the woman and said, "Big eyes mean big vagina!" evoking laughter from the other customers. At these words, the woman quietly retreated into the group with seeming embarrassment. This did not stop *Mami*. "We also have one with tight buttocks. She will surely serve you well!" She called out, "Come over here, Tight Buttocks! Come to the front, Tight Buttocks!" At these words, I saw a pretty woman in a tight cheongsam move to the front. A male customer raised one finger at her, motioning her to come over. The woman almost leaped to the man's side and hung on to his arm. Another customer pointed at a plump woman in the group and shouted at her, "Hey, are those breasts fake or real?" The hostess responded by gently shaking her full figure. The customer, apparently unsatisfied, turned to all the women and cried out, "Whose breasts are the largest? Who wants her breasts to be fondled? Come and sit next to me!"

As shown in this particular scene, one hostess, despite the customer's insulting comments about her breasts, continued her erotic performance to gain the customer's favor. Such a hypersexual image projected the rural women's cultural portrait as sexually promiscuous and available. The woman with tight buttocks also demonstrated her willingness to be sexually dominated by jumping to the embrace of the customer. Insulting the hostesses is also discussed by Anne Allison, for instance, the "breast talk" she analyzes in a Japanese hostess bar.[4] It shows the nature of the hostess and guest relationship as a contest.

To lure clients, hostesses presented a hypersexual and lustful image by winking, wearing revealing clothes, and assuming seductive postures. They purred, laughed, screamed, or moaned when clients preyed on their bodies, and they sang songs to seduce clients and convey their "devotion." For instance, a hostess chose a song titled "Why Do You Love Other Women Behind My Back?" *(weishenmo ni beizhe wo ai bieren)*. As she sang the song, she fondled her client, leaned her whole body over him, and coquettishly asked him the question in the title: "My husband *(laogong)*, why do you make love to other women behind my back?"

Outside of karaoke bars, hostesses sent tantalizing phone messages to their clients, such as "Making love is fun. A woman with large breasts is like a tiger or a wolf. A woman with flat breasts has unfathomably superior techniques. Let's make love." Hostesses commonly boasted to each other about the "whore-like sexuality" (sao) that their clients loved the most.

By allowing their bodies to be sexually fragmented and erotically staged for marketing, hostesses refuse the state's attempt to regulate rural women's promiscuous and transgressive sexuality and to control them for purely reproductive purposes. By flaunting their hypersexualized bodies, hostesses intend to employ the hegemonic portrayal of rural women as the exotic and erotic Other for their individual profit. How well hostesses perform in this task determines how much profit they can extract from male clients.

Did hostesses all "go out"? Eventually all of them did, after submitting themselves to the group value. In one category of exchange, hostesses would not go out when they were involved in certain types of semipermanent, exchange relationships with male patrons. A male patron provided economic benefits—direct cash presents and gifts—in return for more or less exclusive user rights over the body of the hostess. The degree of exclusivity of user rights depended on the level of economic compensation. At one extreme, the male patron was responsible for all of the hostess's living expenses plus entertainment fees and assorted amenities. In exchange, he acquired absolutely exclusive rights. With the terms of the agreement (though not necessarily in reality), the hostess became the sexual property of the male patron for the duration of the relationship. The hostess was obligated to terminate sexual relations with other men and discontinue work at the karaoke bar. In these cases, it is said that the male patron has "contracted" (bao) with the hostess. At the other extreme of a second category, the male patron only enjoyed user rights for the duration of a particular service session. The majority of hostesses' sex-for-money transactions fell into this category of one-time-only deals.

A third category of semipermanent exchange relations fell in between these two polar extremes. Here, the compensation provided by the male patron covered only a portion of the hostess's total living, recreational, and other expenses. Accordingly, the patron obtained partially exclusive user rights: hostesses continued to entertain customers *(zuo tai)* but were obligated not to go out *(chu tai).* These arrangements generated a serious "moral hazard": the hostess would be tempted to supplement her income on the side by furtively going out. To ensure that hostesses adhered to the terms of agreement, male patrons sent friends undercover as regular clients to monitor the hostess's behavior. These spies approached the hostess with propositions for sex-money exchange. If the hostess agreed, her patron would abandon her, and she would lose this source of income.

Particular relations were subject to changes. Hostesses expended great efforts to upgrade customers from less to more permanent types of relationships as a way to stabilize and hopefully increase their income. Hostesses routinely left their contact information with clients. If the client left his name card, the hostess would actively make contact and set up "dates." In addition, hostesses only went out with customers who they were already familiar with or who had been introduced by either the bar boss or other reliable acquaintances (for example, other hostesses and bar bouncers). Propositions from strangers were almost universally rejected, partly because of the danger of being arrested by plain-clothed policemen.

Some hostesses held moral reservations about going out. This situation was more common among newly arrived hostesses who were still virgins. These newcomers often looked down on veteran hostesses who went out. I encountered several expressions of this attitude in KTV bars. For example, a newcomer whose customer wanted to go out stormed into the lobby from one of the private rooms. "This guy is looking for a hostess to go out with him," she yelled. At this prompt, several veteran hostesses bounced up from their seats and filed into the private room for the customer to select. The newcomer took a seat in the lobby and looked on with thinly disguised disapproval.

Pan Suiming observed a similar situation among sex workers in China's hair parlors.[5] He described how sex workers derided those colleagues who "overexert" *(guoyu mai liqi)* themselves in their work. He argued that sex workers internalized mainstream prejudices against sex work. For most people in the general public, the "terror" of being associated with the "abnormal" and "heretic" *("yilei" he "yiduan")* drives them to prove their own purity and decency by condemning sex industry workers and consumers. This psychological dynamic is so powerful that even sex workers themselves are not immune to its influence. Pan concluded that even sex workers long to "stay clean even in the muck" *(chu yu ni er bu ran)*.

Pan's analysis only partially conforms to my own findings. Pan sees sex workers as held under the sway of a hegemonic cultural view. I argue that the experience of sex work itself leads hostesses to revise and eventually abandon mainstream moral values. This is evident in the discrepancy between new and veteran hostesses' views on the issue of going out. Newly arrived hostesses often refuse to go out with customers and even disdain veteran hostesses who do go out. Over time, however, these mainstream values are gradually replaced by a new moral perspective that legitimizes and even encourages the sexual commodification of the body. Thus, Pan's analysis accurately describes the situation of new hostesses but not veteran hostesses. In his work, Pan does not distinguish between new and veteran hostesses. Perhaps he overgeneralizes the situation of new sex workers to the whole of sex workers and therefore fails to see how sex workers' moral views are gradually reshaped by new experiences.

How do more experienced hostesses view sex-money exchanges? The statement quoted below, an excerpt from a veteran hostess's advice to a newly arrived hostess, is representative of veterans' attitudes toward prostitution. Like many newcomers, the recipient of this exhortation was opposed to going out and was resolutely saving herself for her future husband. Zhang, the experienced hostess, advised:

> I used to be as foolish as you. When I first worked in the bar, a client offered me 100,000 *yuan* for my virginity. I refused. Later on, another client manipulated my emotions and took away my virginity for free. Now I regret it so much! Virginity has a price. Who do you keep it for? I always ask myself: How long will I need to work to earn 100,000 *yuan*? Quite a long time! So after that, I did not hesitate to sleep with customers, as long as I could get money. The point is that purity is meaningless. No men are good in this society. If you give them the chance, they will take away your virginity without paying anything and abandon you afterwards. Don't save your purity for anyone. Earn money for yourself and enjoy it. That's the most important thing—to have money in your own pocket! Always remember that money is first and foremost before settling down with a man. I do not want to waste my time with young boys now. They cannot give me anything. No men are trustworthy. We have already experienced enough *[guo lai ren]*.

Zhang's comments directly contest the moral basis for the prohibition against premarital sex and prostitution. This morality tells women to preserve their sexual purity for their true love. To do otherwise degrades the woman's worth and dignity. Zhang turns this moral critique of prostitution on its head. As she argues, the true denigration of women lies in men's free use of the female body under the pretense of romantic love. Adhering to mainstream morality causes women to lose on two counts. First, unscrupulous men obtain sexual pleasure-value without properly compensating women. Two, women fail to capitalize on the economic value of their bodies while preserving their sexual purity. In short, romantic love is a deceptive male tactic to get something for nothing, and purity is a waste of the female body's potential economic value.

Hostess Zhang's views are rooted in the conditions and experiences common to hostesses as a subordinated rural group. These include lack of resources and negative experiences with urban men. As rural migrant women, hostesses lack the education and social contacts necessary to get ahead in life. In a very real sense, their only resource is their bodies. Under these circumstances, the high profits available through body commodification provide powerful incentives for rejecting the legal-moral prohibition against prostitution.

Popular explanations for prostitution often place an exaggerated emphasis on the "temptation of money" (jinqian de youhuo) in a way that condemns sex workers for their greediness and shallow pursuit of material comfort.[6] My fieldwork data, however, suggest that the causal powers attributed to this factor are overstated. As described above, new hostesses rarely, if ever, go out. This clearly indicates that money is only one of multiple factors in the decision to enter into prostitution. If money were the primary or only reason for prostitution, then we would expect to see that poorer hostesses prostitute themselves more than wealthier hostesses. Instead, the relevant crosscut is not based on economic condition (poor–wealthy) but, rather, the amount of time spent working as a hostess (new–veteran). This means that the critical factor for engaging in prostitution is encountered sometime after becoming a hostess and is most likely tied to the experience of hostessing itself.

Further, many hostesses have at some point been cheated or abandoned by men. Others went through the torture of rape and abandonment in the

urban working environment. Hostesses' experience of rape and abandonment taught them not to be duped by men's romantic words and to embrace independence through hostessing. They commented, "Dalian men
try to cheat both our bodies and emotions. Without spending a cent, they
get what they want from us." Hostess Guang served as a domestic maid
in an urban family before hostessing. Within two months, she was raped
three times by her male employer. In another story, hostess Yu was involved
in a romantic relationship with an urban male in Beijing when she was
working as a waitress. He abandoned her immediately after learning that
she was pregnant. Broken-hearted, Yu walked into a karaoke bar and started
working as a hostess.

Hostess Min recounted to me her story of rape and abandonment by
an urban customer when she was working as a waitress in Dalian:

> After the rape, I was pregnant and considered myself his. I completely
> believed him when he promised me that he was going to marry me.
> Every day I was enjoying our romantic and sweet love, yearning for our
> wedding. Until one day the rosy bubbles built up in my dream were
> crumbled and collapsed. That day, I was carrying a dish from the kitchen
> upstairs to attend to the guests. The moment I stepped on the upper level,
> I caught my lover sitting at a table with a woman on his lap flirting and
> laughing. I could not believe my eyes: is this the man who says to me
> every day that he loves me and he cannot wait to marry me? I felt the
> whole world turning in a whirl in front of me. I did not know when I
> dropped the plates and fainted onto the floor. That accident killed the
> baby in my belly and, with it, my romantic dreams.

Min's eyes moistened as she was telling the story. In the end she sighed and
concluded, "Urban men take advantage of us both emotionally and physically. We cannot be too innocent [tai chunjie] or devoted; otherwise, we
will be tricked, used, and abandoned. Only women who are not pure can
protect themselves." While Min's retelling of the story may have appeared
to many readers as melodramatic, it still suggests the motivation turning
many women to hostessing.

Similar stories happened to almost everyone. Hostess Xu was not only
abandoned but also went through virulent humiliation and malicious
abuse from her urban lover and his family members. Xu was in a romantic relationship with a man from a wealthy urban family when she was

working at a factory. Every time she visited his house, his mother treated her very coldly and complained in front of her that ever since they were together, he always asked for money and spent way too much. Xu retorted by saying that she did not need his money as she earned her own. Nonetheless, it did not change his mother's attitude. In fact, Xu's boyfriend was constantly pressured to separate from her, because, as his mother kept warning him, her rural family would be a "bottomless hole" sucking up all his money in the future. In the end, his mother bought him a car, a house, and a business in another city and used it as a bait to lure him away from her. He succumbed to the temptation and left her, taking on the managerial role of the business in another city.

None of the above-mentioned migrant women went directly into the hostessing business upon migrating to the city. Rather, they started out in other employment, such as being domestic maids and restaurant waitresses. While the risk of sexual violation varies between different jobs (maids are perhaps the most at-risk occupational group), migrant women's low social position and lack of economic resources easily make them tempting targets for male sexual assault. Their stories are typical: urban lovers manipulate their emotions and then leave them empty-handed. As rural migrants, their bodies are more vulnerable to male sexual violation and subsequent abandonment.

Working in a male-dominated sector, hostesses are more at risk of sexual violation than women in other occupational sectors. Almost every hostess has excruciating experiences of this power hierarchy and has managed to deal with it in their special ways. These negative experiences have left hostesses extremely cynical toward ideals of love and marriage. As one hostess comments:

> Whomever you are married to, you will face the risk of getting
> divorced because of men's sexual promiscuity. At that time, you will lose
> everything—your love, age, time, beauty, and financial base. What good
> does it do? So get a rich man to marry first so that when you are older,
> you still have money and status in the family.

Thus, for nearly all hostesses, the outright rejection of prostitution represents a transitional phase in which internalized moral prohibitions against sex-money transactions are broken down and replaced by a new moral vision that permits and even encourages prostitution. I purposefully use the term *moral vision* to emphasize that this view is not an ad hoc excuse for immoral behavior. Rather, it represents a fundamental revision of the standard of right and wrong. Specifically, commodification of the body and commodification of romance and intimacy are transformed from a denigration of female virtue into a route to empowerment. Hostesses reject mainstream morality's emphasis on romantic love and sexual purity as a thin disguise for the ugly reality of men's sexual exploitation of women, and actively perform and commodify romantic love and sexual purity for their instrumental purposes.

COMMODIFYING INTIMACY AND ROMANCE

Huang was married to an urban man but still slipped out to do hostessing. She said that she was despised because of her rural background, and everyone in his family treated her as a domestic maid. As a result, she secretly worked as a hostess to earn her own income, and hence her independence, worth, and self-esteem.

Hostess Hua said to me, "I would rather be a mistress *[qingren]* than a wife *[airen].*" I asked her why. She said, "Because I can get much more by being a mistress *[zuo qingren dedao de gengduo].*" She commented:

> What good does love do? What's the use of it *[ai you sha yong ya]*? Can you eat it or drink it *[ai nengchi haishi neng he ya]*? If a man does not give me money and only says he loves me, I don't want this kind of love. What's the use of such a man? If I want sex, I am not looking for you. So many men are waiting in line. I am still young and have my capital *[ziben].* How can I give it to you without any remuneration? I will not be able to say this when I grow old, but at least at this moment I can choose and select. If you don't give me money, only talk love and try to take advantage of me, I will never let you get me. I will tempt you—I will kiss you and hug you to the extent that you cannot stand it, but I will not let you get me. I will make you want to touch me, but I will not allow you to touch me; even if you succeed in touching me, you cannot get me. Until you pay out of your pocket.

Commodifying romance and intimacy is the pervading discourse in the hostesses' coterie. Hostesses feign intimacy and romance with clients and men in general to obtain financial security. By feigning this closeness, hostesses are commodifying not only the physical aspect of intimacy such as sexual contact but also the emotional aspects of intimacy, including devotion, care, considerateness, trust, intimate exchanges, emotional engagement, and love.

Hostess Lin talked about her former hostess friend Fang who exited hostessing and enjoyed the life of being a "second wife." Fang worked for an insurance company during the daytime. According to Lin, insurance companies did not demand any educational or professional background, nor did they pay any monthly income. Employees had to earn their own income by selling insurance policies. Lin said, "Fang joined the company in order to get closer to the powerful men there. Every day she dressed up very womanly *[hen nu ren]* and appeared very gentle and pure in front of the boss"; with these words, Lin was mimicking Fang's demeanor, casting her eyes down and looking very subservient. She continued, "She had the techniques to convey her devotion and romantic feelings to the boss. She finally succeeded in hooking up with him and became his second wife." Needless to say, with her changed status, she obtained financial mobility.

In order to increase the appearance of intimacy and romance, hostesses called their client or nonclient boyfriends "husbands" *(laogong)*. This was tinged with a coquettish, delicate, and charming tone. They commented that such an intimate and romantic address intoxicated men so much that they immediately "forgot who they were and were easily conquered." Most important, this appellation changed the nature of the relationship and reshaped it from an economic transaction into an intimate husband-wife exchange. The reconfigured intimacy instigated men's feelings of responsibility, the same kind of responsibility that they carried for their own wives, such as taking care of them in financial and living terms and protecting them in dangerous and risky circumstances. Thus the intimate address of "husband" shrinks the distance and draws the two parties together.

Hostesses also conveyed their devotion to their lovers by obeying the men's demands. As illustrated above, once they set up a semipermanent or permanent relationship with a client lover, they promised to be faithful and not go out with others. Oftentimes, clients sent their friends to test the hostesses, in which case the hostesses needed to prove their loyalty and fidelity through refusal of other men's sexual advances. Hostesses also catered to their client lovers' tastes in their appearance. Hostess Teng's lover did not like her doing her hair up, because, in his terms, "you looked too loose *[tai sao]* with your hair up." So every time they had a date, she would let her hair down to please him. Most important, she wanted to convey the message to him that she cared about his opinions. Hostesses also accompanied their lovers on business trips and to business banquets.

When their lovers were absent, they would call to remind them that they loved them and were missing them. However, the frequency and content of the calling posed another intractable issue. As the hostesses told me, they should call but never too much. Ling said, "You cannot give him the wrong impression—that you are totally dependent on him—because then he would get scared and leave you. When calling, you have to make him feel like you are always busy, you are not just sitting there waiting for him to come, you have many things to do, yet you still miss him and love him." Ling had been expecting her client lover for a whole week, but when calling him, she said, "I love you and I miss you very much, but if you are busy, you don't have to come." In the end, her client lover came by and took her on a four-day tourist trip to many scenic spots. She said she had a wonderful time. Before he left, he gave her another 3,000 *yuan*. Ling's carefully rehearsed phone calls not only conveyed her devotion despite her "busy schedule," but also expressed her understanding of his work. She knew that her techniques worked, when he came to spend four days with her and left her a handsome amount of money. She compared dealing with men to flying a kite: "You cannot hold on to it too tight, but not too loose either."

In karaoke rooms, hostesses sang romantic songs insinuating or, at times, expressing boldly their romantic feelings toward the men. They also exhibited their love through physical contact. In the karaoke rooms, they gently massaged the men's back and chest, resting their heads on the men's shoulders, singing songs when gazing at the men, or shedding bitter, sad, or happy tears, depending on the nature of the intricate relationship between the two, kissing the men's cheeks or lips, sitting on their laps and embracing their heads and shoulders, dancing with their bodies together *(tie mian wu),* embracing their waist intimately, and so on. Sometimes the aggressive ones would even grasp the men's penis or pull down their pants to invite more sexual intimacy and physical contact, depending on the men's propensities. They also indicated their devotion to the men through serving them food and drinks, peeling fruit skins or melon seeds, and feeding them what they liked.

Once I was singing songs at a karaoke bar with two hostesses and two clients. The two hostesses, Hua and Yeh, had just returned to Dalian from Shanghai and were invited by Liu and Li to sing songs with them at an upscale karaoke bar. Hua and Yeh invited me to come along. At the karaoke room, Hua rested her head on Liu's shoulders and kissed his cheeks and lips; Yeh was sitting on Li's lap and put her arms around his head. Hua and Yeh each selected some romantic, melancholic, and sentimental songs to convey their feelings for Liu and Li, respectively. While Hua was singing, she was so deeply engaged that her tearful big eyes were gazing at Liu, soulfully and affectionately. When Hua and Yeh left for the restroom, Liu and Li sang high praise for Hua and Yeh's sincerity, purity, and devotion. They told me that they trusted these two "girls" because they were "truly devoted friends" (gou peng you):

> When we traveled to Shanghai on a business trip, we were not familiar with the locale and did not have any friends there [rensheng dibushu]. We had the phone numbers of Hua and Yeh on us because we used to play together in Dalian. So we tried calling them. We did not expect that they would receive us so whole-heartedly. We went out to a karaoke bar drinking and singing together throughout the whole night. We drank so much that none of us was sober. We talked nonsense to each other, we exchanged the most personal and intimate stories with each other, and we laughed at our stupidity and funniness together. We really appreciate the two girls' accompanying us in the outside city [waidi]. We were especially moved by their care and consideration when they bought us four boxes of cigarettes before our departure, knowing that we love cigarettes. Four boxes of cigarettes!

Both Liu and Li got so excited that their faces turned red. "They are true friends, indeed!" they claimed. "Ever since then we have always cherished that memory in our hearts. We can never forget their care and devotion to us."

At the beginning, Liu and Li apparently did not expect much from the hostesses because, in their words, they only "tried calling them." I suspect that they thought, or to be more exact, they were afraid that the hostesses would take their previous relationship only as superficial play. After the two hostesses demonstrated their intimacy, love, and devotion through a series of performances in Shanghai, the two men's hearts were melted and completely moved. The fact that the two felt dislocated in a strange city could also have played an important part in enhancing their appreciation of the hostesses' performance of intimacy and warmth. In any event, the relationship now became such a "deep play" that both men felt responsible for the two women. In other words, Hua's and Yeh's commodification of intimacy and devotion bore its fruit.

For Hua and Yeh, however, Liu and Li were no more than another two clients whom they could benefit from, not only temporarily but also in the long run. In fact, Yeh told me that she was thinking about opening a small restaurant selling duck neck meat because she witnessed how hot (*huo*) the business was when she traveled to Wuhan, a southern city in Hubei Province. She was confident that her business would be very successful in Dalian, not only because no one had filled this niche in Dalian yet, but most important, because she did not need to worry about the source of her customers. Her client lovers such as Liu and Li were countless in Dalian and would no doubt form a solid customer base. She said, "They will not only come themselves, but also bring their friends." Her commodification of intimacy and romance earned her not only men's trust and affection, but also a wide social network that she will be able to capitalize on whenever she needs it.

In the coterie of the hostesses, the leading discourse is about how to get the most out of men and give the least. It is taboo to talk about emotional involvement with a man without being compensated. This is inexorably denigrated and ridiculed. For instance, everyone was gossiping about Lili, who was supporting her boyfriend with the money she earned at the bar. She was despised and ostracized from the group. When she was in financial straits, no one was sympathetic and no one was willing to loan her any money. When she was finally abandoned by her boyfriend, everyone was ruthlessly straightforward with her: "You asked for it! It was all because you have been spoiling him with your money! Now you know where it leads to! Now you have learned your lesson!"

Hostesses manipulate romantic love in their dealings with clients to attain rational control. As illustrated in the next section, the untold stories behind this veneer of triumphant rational control are filled with constant struggle, fierce negotiation, subversive contestations, and broken-hearted setbacks.

resisting state control

COMPLEXITIES BEHIND THE VENEER OF RATIONAL CONTROL

My research reveals that while hostesses practice rational control to deal with hierarchical relationships with urban men, they have not forgone their hope for a romantic and financially secure marriage down the road. Caught between a survival strategy to exert control and a persistent dream for a perfect romance, hostesses find themselves actively resorting to supernatural forces for direction and help. At times when they feel they are "losing it," recourse to supernatural force and magic helps them regain a sense of power and control.

tension

To make sure that their lovers are faithful, for instance, hostesses cut out an effigy of the man they are involved with and place it inside their shoes. They believe that through stepping on it every day, they can successfully control their lovers' heart. Such a belief in supernatural power is not limited to the use of magic. Hostesses also employ other supernatural powers to locate their future romantic and wealthy companions. If you enter a karaoke bar around 6 P.M. in the evening when the bar is just open, you will see a team of hostesses burning incense in front of the treasure god, not only to wish themselves good fortune but also, most important, to meet a good man who could take them away and assure them security and happiness in the future.

In another karaoke bar where the treasure god was not available, you could see hostesses in circles playing cards as a form of fortune telling. Every evening before clients started trickling into the bar, hostesses religiously surrounded the hostess who could foretell one's future through card playing and listened attentively to her announcement of what would happen in their future. Every time, the fortune-teller hostess asked, "What do you want to know about your future?" Almost every hostess replied that they would like to know who their future husbands would be. Then the fortune-teller asked the hostess to shuffle the cards three times with her own hands before the fortune-teller hostess became closely engaged in card playing for a while. When the cards were finally ready in front of her, the fortune-teller would start analyzing as she uncovered each card slowly.

Mainly, she would talk about whether the requested hostess could meet her future husband tonight; where he would be from; what profession he would be in; whether he was wealthy, tall, and handsome; whether they would get along; and so on. Hostesses never get tired of such fortune telling. It is a ritual that they religiously and indefatigably participate in every evening with steadfast belief.

Even this daily ritual is not enough. Many of them would even go in groups on a three-hour train ride to a well-known shaman *(da xian)* in a nearby village to learn about their future husbands. As I learned, even though the shaman refused to tell their fortunes because they were hostesses (in a "tainted" profession), some of them insisted on going regularly, hoping one day the shaman would miraculously start talking to them. They commented that the shaman, who was neither a man nor a woman, was really omniscient. In fact, so many people were visiting him/her that they had to start waiting in the front of the shaman's house at three o'clock in the morning. Fan said, "The shaman looked at me and said, 'Why do you have to love a man who already has a wife? Can't you find another man?' and then drove me away. The shaman is truly tough. Just by looking at me once, the shaman already knows my profession and my affair with a married man." Fan continued, "We thought it was because of the way we were dressed. So we chose some really ragged clothes to go again, but the shaman still could tell that we are hostesses." Nonetheless, the shaman's rejection did not make the hostesses retreat. They continued making efforts to ask about their future. Some of them succeeded. Hostess Hui told me that she fell in love with a married client and could not extricate herself from the affair. She went to the shaman. Without her telling the shaman, the shaman already saw what was going on and told her to leave the man immediately because he was not the one. She followed the shaman's words and cut off the relationship.

Besides going to the shaman, hostesses also took trips to southern cities in order to ask for fortunes *(qiu qian)* in the temples. My friend Hong took a trip to Shanghai for this reason. She spent four days in the temples burning incense, after she started dating her boyfriend. She wanted to see if they were going to get married and whether they would be happy together. She met her boyfriend in a real estate office when I accompanied her looking for an apartment closer to the bar we were working in. It so happened that a man was also seeking an apartment in the office. At the suggestion of the manager, they co-rented an apartment and later became a couple. She told him that she was pursuing a degree at a night university and he believed her. He had a very good job in the city and earned a handsome salary. She did not know if he was the one for her, so she spent more than 3,000 *yuan* on the trip to Shanghai to ask for her fortune in numerous temples.

When she came back, she was wild with joy, telling me that when she shook the cylinder vessel full of fortune-telling sticks, the one that fell out said that she was going to get married this year. I congratulated her that she could soon be settled with a nice man. After a week, however, she told me that she had broken up with him because it turned out that her boyfriend had brought another woman back to their apartment after she left and stayed a whole night with her. Her neighbors, who thought they were a married couple, told her when she came back. She immediately broke up with him, not allowing him to explain anything. She said, "He told me he could explain. I said, 'There is nothing to be explained. Whatever has been done is already done. That's the end of it.'" She ended the relationship, quite staunchly and coldly. She moved to another apartment rented by a man who was willing to keep her as a second wife. She stopped coming to the bar. I went to visit her a couple of times and learned that she was working in his store selling refrigerators.

Hong devoutly pursued supernatural rituals to determine her relationship with her lover. Although she was overjoyed when she was told that she was going to get married that year, she made her independent and rational decision to end the romance with her current boyfriend when she saw that this was not an ideal romance. Hong, despite practicing the new model of romance with men in general, still seeks a perfect romance and is not willing to make do with one who only assures financial security but not faithful love.

In fact, Hong's pursuit of an ideal romance has been constant. Before she was a hostess, Hong worked in a company. At that time she was only twenty years old. Her boss was pursuing her, but she refused. Her boss said to her, "One day you will voluntarily walk to me naked." Her boss's words turned out to be true. She said in the end she was completely conquered by his charm and skills and willingly became his second wife for three years. She was enjoying her romance until one day when she went to the seaside with her friends, she caught sight of her boss going into a hotel with a woman and coming out after a couple of hours. She said she told her boss previously that if he had another woman, she would immediately exit the relationship because she could not tolerate the fact that he had another woman beside her. She quit the job and left him after that. No matter how he apologized and asked for her forgiveness, she resolutely adhered to her decision and walked to a karaoke bar. When he learned that she was working as a hostess, he asked her out and gave her 6,000 *yuan,* but she refused. She said, "I was with you because of pure love. There were no material considerations. I cannot stain my pure intention by receiving money. If I received your money now, I would be saying that I was with you for the purpose of money. I was not, so I cannot accept your money."

Hong was condemned in the hostesses' circle as a big fool *(sha zi)* for her refusal of the money. Hostesses commented, "Why not take the money? You should take the money and forget everything else. That's what he owes to you!" To other hostesses, Hong lost it in this relationship because she "followed her true emotions" *(dongle zhen ganqing).* To Hong herself, the idea of true romance remained a sacred hope, albeit with a married man with no possibilities of fulfilling the romance with a marriage. Hong managed to maintain a space in her heart that cherished this pure romance and would not allow it to be "polluted" or "tainted" by money.

Hong's story is not rare in the hostesses' group. Although Fen was elevated as a model for others to follow because she had garnered tens of thousands of *yuan* from her client lovers since starting work as a hostess, once Fen confided to me, "I cannot tell other hostesses that I sometimes also give him [her client lover] small gifts, because otherwise they would despise me. But how can I demand money every time after I have sex with him? After all, he is my lover, right? But I cannot say this in front of other hostesses because I would be scoffed and laughed at."

I was also told a story of a previous hostess who left hostessing because she was kept by a very wealthy man. The man deposited a million *yuan* in her bank account, bought a house under her name, and sent her child to a local aristocrat school. Several months later, however, she escaped with another man whom she loved. That was a very dangerous move because, as the hostesses commented when they were telling the story, if the man ever found out her whereabouts, it would be the day of her doom.

Although hostesses accept the dominant discourse on intimacy, they still save a spot in their hearts seeking ideal romance. At times this dream makes them succumb to what they think is a perfect romance. In dangerous liaisons with clients whose goal is also to strive for rational control, hostesses find that dealing with these types of relationship is like walking on a tightrope, always teetering between losing it and maintaining control. Those who adhere to the strict approach to romance eventually experience its trade-off, either marrying their clients or becoming successful businesswomen in the city. Those who succumb to men's romance get lost in the game and are left broken-hearted. To remind themselves of the nature of the ruthless games that they are embroiled in, hostesses inflict scars on their hands and wrists with a burning cigarette or a knife every time they "lose it" and are abandoned by men. The sight of the ugly scars is eternal evidence, and a constant reminder, of their failures.

The hostesses in my study rejected romance as nothing more than a vehicle for men's sexual exploitation of women, and they insisted that romance obscures its patriarchal characteristics by attributing impossible virtue to women and confining them to a narrow sphere of behavior.[7] Thus the hostesses understood that romance is not a vehicle for their liberation. The romantic ideal encourages women to love unconditionally, but this unconditional love is seldom reciprocated.[8] While the hostesses are clever enough not to question their clients' romantic rhetoric, they are in fact, hard-nosed realists who see the situation with great clarity.

As in America, a common stereotype of women in China is that they are weak and emotional while men are cool and rational. Women live for love and men live for work. Veteran hostesses are not fooled by this stereotype. They typically provide leadership to younger hostesses and initiate them in the realities of male subterfuge. To survive in the world of hostesses, one must be a cool-eyed realist. Their realism is ironic, since it involves a rejection of the male stereotype of an emotional woman. The hostesses play the game of romance and demand cash in exchange for their favors. In this way, they are able to turn the tables on their customers and save themselves from denigration.

By casting aside these illusions, hostesses are able to embrace the commodification of their bodies as an empowering practice. Hostesses reenvision the female body as a repository of economic value ("Virginity has a price"). Sex work, rather than denigrating women, is the realization of this value, allowing hostesses to achieve economic profit and hence independence from unreliable and dishonest men. The new value of sex thus helps them subvert the gender and rural-urban hierarchy by redistributing urban clients' economic and social resources.

ONSTAGE PERFORMANCES
THE DEMURE VIRGIN

When young clients came in, hostesses immediately called out to each other, "Young fellows [xiao huo er]! They love women who are virgins!" They ran into the fitting room to exchange their sexy dresses for more conservative attire, letting their long hair down on two sides in the front and wiping off some facial makeup. By this change of attire and appearance, they were transformed into "virtuous maidens" (shunv). In the karaoke suite, they walked in short steps, seldom drank or talked, sat somewhat far from the clients, knees tight together, their eyes innocently cast down like "pure" and "shy" rural women fresh from the countryside who had just started working here out of desperation and poverty. Offstage, the hostesses often practiced the virgin look through dress, hairstyle, makeup, and manner of talking and walking. "I am a virgin. Good evening, big brother [dage, used to address unfamiliar clients]." A nineteen-year-old hostess, Sheng, was exceptionally skilled at playing the virgin. Younger clients often offered her larger-than-usual tips between 300 and 500 yuan (an average tip was 100 yuan).

Such a pure virginal look required not only more conservative attire, hairstyle, and so on, but also demure manners. First, hostesses had to learn not to be too "bold and desperate" in front of clients. They commented that the more they retreated, the more the client was attracted to them. The knowledge of how and when to retreat projected their virtue and purity. Second, a cultivated manner had to be displayed during socialization with clients. Once I had dinner with hostess Hui in her room. Because I was really hungry, I ate a lot. Feeling quite relaxed, I was shaking my legs a bit under the table. Appalled by my improper manners, Hui said:

You cannot act like this. You have to look like a gentlewoman *[shunv]*. Look, whenever I am with my clients, I always sit very straight, very quiet, never shake my legs, only eat a small amount of food, and preoccupy myself with serving the client the food he cannot reach. Even when extremely tired and starving, I am glad I project an image of a gentlewoman, neither crude nor rough, with good education. Clients really like that.

In addition, hostesses need to act docile and obedient. A twenty-two-year-old hostess from Anshan explained:

When I first came here, fresh from the countryside, I did not know anything. I did not know how to put on makeup, how to dress, how to behave. But I made up my mind to prove myself better than the urbanites. I went through several jobs before coming to the bar. Since working in the bar, I have tried to learn from everybody, how they work, how they use makeup, and how they behave. If the other hostesses earned ten work points, I would earn fifteen. I knew I could do that. Gradually, I learned how to dress up. I learned that customers are God. They are the most important channels through which I can reach my goal and gain my work points. Thereafter, I always put them at the top of my list. Whenever a customer chooses me as a companion, I always serve him whole-heartedly. If I notice that he likes beer, I will always fill up his glass. If he likes to smoke, I will always light his cigarette. I always offer him a toast and drink up a full glass of beer first. Without demanding him to drink the same way, I convey to him my desire to please him. I always help him peel the melon seeds with my teeth until I have a hand full and then serve them to him. It does not take very long, only about ten to fifteen minutes. But he always respects my effort to serve him and often comes back to me, which earns me great respect from the other women and *Mami* for my ability to attract guests.

This hostess's experience illustrates how hostesses in general, to win a client's favor and procure a higher tip, have to compete with each other by projecting the most subservient rural woman's image. As shown in this narrative, the motto of this hostess's service was: "Customers are God. I am here to serve them." She painstakingly offered a loyal and obedient service to her clients by catering to their every need. Such devoted service also involved enduring clients' physical and sexual abuse. For instance, hostesses demonstrated their submission through silence and tolerance in the face of the male customers' degrading remarks about breasts and vaginas. They adopted the image of a compliant rural woman presenting their submissive feminine nature before the clients.

PLAYING CINDERELLA TO PRINCE CHARMING

Hostesses also played upon the stereotype of a poor, rural, vulnerable woman to entice the clients to be their "saviors." I heard many hostesses mention how they told their clients about their horrific experiences of being raped or sexually abused. One hostess said, "I told my client that I, as a rural woman, came to be a hostess because my previous city boyfriend raped and abandoned me. My client was so touched by my story that he was literally in tears!" The other hostesses all laughed. I asked her if this was true, because I often heard clients say that this was the main reason that hostesses "fell" into their profession. When I asked this question, the hostess laughed loudly: "Who ever tells clients the truth? You are a fool if you believe it! Of course, I made it up!" Hostesses created such stories to evoke customers' sympathy and desire to save the "fallen" woman. Most times clients were so moved by the "tragic existence" of such pretty and vulnerable rural women that they offered them larger tips, financed their education, and established enduring sexual and sometimes emotional bonds. As one hostess recollected, she often ended up in fairly long relationships with such caring and sympathetic men, playing the role of a vulnerable rural woman.

I got to know twenty-year-old hostess Tang through her client, a forty-seven-year-old businessman named Ceng. Tang acted as Ceng's mistress for a year and a half. Ceng treated her as a fallen woman to be saved. He sent her to a local university to study law, paying not only for her tuition but also miscellaneous living expenses, such as the fees for hairdressing and cosmetics. Ceng provided Tang with a comfortable standard of living to prevent her from "turning bad." He told me that when they were together, he sent a friend to the bar to test her. It turned out that she refused to sleep with his friend. Ceng proudly told me that Tang was changed to "a better woman" under his guidance. The process though, according to him, required a lot of "preaching and inculcation." He talked about Tang as if he were not only her savior, but also her educator and mentor. Ceng talked about her as if she were a little child, innocent but transgressive, who needed his discipline and direction. He even drew on concepts of "socialist education" to try to instill in Tang "an enthusiasm to surpass others and an enterprising spirit." He acted like a saint who "donated money" to her for nothing but to "turn her good." He said:

> I have helped her a lot with money. She thinks I saved her. I said, "What do I want from you? Nothing. I just want you to be transformed into a good woman. Otherwise, you will not even be able to forgive yourself." Before, you know, she would sleep with her customers. Such mistakes can never be corrected or excused. I feel deeply disconcerted about the matter. Ever since she slept with me and we became lovers, I have been educating her to be a good person, and she has gotten a lot better. I told her if she ever slept with other men again, I would destroy her face. I said, "What could you do without a face?" Right? I said, "You could do nothing without it." I said, "All I want to do for you is to make you become a good woman. If you only want money, you will become a bottomless hole. This way, you will turn worse and worse." I want her to walk the right path.

Ceng's desire to be the "masculine hero" through "reforming" a "naïve and transgressive rural girl" is clearly spelled out in his talk.

I asked Ceng what he thought about Tang as a person. He said:

> I think she is quite a naïve and ignorant rural girl, imagining she can become an urban woman someday. Sadly, the most she can do is to have one foot rooted in the village and one foot in the city, always half-urban and half-rural, caught in between. She is too naïve and ideal, not grounded in reality. Now she has stepped into an abyss of love and cannot drag herself out. She sometimes comes to look for me. She is crying and saying some soft words, and I cannot endure her begging, so I make up with her again.

In Ceng's mind, Tang was nothing but an innocent and fallen rural girl with unreasonable thoughts and unattainable dreams. He assumed a strong patriarchal responsibility for rescuing this "deplorable victim" from "sinking too deep." This kind of rescue, however, brought about not only economic and social advantages but also abuse to Tang. As Ceng's friend told me, Ceng always beat her up and cursed her. Because Tang always came back to him afterwards, Ceng considered it very natural to beat her up. Tang said that Ceng not only beat her up, but also looked into her wallet and checked her tips. If she was offered a larger tip than he considered reasonable, he would interrogate her harshly: "Why are they giving you such a large tip? What have you done to make them offer you so much money?"

INTERNALIZING THE PERFORMANCES?

In this section, I address the question of whether hostesses identify with the characters that they act out in their sex work. Chapkis argues that sex workers are at risk of merging with their work identities. Hostesses, however, maintain a clear and stable distinction between their "true" self and the characters that they portray as part of their erotic services. Several factors contribute to the hostesses' detachment. Some of these lie in the objective circumstances of the karaoke bar sex industry; others reflect a conscious attempt on the part of hostesses to distance themselves from the weak and passive characters of their erotic performances.

As shown in the previous section, onstage hostesses were obliged to fulfill client expectations of rural women's "nature" by acting out their image as portrayed in state and media representations. Offstage hostesses reversed their position in the exploitative onstage relationship by performing the role of clients. They parodied the client's abusive commentary and even reenacted episodes of sexual aggression. On several occasions, I witnessed hostesses removing each other's bras and fondling each other's breasts. Such activities would sometimes escalate to mimicked rape scenes. Hostesses would ride on top each other's bodies, ordering each other to shout and scream.

This behavior should not be interpreted as an expression of homoeroticism. Hostesses do not derive sexual pleasure from these acts. Rather, mimicking their client's sex acts both reflects and helps to create a separate space within which they can construct a "true" and "ideal" identity as distinguished from the characters that they act out in the unequal relations of their onstage lives. By *true,* I mean that hostesses subjectively understand their offstage identity as being real in relation to the set of characters that they act out onstage. By *ideal,* I mean that this offstage identity is in many ways preferable to their onstage characters. Hostesses see their offstage self as their true identity because it offers a stronger, more independent self-image than their onstage characters. Thus, the existence of this offstage space serves as the basis for hostesses' interpretation of their on- and offstage selves as, respectively, fake and real.

Below I explore in detail the specific ways in which this understanding takes shape. Hostesses saw character playing as an instrument for cheating clients out of more money and extra benefits. The view of clients as cash cows to be exploited was a constant theme in offstage conversations. A hostess who had lost her clients' phone numbers exclaimed, "Shit! I lost my clients' phone numbers. Do you know what those numbers mean? They mean money! Clients are Renminbi [Chinese currency]!"

Hostesses derived a sense of empowerment from the idea that they had "cheated" *(pianqu)* clients out of money. To "cheat" a client meant to have extracted benefits (cash and otherwise) beyond the common standard for labor rewards. I put "cheat" in quotation marks because this is the hostesses' own construction of the nature of these transactions. An alternate interpretation would be that these perquisites are a proportional compensation for their labor output; a larger-than-average tip, for example, indicates that the hostess has performed better than average. There are two reasons why hostesses do not adopt this second interpretation, or why it is less available as a way of understanding these transactions. On the one hand, sexual labor is socially not prestigious, thus negating any sense of accomplishment from doing a "good job." On the other hand, casting themselves as "cheaters" gives hostesses the sense that they have gained the upper hand in a transaction in which they are subject to severe abuse. The idea that they "got something for nothing" is both a source of comfort for the abuse they endure in the course of services and seems to prove that they are still able to exert some measure of control over male clients.

Hostesses loved to recount tales of how they were able to fleece gullible clients through well-executed character performances. Hostess Sheng, for example, earned the respect of other hostesses for the large tips she garnered for her demure virgin performances. Sheng was pleased not only by her economic gains and peer recognition but also, and more important, by the fact that her clients had fallen for her ruse. As she repeated many times, "These stupid clients think I am pure and innocent [chun zhen]. They say, 'Look how pure this rural woman is!' Fuck, I am just faking purity [zhuang chun]."

Clients' abusive treatment toward hostesses contributes to the sense that character playing is an acceptable façade to disguise their profit-making aims. Clients physically (pinching, punching) and mentally (denigrating and objectifying commentary) abuse hostesses during onstage services and in their out-of-bar interactions. This treatment naturally engenders resentment and even outright hatred against clients. Hostesses always insisted, "We hostesses are also human beings!" While they express their sexual needs, it is seldom in relation to clients. Once in chatter before going to bed, a hostess named Han said, "Whenever I touch my breasts, my body feels weird." The others laughed and said that she was horny. She laughed, too. During my research, one hostess confided in me that occasionally she had orgasms with some clients, but not often. In spite of these isolated examples, sexual arousal seems to have been rare among the hostesses. There is a popular saying created by the hostesses to express their contempt for their patrons and their ability to turn male exploitation against the exploiters by practicing a cold detachment:

If I want you	[wo xiang he ni chu]
You can't resist me	[shui ye dang bu zhu]
And then I break up with you	[wo xiang he ni huang]
I am so arrogant	[wo jiu zhe mo kuang]
If I break up with you	[huang le wo zai chu]
I go out with other men	[wo jiu zhe mo ku]
And then I screw them and abandon them	[chu le wo jiu shang]
I am so cold	[shang le wo jiu shuai]

Typically the attitude of the hostesses is one of levity toward their clients. This is also illustrated by a conversation among three hostesses returning from their time with clients. They were laughing and teasing each other, joking about their fake screams and orgasms and confiding to each other their intense desire that this experience would be over with as soon as possible. They view sex with clients as a means of making money and hopefully achieving some sort of mobility. Even in cases in which they have established a love relationship with their clients, they still treat sexual intercourse as a business transaction that must be compensated with money or gifts. At the same time, hostesses are prevented from direct expressions of resistance by the imperative to satisfy clients and thus maximize their profits. The inability to forthrightly give voice to these sentiments leads to a strong sense of division or schism between true and false selves. As one hostess described, this condition creates the "bitterness" of a hostess's life:

> I don't like men. I hate them. To get their money's worth, they torture you until you can't stand it anymore. They curse you and treat you as if you weren't a human being. We have to take all this with a smile. Do you know what kind of feeling that is? Only a hostess can understand. It's like we hostesses have two faces—one real face and one fake face. The fake face tries very hard to cheat men out of their money. It is all fake.

This quotation demonstrates how clients' behavior creates powerful emotions that are denied expression by the economics of the server-client relationship. The disjuncture between what is thought or felt and what is expressed leads to a bright-line distinction between a hostess's true self and the falseness of their character playing—the two faces of the hostess.

If economic pressures force hostesses to grin and bear clients' abusive treatment, hostesses' offstage lives give ample opportunity to vent their outrage. The following poem written by and circulated among hostesses concisely combines the themes discussed in this section, namely, the falseness of hostesses' performances, their instrumental purposes, and their antipathy toward clients:

Entering the karaoke room,	[jin men xiao xi xi]
We smile our brightest smile.	[zuo xia xiang fu qi]
Sitting by the clients,	[xiao fei yi dao shou]
We act as if we are their most obedient wives.	[qu ni ma le ge bi]
But as soon as the tip lands in our hands—	
Fuck your mother's cunt!	

While hostesses gain a sense of empowerment from cheating clients, the truth of the matter is that they are still very much at the mercy of clients' whims. One hostess's comments reflect this fact: "If you do not tolerate these small things [clients' abusive treatment], you will encounter a big mess [xiaoburen ze daluan]. Hold your nose and do whatever he says. Always be compliant. Never act against his will. Then, he will definitely give you a 200-yuan tip. Otherwise, you will suffer the worst consequences."

This chapter illustrates how hostesses juggle multiple identities in the kara-oke bar setting. They are forced to play a role to access their clients' social, cultural, and economic resources. It is not that hostesses are naturally subversive; rather, the conditions of the bar's labor industry structure the hostesses' experiences of these images in such a way that they appear to be false. At the same time, the expressive freedom enjoyed by the hostesses in their offstage lives allows them to construct a "true" and "ideal" self. If the onstage hostess is a weak and vulnerable victim, the offstage hostess is a strong and aggressive manipulator.

As more and more women are sucked into this trap only to discover the unbalanced power too late, veteran hostesses have established the sex-value system to defy male supremacy and subvert the existing power hier-archy. Fully aware of the power structure and men's manipulative techniques of romance, hostesses assume control by quantifying men's romantic lean-ings into monetary gains and benefits. This rational control puts them in a superior position not only over hypocritical men, but also over other women who are duped by men's romantic ploys. Such rational control up-sets the hierarchical emotional discourse of "weak and emotional women" and "cool and rational men."[9] Such rational control overthrows the myth that women live for love and men live for work.

Hostesses' value transition in their discursive practice is a political act of rebellion and negotiation over resources and power. Refusing to be duped into urban men's myths of romance, hostesses form a new sex-value system and indoctrinate it into newcomers' minds. By trivializing men's romance and demanding its quantified monetary gains, hostesses upset the gender and social hierarchy and realize their body's commodified value as an empowering practice. Behind the veneer of rational control lie the complexities of the hostesses' constant negotiations, heartbreaking setbacks, and religiously persistent recourse to supernatural forces to gain power. Despite the practice of the new model of romance, some still steadfastly hold on to the dream of an ideal romance and will not let it go, even when it means possible heartbreak.

In defiance of the state's opposition to prostitution and of patriarchal control over their bodies and sexuality, hostesses market their bodies for their own independent, autonomous, and instrumental uses. Their work entails not just the sale of sex but also the sale of a performance in which they act out male stereotypes of rural migrant women: the unruly whore, the docile virgin, or the victimized peasant woman. We have seen that manipulation of rural women's images not only enables hostesses to become active commodity consumers and debunk their image as country bumpkins but also gives them access to their clients' social networks in order to reap cultural capital, social advancement, and economic security. Through their performances, they have come to constitute an important part of Dalian's economic system, redistributing vast amounts of wealth to immigrants who otherwise would be impoverished.

Consumption and body culture constitute the available cultural repertoire, which hostesses appropriate for their social advancement. Their dual cultural strategies are manifested through rather than outside of the constraining and enabling masculine state structure. In this sense, their very agency paradoxically binds and limits them by reinscribing and reproducing the hegemonic state discourse that legitimizes and naturalizes the docile virgin/promiscuous whore split image. Thus, their agency becomes what is held against them and reinforces their marginality and low status.

Afterword

FROM ENTERTAINER TO PROSTITUTE

THIS STUDY HAS BEEN A VOYAGE of discovery for me, but not of resolution. Like the hostesses, I grew up in a patriarchal China that defined me as a filial daughter. For the hostesses, filiality represents an unchallenged value, accepted and practiced, and the traditional value foundation on which the house of their reconstructed identity has been built. My journey has taken me to America, a place where I can stand and see China for the first time. It is a place outside myself where I can see myself for the first time. This is an advantage, or a curse that differentiates me from my hostess friends. My study of the social sciences allows me to understand that the deep cultural values of filiality are socially constructed values that are immutable truths only in China.

This year I became an American citizen. I look back to the confrontation with my classmates in Iowa over my criticisms of single mothers and smile. Yet my newfound ability to intellectualize my past world has not freed me from it. Like the hostesses, I continue to be a filial daughter; unlike the hostesses, I have to live with the contradiction between my understanding and my feelings.

But this is not my story. I now live in a safe world where I am free to think and speculate about my past. The hostesses continue to live and struggle in the dangerous world of state patriarchy. This song that was often sung to me during breaks in the karaoke room reminds me of their courageous struggle:

Leaving parents and friends,
Waving them good-bye with hot tears in my eyes,
Although buffeted by wind and pelted by rain,

I will still march on
Along that long and arduous road
That I silently walk alone.
How many winters, summers, springs, and falls,
Have I faced the streams of traffic amid tall buildings,
As I searched and searched in the sea of people,
For the happiness I crave is difficult to find.

On March 3 and September 9,
Sweat and tears pour down my body,
As the sun scorches and the freezing breeze blows,
Relatives' smiles appear only in my dreams.

On March 3 and September 9,
I let my bitterness flow only inside my heart.
Marching east and marching west,
I have more sorrow than I can express.

Hostesses sang it with such emotion that it brought tears to my eyes. They loved to sing this song because it vividly portrayed their life of struggle as both migrant women and hostesses in the city. "For the happiness I crave is difficult to find," they sang. Yet they do not back down in the face of adversity: "Buffeted by wind and pelted by rain, I will still march on." Their sweat and tears, their sorrow and bitterness, are signs of their persistent struggle in the city's harsh environment.

In the summer of 2004 when I returned to Dalian, I was told that karaoke bars had changed their tactics. Hostesses, when singing and dancing with the clients, were completely naked. My friends explained to me that this was due to the sluggish business in the bars. The naked hostesses danced, sang, and touched clients' genitals to "see their reactions." This new service counteracted the economic slump and boosted the karaoke bar business. In fact, naked hostesses attracted so many customers that there were hour-long lines outside of the bars.[1] This seems to offer a hint about the future trends in the karaoke bar industry. Japan, faced with a similar decline in the karaoke bars, took a very different approach. They attempted to broaden the appeal by adding dancing games, electric musical instruments to accompany singing, banquets, a children's entertainment area, and communal bathtubs with warm spring water to attract long queues of clients.[2] While Japan has solved this problem by broadening its appeal to include even families, the approach in Dalian has been to offer rawer, hardcore sex. In Dalian to this day, the number of clients in karaoke bars far exceeds the number of people in bowling alleys and on golf courses. Sex consumption in karaoke bars in the twenty-first century continues to manifest its vitality while maintaining class distinctions between men. It continues to be a vehicle for men to affirm a new and more aggressive masculine identity.

Although local government's attitudes toward the karaoke bar continue to display the ambivalence we have seen from the 1920s and 1930s, the future of karaoke bars in Dalian seems assured. They not only provide sexual services, but they are an essential source of municipal government revenues. In Dalian, taxes paid by the entertainment industry are the largest source of local revenue. Karaoke bars are required to pay 33 percent of their net income and an additional 20 percent operating tax. This far exceeds the 5 percent tax rate on all other local businesses. The fact that local revenue depends on the karaoke bars guarantees that they will continue to be an important part of the Dalian economy.

As we have seen, masculine identity has undergone dramatic changes from classical China to the present. The most dramatic change has taken place in the twentieth century. There was a time in China when sexual services were the least significant part of a sophisticated interaction between courtesans and the scholars who sought their services. The Western challenge to classical China produced a new Chinese masculine ideal—the patriotic man. Patriotic men were defined by rebellion from classical norms, which were felt to be emasculating. During the Maoist era, with the establishment of an independent China, we had the rise of the bureaucratic man. Power was in the hands of the political commissars. And finally, the post-Mao era has given us the entrepreneurial man. A consistent pattern through all four stages has been a coarsening of masculine identity. The demand for naked hostesses is a long ways from the scholar's relationship with the courtesans in classical China.

This image of naked hostesses shows the crude quality of desire that now defines entrepreneurial manhood. It also shows us the most serious challenge to the hostesses, whose job is not just to exploit their bodies for wealth but also to hang on to some shred of dignity.

Working and living with the hostesses changed my views of these women. Before my research, I was intimidated by their glamour but considered them only women who had discarded their self-esteem in order to serve as exploited sexual objects for men. After my research, I came to see them as not so different from other Chinese women who wrestle with patriarchy on a daily basis, although their fight is much more fierce and violent due to the extreme masculine environment in which they work. I have a great deal of respect for these women because they are the most tenacious and brave women I have met in China. When the state, scholars, and popular opinions expunge them from the city by emphasizing their inability to become full-fledged urbanites, these women assert loudly that they can become not only real urbanites but also trendsetters on the cutting edge of urban style and fashion.

Hostesses face the dilemma of working within a male-defined system, and it is their task to turn this system to their own advantage. Most of these immigrant women had been ruthlessly exploited by men before becoming hostesses. As hostesses now, by exchanging humiliation for monetary gain, the women are exploiting the contradiction of the modern patriarchal orientation. Men achieve a sense of identity that is rooted in violating the mainstream values of female chastity: that is, they possess and humiliate the women, thus displaying their power. But in doing so, they allow the hostesses to practice an aggressive capitalism at their expense. The hostesses reject the value system that is the basis of their exploitation and choose to define themselves as modern entrepreneurs. In this way, they retell the story of their exploitation in such a way as to allow their triumph over the men who are exploiting them.

As we have seen, hostessing is also an expedient route for rural women to achieve a certain degree of social mobility with the acquired cultural, economic, and social resources. For these women, hostessing is not a lifetime occupation but a means to an end. Every year when I returned to continue my research, I found more hostesses married to their clients or having opened their own businesses such as gift shops, butcher shops, cosmetic shops, and clothing shops. Sometimes I ran into them when I went shopping myself. In the summer of 2004, while I was shopping at the largest underground mall at the train station, I bumped into a hostess

I had worked with. She was selling cosmetics and told me that she made considerable profit every day. She did not have a boyfriend and had been enjoying herself as an independent entrepreneur in Dalian.

In general, for the fortunate, opportunities for a better life lead them down these paths. The less fortunate are pushed into retirement as their increasing age puts them at a disadvantage with younger hostesses. Although some ex-hostesses stay on as madams and bar owners, most withdraw from the bars entirely. The hostesses' ideal exit strategies include marrying into an urban family, becoming the second wives *(ernai)* of wealthy businessmen or officials, or becoming independent businesswomen. These strategies are adopted with varying degrees of success. It is not uncommon for a hostess to exit and reenter hostessing work many times before escaping for good.

Regardless of which exit strategy is adopted, a hostess's ability to extricate herself from the karaoke bars and start a new life with a new identity is hindered by the lingering shadow of her past occupation. Ex-hostesses live with the constant dread that their new lives will be destroyed by the exposure of their history in the karaoke bars. An ex-hostess whose vending stall I helped tend when she was ill swore me to secrecy on several occasions not to out her to the other vendors. Her anxiety is universally shared by ex-hostesses in all familial and occupational situations. Whether the wife of an urban man, a government official, or repatriated countryside entrepreneur, ex-hostesses must cover up their pasts under the threat of losing their hard-earned new lives.[3]

Are hostesses able to achieve upward mobility within urban society with a sense of personal dignity? As we have seen, hostesses define themselves as modern entrepreneurial women. By personally rejecting patriarchal attitudes toward chastity, they freed themselves from the constraints that were imposed on women in general. Still, they must live in a modern world—and a modern China full of many contradictions. While they have rejected the internalization of patriarchal sexual values, the larger society that they seek to join continues to hold on to these values. The story of the Dalian hostesses is the age-old story of marginalized people. They struggle for economic survival and, equally important, strive to achieve for themselves a sense of identity within a larger culture where they live on the margins. It is a story of hope, struggle, defeat, and occasional victory.

Acknowledgments

NUMEROUS PEOPLE HELPED ME locate the field sites, protected my safety in the field, and acted as important informants for my research. I am indebted to the political officials, bar owners, bouncers, and hostesses for their safety advice and, at crucial moments, direct interventions. Without their sacrifices, my research in the bars would have been too dangerous to continue.

During the years of my research and writing on karaoke bar hostesses, I accumulated immense debts to my primary thesis adviser, Helen F. Siu, as well as to Deborah Davis, Harold W. Scheffler, William W. Kelly, and Susan Brownell. Helen Siu first encouraged me to pursue my interest in migrant women in urban China; I am grateful for her support throughout the process of my fieldwork and writing. This project would not exist without her intellectual inspiration, invaluable comments, and persistent quality requirements. She and William Kelly are responsible for obtaining funds to subsidize one of the most important parts of my writing: editing. During the most dangerous period of my fieldwork, Helen Siu and Deborah Davis were so concerned about my safety that they brought me back from the field. Deborah Davis's warm encouragement, intellectual inspiration, and appreciation of my work have always provided motivation and energy, and her professional advice and positive support continue to be a major part of my professional life. Harold Scheffler has offered me continuous intellectual and emotional support. He never tired of reading drafts and meticulously editing each sentence of each chapter. His intellectual support has been an important source of my persistence through most difficult times. Even after I graduated from Yale, he continued to support my intellectual development by offering me professional advice and editing drafts of journal articles. William Kelly's constructive comments, detailed suggestions, and special enthusiasm for my project were very precious and helpful to me during my fieldwork and my writing.

I benefited enormously from Susan Brownell. She generously assisted me in formulating my dissertation prospectus and designing the protocol for the human subject committee. She is an amazingly generous, insightful, and indefatigable mentor who helped me revise my dissertation into this book. She invested an immense amount of time and energy in the manuscript, not only making detailed corrections but also offering me thorough criticism and incisive suggestions that considerably sharpened and improved the whole project. The manuscript was reordered, reshaped, and rewritten according to her exceedingly clear guidelines. I thank her for her extraordinarily careful work, for her excellent suggestions, and for her warm encouragement. The present form of the book would have been impossible without her tirelessly incisive and generous comments.

I thank my teacher and mentor in China and in the United States, Jack Wortman. He not only contributed tremendously to my academic development but also helped me make the transition from a linguistics graduate student to a professional cultural anthropologist in the United States. He introduced me to the discipline of anthropology, inspired my strong interest in it, and encouraged me to study abroad. His generous support enabled me to come to the United States to study. For many years he has been a continuous intellectual and emotional support for me in every step of my intellectual development. During my most difficult years in the United States, he was my most faithful listener and selfless adviser, offering me time, advice, and, most important, faith. He tirelessly helped me edit the entire manuscript and engaged in inspiring and insightful discussions on its materials. I thank him for his extraordinary insights and his most generous and incessant emotional and academic support. My small achievement today would be impossible without his consistent mentorship. My debts to him and all above-mentioned mentors can never be repaid.

My writing also benefited from Dorothy Solinger, Vanessa Fong, Arianne Gaetano, Tamara Jacka, William Jankowiak, Andrew Kipnis, Ching Kwan Lee, Rachel Murphy, Louisa Schein, Emily Schultz, Mark Selden, Suisheng Zhao, and other anonymous reviewers for insightful comments and publication of earlier versions of selected chapters. I thank Marc Blecher and Li Zhang for their favorable review of my early publications, and I thank Xin Liu, Deborah Davis, and William Kelly for inviting me to their schools to present selected chapters. My gratitude also goes to Lisa Hoffman for her helpful suggestions before I embarked on my fieldwork in Dalian.

My special gratitude also goes to the following people. My parents provided emotional encouragement and great assistance to my fieldwork. I am grateful for Lawrence and Frank Szmulowicz, who industriously edited various parts of the book, provided insightful food for thought, and served as exciting and provoking intellectual interlocutors. My thanks go to Dave Grass, who carefully edited the language of the introduction. I am especially grateful to my editor at the University of Minnesota Press, Jason Weidemann, for his enthusiasm and support in guiding me through book preparation and production.

Various stages of this project were funded by the Yale Center for International and Area Studies; the Council on East Asian Studies of Yale University; and the Williams Fund and the Mellon Fund of Yale University's Department of Anthropology. I thank Elizabeth Russell and Mark Prus for offering me conference grants to present selected chapters.

$\mathcal{Notes}$

Introduction

1. Shaoguang Wang, "The Politics of Private Time: Changing Leisure Patterns in Urban China," in *Urban Spaces in Contemporary China,* ed. Deborah Davis et al. (Cambridge: Cambridge University Press, 1995). Wang argues that with the strict regulation of leisure time as a space, only very few leisure activities were organized by "work units" to demolish any bourgeois "counterrevolutionary decadence."

2. Ibid., 156.

3. Ping Jian, "Caifang Shouji: Jingyan Dalian" (interview memoirs in Dalian), *Xinzhoukan* (New weekly) 10 (2001): 44.

4. Gan Wang, "Conspicuous Consumption, Business Networks, and State Power in a Chinese City" (Ph.D. diss., Yale University, 1999).

5. Jian, "Caifang Shouji."

6. Courtesan houses, or public places where courtesans were summoned as professional entertainers, formed an integral part of the official and business routine where social relations of officials, literati, artists, and merchants were conducted. Every official entertained his close colleagues—superiors, inferiors, and merchants—to conclude or negotiate deals. An official could ensure his promotion by introducing his superior or an influential politician to a discreetly chosen courtesan, and by the same means a merchant could obtain much-needed credit or an important order. R. H. Van Gulik, *Sexual Life in Ancient China* (Shanghai: Shanghai People's Publishing House, 1990).

7. Gail Hershatter, *Dangerous Pleasures: Prostitution and Modernity in Twentieth-Century Shanghai* (Berkeley: University of California Press, 1997), 69–102.

8. While Karl Marx emphasized economic factors as determinants of social class, Max Weber showed how class, status, and bureaucracy could operate independently. Weber identified the second dimension of stratification and status as

honor or prestige—as elite groups strived to monopolize the markers of prestige and deny access to others. In his work, Weber related a pertinent case of the elite class in the imperial China: "For twelve centuries social rank in China has been determined more by qualification for office than by wealth." Quoted in Terry Nichols Clark and Seymour Martin Lipset, *The Breakdown of Class Politics: A Debate on Post-Industrial Stratification* (Washington, D.C.: Woodrow Wilson Center Press, 2001), 123. Scott Sernau, *Worlds Apart: Social Inequalities in a New Century* (Thousand Oaks, Calif.: Pine Forge Press, 2001), 143.

9. The literati model, as a symbol of prestige and power, became an aspiration that nonliterati wished to emulate. Joseph Esherick and Mary Backus Rankin, "Introduction," in *Chinese Local Elites and Patterns of Dominance,* ed. Joseph Esherick and Mary Backus Rankin (Berkeley and Los Angeles: University of California Press, 1990), 1–26. Helen Siu, "Recycling Tradition: Culture, History and Political Economy in the Chrysanthemum Festivals of South China," *Comparative Studies in Society and History* 32 (1990): 765–94. "Where Were the Women," *Late Imperial China* 11 (1990): 32–62.

10. David Faure, "The Lineage as a Cultural Invention: The Case of the Pearl River Delta," *Modern China* 15 (1989): 4–36. Helen Siu and David Faure, *Down to Earth: The Territorial Bond in South China* (Stanford, Calif.: Stanford University Press, 1995).

11. According to China scholars, the defense of the elite's privileged position and the merchants' conversion into the gentry class hindered technical modernization and economic development. Esherick and Rankin, *Chinese Local Elites,* 3–9.

12. John Fitzgerald, *Awakening China: Politics, Culture, and Class in the Nationalist Revolution* (Stanford, Calif.: Stanford University Press, 1996).

13. Wendy Larson, "The Self Loving the Self: Men and Connoisseurship in Modern Chinese Literature," in *Chinese Femininities, Chinese Masculinities,* ed. Susan Brownell and Jeffrey Wasserstrom (Berkeley and Los Angeles: University of California Press, 2002), 175–94.

14. Tiantian Zheng, "Embodied Masculinity: Sex and Sport in a (Post) Colonial Chinese City," *China Quarterly* 190 (2007): 1–20.

15. Helen Siu, *Agents and Victims* (New Haven, Conn.: Yale University Press, 1989), 292.

16. Ibid. These state agents established not only the social hierarchies of class, revolution, and socialism, but also the party-state power in people's daily lives. While peasants and workers were leading the communist revolution as the proletariat, the landlord and bourgeoisie class were attacked and persecuted as the "enemies of the people" in class struggles.

17. G. William Skinner, "Marketing and Social Structure in Rural China," *Journal of Asian Studies* (AAS Reprint Series no. 1) (1964): 24. Jonathan Spence, *The Search for Modern China* (New York: Norton, 1990).

18. These benefits included almost cost-free housing, medical care, pensions, staples, job assignments, grain, hardship allowances, and other perquisites. Wenfang Tang and William L. Parish, *Chinese Urban Life under Reform: The Changing Social Contract* (Cambridge: Cambridge University Press, 2000), 13–24.

19. Concomitant with the Communist broad-based restructuring of society, the "peasantry" as a derogatory cultural category and revolutionary mainstay was further refined and concretized. First appearing in its modern form during the New Culture movement (1905–23), the figure of the peasant came to embody the old, "totally objectionable" regime that avowedly had been overthrown by the Communist revolutionary ascendance to power and replaced by the new socialist order. The Maoist government's portrayal of the countryside in terms of peasant administrative categories, involving the house registration system and mobility restrictions, reinforced the cultural stereotypes of rural identities, segregating and branding peasants as the reservoir of backward feudalism and superstition, and as a major obstacle to national development and salvation. Myron Cohen, "Cultural and Political Inventions in Modern China: The Case of the Chinese 'Peasant,'" *Daedalus* (spring 1993): 151–70.

20. The state policy of segregation between city and countryside exacerbated the urban-rural divide, with most resources concentrated in the urban areas. Dorothy Solinger, *Contesting Citizenship* (Berkeley: University of California Press, 1999).

21. Margaret M. Pearson, *China's New Business Elite: The Political Consequences of Economic Reform* (Berkeley and Los Angeles: University of California Press, 1997).

22. Victor Nee, "The Emergence of a Market Society," *AJS* 101 (1996): 908–49.

23. Yanjie Bian and John R. Logan, "Market Transition and the Persistence of Power: The Changing Stratification System in Urban China," *American Sociological Review* 61 (1996): 739–58. Xueguang Zhou, *The State and Life Chances in Urban China: Redistribution and Stratification, 1949–1994* (Cambridge: Cambridge University Press, 2004). Douglas Guthrie, *Dragon in a Three-Piece Suit: Foreign Investment, Rational Bureaucracies, and Market Reform in China* (Princeton, N.J.: Princeton University Press, 2000).

24. Yunxiang Yan, "The Impact of Rural Reform on Economic and Social Stratification in a Chinese Village," *Australian Journal of Chinese Affairs* 27 (1992): 1–23.

25. Wenfang Tang and William L. Parish, *Chinese Urban Life under Reform: The Changing Social Contract* (Cambridge: Cambridge University Press, 2000), 141.

26. Ibid. Hill Gates, "Owner, Worker, Mother, Wife: Taibei and Chengdu Family Businesswomen," in *Putting Class in Its Place: Worker Identities in East Asia,* ed. Elizabeth J. Perry (Berkeley: University of California Press, 1996), 127–66.

27. State clientelism served the interests of the central state and of individual officials, while helping the entrepreneurs carve out a niche for themselves despite a lack of formal channels.

28. Mayfair Mei-hui Yang, "Introduction," in *Spaces of Their Own: Women's Public Sphere in Transnational China,* ed. Mayfair Mei-hui Yang (Minneapolis: University of Minnesota Press, 1999), 10.

29. Ibid.

30. David Gilmore's cross-cultural study of various masculinities and R. W. Connell's call for both international and local approaches to the study of masculinity have generated much interest. Zhong Xueping and Kam Louie examine masculinity through in-depth readings and intricate analysis of Chinese films and literary works that were produced throughout the crucial historical junctures in China. Zhong utilizes a feminist psychoanalytic lens to argue that Chinese men feel "besieged" in post-Mao China and attempt to negotiate an image of strong men vis-à-vis women and the state as a part of the effort to create a geopolitically strong Chinese nation. Kam Louie traces the historical changes of the dyad *wen-wu* (cultural attainment–martial valor) and argues that this dyad is an analytical tool and theoretical construct facilitating the conceptualization of Chinese masculinities. Brownell and Wasserstrom's edited book takes an anthropological and historical approach to evoke how femininity and masculinity in China are mutually constructed and have changed over time. See Michael S. Kimmel, "The Birth of the Self-Made Man," in *The Masculinity Studies Reader,* ed. Rachel Adams and David Savran (Malden, Mass.: Blackwell, 2002), 135–52. R. W. Connell, "Masculinity Politics on a World Scale," in *The Masculinities Reader,* ed. Stephen M. Whitehead and Frank J. Barrett (Malden, Mass.: Polity, 2001). "The History of Masculinity," in *The Masculinity Studies Reader,* ed. Rachel Adams and David Savran (Malden, Mass.: Blackwell, 2002), 245–61. Susan Bordo, *The Male Body* (New York: Farrar, Straus and Giroux, 1999). Brian Pronger, *The Arena of Masculinity* (New York: St. Martin's, 1990). David Gilmore, *Manhood in the Marking: Cultural Concepts of Masculinity* (New Haven, Conn.: Yale University Press, 1990). Kam Louie, *Theorising Chinese Masculinity: Society and Gender in China* (Cambridge: Cambridge University Press, 2002), 42–57. "Chinese, Japanese and Global Masculine Identities," in *Asian Masculinities: The Meaning and Practice of Manhood in China and Japan,* ed. Kam Louie and Morris Low (London: Routledge/Curzon, 2003), 1–16. Xueping Zhong, *Masculinity Besieged? Issues of Modernity and Male Subjectivity in Chinese Literature of the Late Twentieth Century* (Durham,

N.C.: Duke University Press, 2000). Susan Brownell, "Strong Women and Impotent Men: Sports, Gender, and Nationalism in Chinese Public Culture," in *Spaces of Their Own,* ed. Mayfair Mei-hui Yang (Minneapolis: University of Minnesota Press, 1999). Susan Brownell and Jeffrey Wasserstrom, eds., *Chinese Femininities, Chinese Masculinities* (Berkeley and Los Angeles: University of California Press, 2002). Nancy Chen, "Embodying Qi and Masculinities in Post-Mao China," in *Chinese Femininities, Chinese Masculinities,* 315–30. William Jankowiak, "Proper Men and Proper Women: Parental Affection in the Chinese Family," in *Chinese Femininities, Chinese Masculinities.*

31. Susan Brownell, *Training the Body for China: Sports in the Moral Order of the People's Republic* (Chicago: University of Chicago Press, 1995), 215.

32. Ibid., 241. Drawing on Foucault, Brownell sees a distinction between a Chinese emphasis on alliance, a technique of the body that is characteristic of societies oriented by kinship, and a Western emphasis on sexuality, a technique of the body that is characteristic of the modern Western state.

33. Ibid., 243.

34. Ibid., 244–48.

35. Michel Foucault, *History of Sexuality: Vol. I* (New York: Random House, 1978).

36. The May Fourth movement was the first mass movement in modern Chinese history. On May 4, 1919, about five thousand university students in Beijing protested the Versailles Conference (of April 28, 1919), which awarded Japan the former German leasehold of Shandong Province. A nationwide boycott of Japanese goods followed this movement. The May Fourth movement marked the upsurge of Chinese nationalism. Intellectuals attacked Chinese cultural traditions as the roots of China's backwardness and embraced Western ideas and ideologies.

37. Frank Dikotter, *Sex, Culture and Modernity in China: Medical Science and the Construction of Sexual Identities in the Early Republican Period* (London: Hurst, 1995), 20.

38. Ibid., 9.

39. Harriet Evans, *Women and Sexuality in China: Dominant Discourse on Female Sexuality and Gender since 1949* (London: Polity Press, 1997). Christina Gilmartin, Gail Hershatter, Lisa Rofel, and Tyrene White, eds., *Engendering China: Women, Culture, and the State* (Cambridge, Mass.: Harvard University Press, 1994). Tamara Jacka, *Women's Work in Rural China: Change and Continuity in an Era of Reform* (Cambridge: Cambridge University Press, 1997), 82–83. Chou Wah-shan, *Tongzhi: Politics of Same-Sex Eroticism in Chinese Societies* (New York: Haworth Press, 2000). Dorothy Ko and Wang Zheng, "Introduction: Translating Feminisms in China," *Gender and History* 18, no. 3 (2006): 463–71.

40. Following the May Fourth movement in 1919, the New Culture movement attributed the failure of the Revolution of 1911 to the suppression of individualism in China's Confucian tradition. The movement called for a complete reevaluation of Chinese culture. Writings by Chen Duxiu, Hu Shih, and others in *New Youth* advocated the liberation of the Chinese people from the yoke of Confucianism and the adoption of Western culture, especially "Mr. Science and Mr. Democracy." They argued that only by releasing the strength of the individual could the nation as a whole be empowered. To secure the survival of China, Chinese culture, indeed the entire Chinese past, had to be recast. In a nutshell, the New Culture movement targeted the Chinese values, principles, and culture that are deemed responsible for the backwardness of the nation.

41. Harriet Evans, "Past, Perfect or Imperfect: Changing Images of the Ideal Wife," in *Chinese Femininities, Chinese Masculinities.*

42. Hershatter, *Dangerous Pleasures,* 374.

43. Yang, *Spaces of Their Own,* 10.

44. Xing Yuan et al., "Nudaxuesheng Jianli Fu Banluo Xiezhen Zhao" (Due to pressure in job market, female college students attach seminaked pictures to résumé), *Xinhua Newspaper,* February 28, 2003.

45. Hershatter, *Dangerous Pleasures,* 374.

46. One Shenzhen secretary was quoted (in Hershatter): "In Shenzhen, if a woman secretary has not slept with her manager, the manager is definitely impotent or gay" (ibid.). Even female graduates of elite universities in China face this dilemma. One example comes from an M.A. graduate from a key university in Beijing who addressed this problem in an article about her first day of employment in a newspaper agency. Because she had been told by her professors that it was an excellent agency, she accepted the job. On the first day she was invited to a restaurant to "talk about formal business." She was appalled to find out that there was no formal business to discuss at all. Indeed, sitting at the table, she was forced to drink alcohol and smoke cigarettes, and in one particularly embarrassing incident, she was forced to share a cigarette with her older boss in a way that suggested intimacy. She wrote, "I am a graduate student from a famous university, although a young and inexperienced girl. . . . Do these men think women are objects that men can play with after drinking?" She wrote that the leader shook her hands for a long time and would not let go, saying, "I have a lot of strength, you know!" The author reported that she had learned at this meeting with these so-called "elite reporters" that "it is difficult for a woman to survive in this society without experiencing a loss of esteem. I am not willing to sell myself for survival." However, in the end, she chose to stay because she was advised by her professors that this was a valuable opportunity. Anonymous, "Xia Fengchennu

Yiyang Peijiu" (Accompany drinking men like a prostitute), *Wenxue City*, January 17, 2003.

47. Meiyuan Liu, "Bao Ernai Yu Fanfubai" (Keeping second wives and anti-corruption), *Can Kao Xiao Xi* (Information and news), August 9, 2001, 8. Jiexi Yu, "Bei Cha Tan Guan Zhong Jiu Cheng 'Bao Er Nai'" (Corruption and "keeping the second wife"), *Dalian Wanbao* (Dalian evening newspaper), January 10, 2001, 10.

48. Fengqing Jiang, "Zise Jiushi Liliang" (Beauty is power), *Dalian Ribao* (Dalian daily), February 17, 2001, 11. Shaozhen Sun, "Lun Meinu de Wuqi" (A discussion of the weapon of beauty), *Dalian Ribao* (Dalian daily), February 3, 2001, 11.

49. Xianghan Wu, "Xinghuilu Weihai You Duoda?" (How much harm does sexual bribery produce?), *Zhongguo Qingnian Bao* (Chinese youth daily), April 2, 2001, 2.

50. This information comes from my interviews with political officials.

51. Hostesses are portrayed as seducing and infecting men with sexually transmitted diseases (STDs) and HIV/AIDS. Shan Guan, "Buxiangxin Yanlei" (I do not believe in tears), *Yi Lu Ben Zou* (Marching on) (Beijing: Huayi Publishing House, 2001). Yaling Li, "Kaojin Mingpai Daxue Liangcaizi Bei Xiaojie Yinyou Ranshang Linbing" (An outstanding student in a key university is seduced by a hostess and contracted an STD), *Chengdu Shangbao* (Chengdu commerce newspaper), August 12, 1999, 2. Jianlin Liu, "Sanpeinu Chengwei Fanzui Gaofa Qunti" (The highest crime rate is found in the group of bar hostesses), *Zhongguo Qingnianbao* (Chinese youth newspaper), August 20, 1999, 3. Wei Shen, "Gonggong Zaiqu E'xi Shi Ci Mousha Momo" (The malicious second wife attempts to murder her man's wife ten times), *Xin Shang Bao* (New commerce newspaper), May 24, 2001, 20. Liu Xiao, "Siwang Yinying Longzhao 'Xiaojie' Qunti" (Hostesses are shadowed by death), *Dalian Wanbao* (Dalian evening newspaper), September 9, 2001, 18. Jiexi Yu, "Bei Cha Tan Guan Zhong Jiu Cheng 'Bao Er Nai,'" 10.

52. Junzhang Zhang and Gao Xiao, *Hong Zhi Zhu* (Red spider) (Guangzhou: Guangzhou Audiovisual Publishing House, 1998).

53. *Fox* here refers to the traditional superstitious view that foxes can in fact turn into beautiful women in order to seduce men. Anonymous, "Kantou Hulijing de Ershida Tezheng" (Twenty traits of vixen), *Yacou Fashion*, March 29, 2004.

54. Ren Xu, "China," in *Prostitution: An International Handbook on Trends, Problems, and Policies,* ed. Nanette J. Davis (Westport, Conn.: Greenwood Press, 1993), 102.

55. Zhaorui Chu, "Shichangjingji Tiaojianxia Ganqing Yu Lizhi de Liangnan Xuanze" (The dilemma between sentiment and reason under market economy), in *Zhongguo Hunyin Jiating Bianqian* (The changes of marriage and family in

China), ed. Dalin Liu, Yingjie Liu, and Qizai Zhang (Beijing: Chinese Society Publishing House, 1998), 229–30, 240. Dalin Liu, "Zhongguo Shehui De Xingwenti: Guoqu He Xianzai" (The sex problem in Chinese society: The past and present), in *Zhongguo Hunyin Jiating Bianqian*, 29–32.

56. Xiaosheng Liang, *Ningshi Jiuqi* (Reflections of 1997) (Xian: Shanxi Tourism and Economic Daily Publishing House, 1997).

57. Chu, "Shichangjingji Tiaojianxia Ganqing," 240.

58. Liu, "Zhongguo Shehui De Xingwenti," 241.

59. Jinling Wang, and Sisun Xu, "Xinsheng Maiyinnu Xinggoucheng, Shenxin Tezheng Yu Xingwei Zhiyuanqi" (The psychological and physical characteristics of sex workers), in *Pingdeng Yu Fazhan* (Equality and development), ed. Xiaojiang Li, Hong Zhu, and Xiuyu Dong (Beijing: Sanlian Bookstore, 1997), 283–86.

60. Ibid., 286–88.

61. Hershatter, *Dangerous Pleasures*, 368.

62. Ibid.

63. More and more public sector workers were laid off as state-owned sectors declined. Autonomous trade unions were not allowed and workers' interests had to be articulated through various forms of protests. Chaolin Gu and Haiyong Liu, "Social Polarization and Segregation in Beijing," in *The New Chinese City: Globalization and Market Reform,* ed. John R. Logan (Malden, Mass.: Blackwell, 2002), 198–211.

64. Anita Chan points out that the threat to the CCP and political stability derives from the peasantry, workers, and dissidents. Peasant migrants in the city constitute a "periphery flexible workforce," held in "forced and bonded labor." They suffer an abuse of labor rights in "sweatshop socialism," putting up with huge deductions of payments, physical abuse, control of bodily functions, and so on. Yet there have been no measures taken to limit their working hours or prohibit their bodily abuses. Many experienced corporal punishments and physical assaults as an integral part of a militarized management style. Chan tells of a typical incident in a joint venture footwear enterprise that had, in effect, imprisoned the migrant workers by holding their residential permits and employment fees for the duration of their contracts and locked them into the factory compound with a hundred security guards. Workers were physically and verbally abused and were required to work overtime five nights a week without compensatation for injuries or overtime work. There was no adequate system of regulation to enforce justice. Fei-ling Wang, *Organizing through Division and Exclusion: China's Hukou System* (Stanford, Calif.: Stanford University Press, 2005). Emily Honig, "Regional Identity, Labor, and Ethnicity in Contemporary China," in *Putting Class in Its Place: Worker Identities in East Asia,* ed. Elizabeth J. Perry (Berkeley: University of

California Press, 1996), 225–43. Helen Siu, "The Politics of Migration in a Market Town," in *Chinese Society on the Eve of Tiananmen,* ed. Deborah Davis (Cambridge, Mass.: Harvard University Press, 1990). Anita Chan, "Revolution or Corporatism? Workers and Trade Unions in Post-Mao China," *Australian Journal of Chinese Affairs,* January 29, 1993, 31–61. Anita Chan, "The Changing Ruling Elite and Political Opposition in China," in *Political Oppositions in Industrializing Asia,* ed. Garry Rodan (London: Routledge, 1996). Anita Chan, "Labor Standards and Human Rights: The Case of Chinese Workers under Market Socialism," *Human Rights Quarterly* 20, no. 4 (1998): 886–904. Anita Chan, *China's Workers under Assault: The Exploitation of Labor in a Globalizing Economy (Asia and the Pacific)* (New York: East Gate Books, 2001). Anita Chan and Robert A. Senser, "China's Troubled Workers," *Foreign Affairs* 76 (1997): 104–17.

65. Kamala Kempadoo, *Trafficking and Prostitution Reconsidered: New Perspectives on Migration, Sex Work, and Human Rights* (Boulder, Colo.: Paradigm, 2005).

66. Gilbert Herdt, *Sexual Cultures and Migration in the Era of AIDS: Anthropological and Demographic Perspectives* (Oxford: Clarendon Press, 1997). Steven Stack, "The Effect of Geographic Mobility on Premarital Sex," *Journal of Marriage and the Family* 56 (1994): 204–208. Cheng Sim Hew, *Women Workers, Migration and Family in Sarawak* (London: Routledge/Curzon, 2003). Evelyne Micollier, ed., *Sexual Cultures in East Asia* (London: Routledge/Curzon, 2004).

67. Lee's comparative study of women workers in two factories demonstrates that migrant women are routinely subject to harsh labor discipline and abuse within the family. Lee also points out that migrant women in urban areas are the most vulnerable players in the market economy because they receive unfavorable treatment in benefits such as insurance, medical care, wages, and bonuses partly because they lack marketable skills and social connections. Ching Kwan Lee, "Labor Politics of Market Socialism," *Modern China* 24, no. 1 (1998): 3–34. Ching Kwan Lee, *Gender and the South China Miracle: Two Worlds of Factory Women* (Berkeley: University of California Press, 1998). Delia Davin, "Gender and Migration in China," in *Village Inc.: Chinese Rural Society in the 1990s,* ed. Flemming Christiansen and Junzuo Zhang (Richmond, Surrey: Curzon, 1998), 230–40. Ngai Pun, "Becoming *Dagoingmei* [working girls]: The Politics of Identity and Difference in Reform China," *China Journal* 42 (1999): 1–18. Alice Goldstein et al., "The Relation of Migration to Changing Household Headship Patterns in China, 1982–1987," *Population Studies* 51 (1997): 75–84.

68. Hairong Yan, "Neoliberal Governmentality and Neohumanism: Organizing Suzhi/Value Flow through Labor Recruitment Networks," *Cultural Anthropology* 18 (2003): 493–523. Nicole Constable, "At Home but Not at Home: Filipina Narratives of Ambivalent Returns," *Cultural Anthropology* 14 (1999): 203–28.

69. I conducted my fieldwork in Dalian karaoke bars during four segments of 1999, 2000, 2001, and 2002.

1. Patriarchy, Prostitution, and Masculinity in Dalian

1. Mingyi Gu et al., eds., *Dalian Jin Bai Nian Shi* (Dalian in the past hundred years) (Dalian: Liaoning People's Publishing House, 1999). Robert John Perrins, "Great Connections: The Creation of a City, Dalian, 1905–1931, China and Japan on the Liaodong Peninsula" (Ph.D. diss.) (York University, 1997).

2. Perrins, "Great Connections."

3. Anonymous, "Dongbeiren Fachu Fennude Housheng: Dongbei Yaoduli" (People in the northeast angrily claim: We want independence), www.secretchina. com (accessed on January 23, 2003).

4. Ibid.

5. Kirou Shinosaki, *Dalian* (Osaka: Osaka Wuhao Bookstore, 1921). Ryosen Takahashi, *Dalian Shi* (Dalian city) (Manchuria: Mainland Publishing Association, 1931).

6. The first Japanese prostitutes arrived in 1905 from Amakusa and Shimabara. By 1930 there were fifty-five brothels run by Japanese and fifteen by Koreans. They housed eight hundred courtesans and hostesses. Fengban Street housed 354 courtesans and 475 hostesses. Xiaogangzi housed 99 courtesans, all from Japan. Among the 120 hostesses, 92 were Koreans. The total number of 1,543 included 839 Japanese courtesans and 174 hostesses. About one in thirty-one Japanese female residents were courtesans or hostesses. Ibid. Zidun Shen, *Dalian Yaolan* (Overview of Dalian) (n.p.: Taidong Daily Agency, 1918).

7. Shinosaki, *Dalian*. Takahashi, *Dalian Shi.*

8. Ibid.

9. Ibid. Two notable exceptions to this pattern were Lavender Moon *(danyue)* and Lake Moon *(huyue),* where brothel and entertainment were combined in the same place. Both of these establishments enjoyed a good reputation for food and entertainment. Music provided by courtesans included ancient instruments such as *sha mi sen;* courtesans also sang traditional songs.

10. "Chedi Zhengdun Fenghua" (Regulate social ethos completely), *Shengjing Times,* October 11, 1936, 12. "Fanguan Guyong Nuzhaodai, Jingting Chuanxun Yingyezhu" (Restaurants hire hostesses, police investigate operators), *Shengjing Times,* March 18, 1936, 8. "Jiguan Yingye Xiaotiao, Anchang Rijian Huoyue" (Brothel business is slacking, clandestine prostitution is flourishing), *Shengjing Times,* October 5, 1936, 3. "Qudi Nuzhaodai, Chefa Daijianwu" (Abolish hostesses, remove single rooms), *Shengjing Times,* September 4, 1936, 7. "Qudi Wuchang

Fengji, Yanjin Wunu Waisu" (Abolish dancing halls, prohibit dancers to engage prostitution), *Shengjing Times,* April 9, 1936, 12. Yunjie Han, "Youshang Fengji Ling Tingye" (Order end of business), *Shengjing Times,* August 11, 1936, 11.

11. Mu Zi, "Zhiye Zhenxian Shangde Nuzhaodai" (Hostesses on the professional forefront), *Shengjing Times,* June 19, 1936, 5. "Lingmaisuo Yulechanghua" (Opium shops are entertainment), *Shengjing Times,* August 4, 1936, 4. "Xianshuo Nuzhaodai" (Comment on hostesses), *Shengjing Times,* November 28, 1936, 7. Yunjie Han, "Yanguan Changji Fangzhice" (Strategies of prostitutes in opium shop), *Shengjing Times,* September 3, 1936, 11.

12. "Naji Weishi Nanmian Tuofu" (Loss of bliss by taking prostitute home), *Shengjing Times,* March 14, 1936, 7. "Suiren Congliang, Youlian Gujiao" (Follow the good with a new man, still love the previous man), *Shengjing Times,* February 5, 1936, 7.

13. "Lianji Cangjiao Jinwu, Beiqi Bide Zisha" (Take prostitute home, forced to suicide by wife), *Shengjing Times,* September 2, 1936, 12. "Jike Zisha Yisiy-isheng" (Customer commits suicide), *Shengjing Times,* September 30, 1936, 7. "Suiji Zisha Fufusheng" (Commit suicide with a prostitute), *Shengjing Times,* October 15, 1936, 8. "Keren Jinu Qingsi An Lianri Cengchu Buqiong" (Frequent suicide cases of customers and prostitutes), *Shengjing Times,* November 28, 1936, 7. "Naji Weiqie, Quzhu Faqi" (Take prostitute as a concubine, banish wife), *Shengjing Times,* November 28, 1936, 7. "Waichengke Guanzou Yanhuaxiang, Zaoshibai Yisi Bao Zhiyin" (Customer from outside frequently visits brothel, commits suicide for his lover), *Shengjing Times,* September 14, 1936, 3. "Wang-laoke Yuhuaji Qingsian Yigao Jieshu" (An end to love: Suicide of customer wanglao and prostitute yuhua), *Shengjing Times,* September 21, 1936, 3.

14. "Fanguan Guyong Nuzhaodai, Jingting Chuanxun Yingyezhu" (Restaurants hire hostesses, police investigate operators), *Shengjing Times,* March 18, 1936, 8.

15. Guandongzhou Guanfang Wenshu Ke (Office of Guandong), *Guandongzhou Yaolan* (Overview of Guandong) (Manchuria: Manchuria Daily News Agency Publishing House, 1942). Guandongzhou Guanfang Wenshu Ke (Office of Guandong), *Guandongzhou Yaolan* (Overview of Guandong Bureau) (Manchuria: Tuban Publishing House, 1940).

16. Ibid. After the Manchurian incident, the Japanese military administration tightened the regulation of dance halls. (The incident, occurring on September 18, 1931, was a feigned Japanese attack on a section of railroad controlled by the Japanese as a pretext to seize Manchuria and create a puppet state of Manchukuo.) By the end of October 1940, dance halls were abolished and transferred to other businesses. The government also regulated and licensed Manchurian prostitutes and brothel owners in Dalian and other occupied areas. The regulations restricted

the residence and movement of the prostitutes and enforced periodic physical examinations for venereal diseases in the newly established Dalian Female Hospital at Langsu Street (currently Tianjian Street). The intention was to protect the security of the Japanese army.

17. "Xigang Chedi Qudi Yanji" (Completely abolish opium prostitutes in Xigang), *Shengjing Times,* September 14, 1936, 3. "Jiwu Yingye Xuke YouGan Xuedai Jinu" (Not only hold no operating license, but also abuse prostitutes), *Shengjing Times,* July 27, 1936, 3.

18. James McClain, *Japan: A Modern History* (New York: Norton, 2002).

19. "Qizi Suiren Qiantao, Qiguo Yuanzai Zhangfu" (Wife escapes with others; it is husband's fault), *Shengjing Times,* December 19, 1936, 7. "Heshinu HeqiBuxing" (How unfortunate the woman is), *Shengjing Times,* October 12, 1936, 3.

20. Ibid.

21. Ibid.

22. Yosuke Matsuoka, cited in Harold S. Quigley, *Far Eastern War: 1937–1941* (Boston: Putnam's, 1942), 59–60.

23. Jiangke Hua, "Yanlou Suohua"(Description of opium building), *Shengjing Times,* May 21, 1936, 7.

24. Ibid. "Guailai Guxiang Younu" (Abduction of hometown young girls), *Shengjing Times,* February 5, 1936, 7. "Qingren Congliang Qule" (Lover follows the good), *Shengjing Times,* December 28, 1936, 3. "Jiejie Jinu Chushen, Meimei Zehui Fanren" (Elder sister is prostitute, younger sister traffics people), *Shengjing Times,* December 28, 1936, 3.

25. Dalian Difangzhi Bianzhuan Weiyuanhui Bangongshi (The editing committee of Dalian history), *Dalian Shi Zhi* (Dalian city history) (Dalian: Dalian Publishing House, 1993).

26. Ibid.

27. Ibid.

28. Ibid., 698–99.

29. Zi, "Zhiye Zhenxian Shangde Nuzhaodai," 5.

30. Fang-fu Ruan Lau and M. P., "China: Demographics and a Historical Perspective," in *The International Encyclopedia of Sexuality,* ed. Robert T. Francoeur (New York: Continuum, 1997).

31. Zi, "Zhiye Zhenxian Shangde Nuzhaodai," 5.

32. Dalian Difangzhi Bianzhuan Weiyuanhui Bangongshi, *Dalian Shi Zhi.*

33. Ibid.

34. In 1908, the Dalian subdivision of the Chinese Women's Relief Group *(jiuji furu hui)* was also founded to save abducted women. Each year they helped about a hundred women return home.

35. Changchi Zhou, *Daode Yulu* (Morality quotation) (Andong: Hongdaoshan Bookstore, 1936).

36. "Daode Hui Wuxian Fang Song: Jiangyan: Fufu Dao" (Morality Organization delivers talks on conjugal morality), *Shengjing Times,* September 14, 1936, 3. "Daode Jiangyan Zhi Fang Song: Zuo Nu Xue Xi Gu Niang Dao" (Morality Organization delivers talks on the morality of daughters and daughters-in-law), *Shengjing Times,* September 21, 1936, 3. "Forward," *Shengjing Times,* December 19, 1936, 7.

37. *Manzhouguo Daodehui Zhang Ze Hui Lan* (Stipulations of the Manchu morality) (n.p.: Dalian Manchu Organization of Morality, 1941).

38. Zhou, *Daode Yulu.*

39. Tiantian Zheng, "Embodied Masculinity: Sex and Sport in a (Post) Colonial Chinese City," *China Quarterly* 190 (2007): 1–20.

40. Ibid.

41. Kuniaki Koiso, *A Report of the Manchu Women Union* (in Japanese) (Dalian: East Asian Publishing House, 1933).

42. Ibid.

43. "Guofang Funv Fengtian Zhibu Yi Yu Zuori Jiecheng Yi" (Fengtian division of the National Women's Union was established yesterday), *Shengjing Times,* September 11, 1936, 4.

44. "Guofang Funv Hui Yi Yi Wuxi Mu Lu" (The National Women's Union raises money), *Shengjing Times,* August 17, 1936, 3. "Junren Jingquan Ying Hua, Guo Fang Fu Hui Wei Wen" (National Women's Union consoles the soldiers), *Shengjing Times,* September 5, 1936, 12. Xiao Ji Guo Zhao, *A Report of the Manchu Women Union* (in Japanese) (Dalian: East Asian Publishing House, 1933).

45. Xun Sun, *Wei An Fu Xue Lei* (The blood and tears of comfort women) (Xi An: Taibai Arts Publishing House, 2001). Duara Prasenjit, *Sovereignty and Authenticity: Manchukuo and the East Asian Modern* (Lanham, Md.: Rowman & Littlefield, 2004), 151.

46. Zong Du, *Nanyi Yiwang de Lishi—Weianfu* (Unforgettable history—comfort women), www.muzi.com (accessed in 2004).

47. Qiulan Chen, "Toushi Zhongguo 'Weianfu' Zhenxiang" (Inside view of Chinese "comfort women"), www.c422df.126.com (accessed in 2004).

48. From 1917 until 1921, Japan occupied Siberia.

49. Zhiliang Su, *Rijun Xing Fulei* (Sexual slaves of the Japanese army) (Beijing: People's Publishing House, 2000).

50. Most of the Korean women were virgins, so there was no worry about venereal disease. From 1943 to 1945, two hundred thousand Korean women were mobilized into *ting shen* teams. Among them about seventy thousand served as comfort women.

51. Du, *Nanyi Yiwang de Lishi.*

52. Prasenjit, *Sovereignty and Authenticity,* 160.

53. Ibid., 159.

54. Ibid., 158.

55. Mure Dickie, "Dalian's Old Relationship Brings Prosperity to a Rust-Belt Centre," www.daliannews.com (accessed on April 2, 2004).

56. Dalian Difangzhi Bianzhuan Weiyuanhui Bangongshi, *Dalian Shi Zhi.*

57. Ibid.

58. "Qiong Ren Zhushang Le Xinfang" (Poor people now live in new houses), *Dalian Daily,* July 21, 1946, 1.

59. Siu, *Agents and Victims.*

60. Anonymous, "Northeastern People Claimed Angrily: We Want Independence" (translated from Chinese), www.secretchina.com (accessed on September 20, 2005). This Web site is accessed by people both inside and outside of China. It is a popular Web site in China.

61. During the 1960s, industrialization of the interior of China required building the "three lines"—national defense, technology, and transportation.

62. For instance, the Anshan Steel Company, which used to be the most advanced steel company in the country, was required to turn in three and a half times more tax than the Wuhan Steel Company, and six and a half times more tax than the Beijing Steel Company. Anshan Steel dropped from the most profitable to the seventh most profitable steel company in the country, earning only a fraction of the profit earned by Beijing Steel. The most difficult time for Anshan Steel was the beginning of the 1990s. Staff members had to donate money, but taxes remained high. At the same time, the taxes turned in by Beijing Steel were not only returned to them, but the company also granted large state loans to construct modern furnaces and buy more iron mines.

63. It is true that Mao was moving some industries to the interior because of his concern with defense. However, the fact that much of the development that was taking place at this time was in coastal areas such as Shanghai and Guangdong makes it clear that this was only a minor factor.

64. On the other hand, under the influence of intense nationalism during this period, some Japanese women willingly served the soldiers as prostitutes.

65. Feng Ling, "Quanqiu Diyi Changjidaguo" (The biggest prostitution state in the whole world)," *Renmin Bao* (People's newspaper), October 14, 2003, 1.

2. From Banquets to Karaoke Bars

1. Helen Siu, "Socialist Peddlers and Princes in a Chinese Market Town," *American Anthropologist* 16 (1989): 195–212. Helen Siu, "The Reconstitution of

Brideprice and Dowry in South China," in *Chinese Families in the Post-Mao Era,* ed. Deborah Davis and Steven Harrell (Berkeley: University of California Press, 1993). Wang, "Conspicuous Consumption, Business Networks, and State Power in a Chinese City."

2. James Farrer, "Dancing through the Market Transition," in *The Consumer Revolution in Urban China,* ed. Deborah Davis (Berkeley and Los Angeles: University of California Press, 2000).

3. Ibid.

4. Ibid., 230.

5. Reconstructing the history of karaoke bars in Dalian proved to be exceedingly difficult. A combination of official denial and embarrassment has ensured that no publicly open records have been kept on the subject and undoubtedly dissuaded any interested parties from prying. To piece together the story, I was therefore forced to rely entirely on the oral accounts of government officials in different divisions of the municipal Bureau of Culture.

6. Joseph Straubhaar and Robert LaRose, *Communication Media in the Information Society* (Belmont, Calif.: Wadsworth, 1996).

7. Casey Man Kong Lum, *In Search of a Voice: Karaoke and the Construction of Identity in Chinese America* (Mahwah, N.J.: Lawrence Eribaum, 1996).

8. Brownell, *Training the Body for China,* 253.

9. Ibid., 260.

10. Mayfair Yang, *Gifts, Favors, and Banquets* (Ithaca, N.Y.: Cornell University Press, 1994).

11. Brownell, *Training the Body for China,* 260.

12. Ibid.

13. Suiming Pan, *Cun Zai Yu Hunag Niu: Zhong Guo Di Xia "Xing Chan Ye" Kao Cha* (Existence and irony: A scrutiny of Chinese underground sex industry) (Beijing: Qunyan Publishing House, 1999). Suiming Pan, *Sheng Cun Yu Ti Yan* (Subsistence and experience) (Beijing: Chinese Social Science Publishing House, 2000).

14. Hershatter, *Dangerous Pleasures,* 366.

15. Xiaobo Liu, "Qing Se Kuang Huan-Zhongguo Shangye Wenhua" (Chinese commercial culture), *Minzhu Zhongguo* (Democratic China) 131 (2004). The intensity of this nationalistic response reminds us of Marshall McCluhan's analysis of the 1950s as a period dominated by hot mediums and the transformation during the 1960s to a cool medium. According to McLuhan, in his *Understanding Media: The Extensions of Man* (coauthored with Lewis H. Lapham [Cambridge, Mass.: MIT Press, 1994]), hot media provides complete involvement without considerable stimulus, emphasizing one sense such as sight or sound over others.

Radio, film, lectures, and photography are examples of hot media. Cool media provides little involvement with substantial stimulus and requires more active participation on the part of the user. Examples are television, seminars, and cartoons. In light of these terms, it is hard to read the Internet comments without recognizing that Chinese nationalism is itself something that is being openly expressed as a hot medium, and perhaps there is not yet enough distance for these male nationalists in China to communicate their anger in an ironic or satirical form.

16. Dickie Mure, "Dalian's Old Relationship Brings Prosperity to a Rust-Belt Centre," www.daliannews.com, April 2, 2004.

17. Kenichi Ohmae, "Capitalism with Chinese Characteristics," *Daily Times,* October 30, 2004.

18. Mure, "Dalian's Old Relationship."

19. Xueyou Sun, "Liangming Riben E Nan Zai Dalian Ba Liangming Zhongguo Nushi Dacheng Naozhendang" (Two vicious Japanese men beat up two Chinese women, cause cerebral concussion), *Shidai Shangbao* (Times Commercial), May 9, 2004, 2.

20. Jia Za, "Ri Ben Ren! Nimen Daodi Xiang Ganshenmo" (Japanese people! What on earth do you want to do?), www.zajia.net (accessed in 2004).

21. Various commentators, "Dalian Bao Ou Funu An, Shuizai Baobi Xiongshou" (The abuse of women in Dalian: Who is protecting the perpetrator?), www.163.com (accessed in 2004). Various commentators, "Dalian Beida Nuzi: Riben Daren Nazi Zhijin Meilai Tanwang Daoqian" (abuse of women in Dalian: Japanese perpetrators have not visited or apologized until today), www.qq.com (accessed in 2004).

22. Ibid.

23. Mure, "Dalian's Old Relationship."

24. Mao Zedong, "Xin Min Zhu Zhu Yi Lun" (New theory of democracy)," in *Mao Zedong Xuan Ji* (Beijing: Beijing Xinhua Publishing House, 1991), 867.

25. Ibid., 695.

26. This perspective was drawn from my interviews with government officials during my fieldwork in 2001.

27. Here the concept of culture is different from its definition in the discipline of anthropology.

28. *Falungong* practices have been denounced, outlawed, and suppressed as antisocialist, anti-CCP, and counterrevolutionary activities since 1999.

29. The Chinese gross domestic product in 1998 and 1999 was 7.8 trillion *yuan* and 8.3 trillion *yuan,* respectively.

30. The films included such war movie classics as *Tunnel War (didao zhan), Land Mine War (dilei zhan), Railway Guerilla Team (tielu youjidui),* and *Heroes' Sons and Daughters (yingxiong ernv).*

31. Elaine Jeffreys, *China, Sex, and Prostitution* (London: Routledge/Curzon, 2004), 157.

32. Ibid., 151.

33. Anonymous, "Sanpei xiaojie de Falu Baohu Wenti" (Legal protection of hostesses), *Shenzhen Fazhi bao* (Shenzhen law newspaper), June 25, 2002.

34. Shaoguang Sun, "Dalian E Mo Ba Xiaojie Fenshi Shiyi Kuai" (A man in Dalian divided a hostess' dead body into eleven pieces), *Dongbei Xinwen Wang* (Northeastern news net), December 12, 2003.

35. It is reported that entrepreneur Lai Changxing, head of Xiamen Yuanhua Group, was accused of smuggling $6 billion worth of cars, oil, luxury goods, and cigarettes; he invested 1,500 million *yuan* in the Red Mansion to entertain officials who eventually worked as his "running dogs." The Red Mansion houses plush apartments with luxury spas, king-sized beds, a banquet room, a cinema, a karaoke and a dance hall, a sauna center, and gym rooms "filled with money, alcohol, and sex." More than forty hostesses "like beauty models" were selectively chosen from Jiangsu and Zhejiang, trained to sing, dance, and give massage. Jianping Wang et al., "Yuanhua An Hou Fang Xiamen, Ji Zhe Yan Zhong de 'Hong Lou'" (The Red Mansion in a reporter's eyes, Yuanhua's base in Xiamen), *Renmin Ribao* (People's daily), October 18, 2001, 1.

36. The economist Yang Fan estimates that with the implementation of the "Regulations on the Management of Places of Entertainment" issued by the State Council during the latter half of 1999, the Chinese gross domestic product dropped by 1 percent. Wei Zhong, "A Close Look at China's 'Sex Industry,'" *Lianhe Zaobao* (Lianhe morning post), October 2, 2000, 3.

37. One might note similarities between the effect of this and the effect of the Eighteenth Amendment to the Constitution of the United States, which made the manufacture and consumption of alcohol illegal. In both cases, a highly lucrative market was created for illicit activities.

38. This bar owner was a woman. It is quite unusual for karaoke bar owners to be female.

39. Richard Brubaker, "City Report: Dalian," in *All Roads Lead to China,* www.allroadsleadtochina.com (accessed in 2008).

40. Ibid.

3. Fierce Rivalries, Unstable Bonds

1. At a pottery bar, drinks are served together with all kinds of games such as cards, Chinese chess, and military chess. The main theme, however, is pottery making. In an adjacent room, a tutor helps you make all kinds of pottery.

2. Jun Wang, "'Qiujiu Duanxin' Fasong Chenggong, Jingfang Jiejiu Bei

Guaimai Funu" (Successful "SOS short message": The police rescue abducted women), *Liaoshen Wanbao* (Liaoshen evening newspaper), May 16, 2003, 2.

3. Some unattractive hostesses tried going to other bars but eventually returned: they could not thrive in those bars. Other pretty hostesses were quite successful at switching. During my research period, two fled to the high-tier bar Colorful Century together, two fled to other high-tier bars, and seven to medium-tier bars. They normally went together with their friends to cope with the antagonistic attitude toward new hostesses in the new bars. Those who did not go in groups had their clients or friends introduce them to a madam in a new bar. This connection with the madam helped sustain and secure their status in the new bar. Madams and hostesses sometimes left together. Once a madam decided to leave a bar, she often took a handful of hostesses to the new bar with her. Thus, madams could form a strong and powerful circle around themselves, which helped sustain their power in the new bar.

4. Emily Honig, *Sisters and Strangers: Women in the Shanghai Cotton Mills, 1919–1949* (Stanford, Calif.: Stanford University Press, 1986). William T. Rowe, *Hankow: Commerce and Society in a Chinese City: 1796–1889* (Stanford, Calif.: Stanford University Press, 1984). David Strand, *Rickshaw Beijing: City People and Politics in the 1920s* (Berkeley: University of California Press, 1989). Gail Hershatter, *The Workers of Tianjin, 1900–1949* (Stanford, Calif.: Stanford University Press, 1986). Lee, *Gender and the South China Miracle: Two Worlds of Factory Women.* Li Zhang, *Strangers in the City: Reconfigurations of Space, Power, and Social Networks within China's Floating Population* (Stanford, Calif.: Stanford University Press, 2001). Ngai Pun, *Made in China: Women Factory Workers in a Global Workplace* (Durham, N.C.: Duke University Press, 2005).

5. Ngai Pun, *Made in China,* 56.

6. Ibid., 60.

7. Ibid., 123.

4. Turning in the Grain

1. Arthur and Joan Kleinman, "Somatization: The Interconnections in Chinese Society among Culture, Depressive Experiences, and the Meanings of Pain," in *Culture and Depression: Studies in the Anthropology and Cross-Cultural Psychiatry of Affect and Disorder,* ed. Arthur Kleinman and Byron Good (Berkeley: University of California Press, 1985), 429–90.

2. Brownell, *Training the Body for China,* 45.

3. K. C. Chang, *Food in Chinese Culture* (New Haven, Conn.: Yale University Press, 1977).

4. Ibid., 17–18.

5. M. C. Yang 1945, quoted in Elisabeth Croll, *The Family Rice Bowl: Food and the Domestic Economy in China* (Geneva: United Nations Research Institute for Social Development, 1982).

6. Cited in Chang, *Food in Chinese Culture*, 301. The Hsus either are unaware or neglect to mention the restrictions I describe here, thereby treating the difference in *liang* consumption between Japanese and Chinese as a naturally occurring phenomenon.

7. Brownell, *Training the Body for China*, 242.

8. Several wives of my interviewees told me that they wished to control their husbands' sexuality by appropriating their semen.

9. Dalin Liu, *Zhongguo Gudai Xing Wenhua* (The sex culture of Ancient China) (Yinchuan: Ningxia People's Publishing House, 1993), 329.

10. Van Gulik, *Sexual Life in Ancient China*, 64–65.

11. As explained earlier, this paranoia comes from men's intense experience of emasculation under Mao; men misunderstood women's desperate attempt to hold on to their husbands through sexually engaging them. Rather than experiencing this as joyful liberation, they equated their wives' actions with the control that they had experienced under the Maoist regime. Rebellion against Maoism left them with no meaningful social purpose, and rebellion against the imagined authority of their wives left them without meaning within the marriage. The final result was a nihilism that led to an even more complete hedonism.

12. The other two themes were steel making and workers' nondemand of wages.

13. Pinghan Luo, *Daguofan: Gonggong Shitang Shimo* (Big bowl of rice: The beginning and end of commune dining halls) (Nanning Shi: Guangxi People's Publishing House, 2001), 74.

14. Ibid.

15. Note that the Communists also concluded that the way to the people's heart was through women, as they were quite concerned about getting a woman to each man, including poor peasants, because the previous system of polygamy/hypergamy had deprived poor men of wives. *Polygamy* refers to the system in which a man has more than one wife at a time. *Hypergamy* refers to the phenomenon in which women tend to marry men of higher social status than themselves.

16. Although these slogans are absent from today's private eateries, they can still be found in some student cafeterias.

17. Susan Brownell, "Gender and Nationalism in China at the Turn of the Millennium," in *China Briefing 2000*, ed. Tyrene White (Armonk, N.Y.: M. E. Sharpe, 2000), 221–22.

18. Mayfair Mei-hui Yang, "From Gender Erasure to Gender Difference: State Feminism, Consumer Sexuality, and Women's Public Sphere in China," in *Spaces of Their Own,* ed. Yang, 35–67.

19. Brownell, "Gender and Nationalism in China," 225.

20. For instance, Suiming Pan, the sexology and sociology professor at the People's University at Beijing, in his report titled "The Issue of Sex in China in the 21st century" at Guangdong Science Museum in 2004, points out that wives should learn sexual techniques from hostesses. Cited in Qianhua Fang, "Xing-xuejia Yuchu Jingren: Xiaojie Xingjiqiao Youke Jiejian Zhichu" (The sexologist's astonishing words: Hostesses' sexual techniques can be borrowed), *Nanfang Ribao* (South daily), November 9, 2004.

21. Judith Farquhar, *Appetites: Food and Sex in Post-Socialist China* (Durham, N.C.: Duke University Press, 2002), 269.

22. Jian Xu, "Body, Discourse, and the Cultural Politics of Contemporary Chinese Qigong," *Journal of Asian Studies* 58, no. 4 (1999): 975.

23. This runs counter to Marc Blecher's argument that workers in China have accepted the hegemonic views of the state as a benevolent patriarchy. Marc Blecher, "Hegemony and Workers' Politics in China," *China Quarterly* 170, no. 2 (2002): 283–303.

24. Pan Suiming, *Cun Zai Yu Hunag Niu* (Existence and irony); Pan, *Sheng Cun Yu Ti Yan* (Subsistence and experience).

25. Pan, *Sheng Cun Yu Ti Yan,* 344.

26. Ibid., 341.

27. Ibid., 344, 343.

28. Ibid., 241.

29. Karen Kelsky, "Intimate Ideologies: Transnational Theory and Japan's 'Yellow Cabs,'" *Public Culture* 6 (1994): 465–78.

30. Ibid. Karen Kelsky, *Women on the Verge: Japanese Women, Western Dreams* (Durham, N.C.: Duke University, 2001).

31. Kelsky, *Women on the Verge,* 2, 10.

32. Ibid., 132.

33. Ibid., 154.

34. Ibid., 4.

35. Hui Wei, *Shanghai Baby,* trans. Bruce Humes (New York: Pocket Books, 2001).

36. Brownell, "Gender and Nationalism in China," 229.

37. Mayfair Yang, "From Gender Erasure to Gender Difference."

38. Brownell, "Gender and Nationalism in China," 230.

39. Faquhar, *Appetites*, 272–73. In her analysis of the 1994 film *Ermo,* Faquhar notes that Ermo's husband, a retired Communist cadre, formerly the village head and still called Chief, is impotent. In the new rural entrepreneurism, everyone must do business to live, and the chief's bureaucratic skills are useless. Ermo's neighbor, Blindman, on the contrary, owns a truck and has access to urban distribution networks through which Ermo sells her noodles. Ermo and Blindman, who are linked by business interests, engage in an affair. Ermo is married to a useless past, but the future that Blindman offers is corrupted by his eagerness to make her his dependent. "Outside of Ermo's troubled home she sees only lonely competition and relations based on the exchange of cash," writes Faquhar. She argues that in China's "rapid plunge into global modernity," Ermo is trapped between "an impotent old husband and a profligate new lover, neither of whom offers her a viable alternative to the unending labor of domestic production and petty commerce." This should be read as "a denunciation of the failures of the past and the banality of the future for a China that has committed itself at every level, even the most domestic, to millennial capitalist relations of production. Impotence in this domain is serious indeed."

40. Brownell, "Gender and Nationalism in China," 230.

41. Ibid.

42. David Wank argues against the traditional critique of clientelism as an inefficient form of resource allocation. The efficiency of a particular institution, he argues, must be evaluated in relation to the total institutional environment within which it is embedded. He finds that in China's case, clientelism promotes marketization by reducing the uncertainty faced by entrepreneurs in an unstable policy environment. Entrepreneurs in the private sector depend on patrons in the state sector for resources (for instance, low-interest loans from state-owned banks, state licenses, and the like) and protection from the predatory behavior of other state agents. Official patrons likewise benefit from their ties to clients by gaining new sources of revenue in a period of dwindling state funding and rising inflation. The reciprocal nature of these ties leads Wank to define *clientelism* as a form of "social trust" in Chinese client-patron ties and a harmonious convergence of interests. David L. Wank, "The Institutional Process of Market Clientelism: Guanxi and Private Business in a South China City," *China Quarterly* 147 (1996): 820–38.

43. Yang, *Gifts, Favors, and Banquets.*

44. Ibid., 320.

45. Ping Jiang argues that changes in risk management techniques follow a linear, evolutionary trajectory from subjective to objective standards. In small-scale societies, evaluations of PBPs are based on personal characteristics, such as

family conditions, moral conduct, etc. This technique is made possible by the fact that the evaluator and the PBPs are members of the same community and likely to be already familiar with each other prior to a transaction. With increases in the scale of business, however, this technique is rendered impractical. New forms of appraisal are developed, based on objective information regarding PBPs' past business performance, asset-debt ratio, etc. Evaluations are no longer made by the entrepreneur himself, but by specialized appraisal institutions. Ping Jiang, *Jiangping Wenji* (The collective works of Jiangping) (Beijing: Chinese Law Publishing House, 2000).

46. Pierre Bourdieu, *Distinction: A Social Critique on the Judgment of Tastes* (Cambridge, Mass.: Harvard University Press, 1984).

47. Yang, *Gifts, Favors, and Banquets,* 123. Yang sketched out a scale of social relationships, in which *guanxi, renqing* (human sentiment), *yiqi* (loyalty or ethics of the righteous), and *ganqing* (emotional feeling) are the most filled with emotional content. On the next level of the scale of social relationships is "diffuse obligation and indebtedness."

48. Ibid. This is because the system values impersonal values more than personal values such as mutual loyalty, shared sentiments, and obligation. Thus *guanxi* is highly valued because it is expressed and accomplished through social bonds of obligation, feeling, and sentiment.

49. This collective fiction that it is men's charm and sex appeal, not money, that win over hostesses is also true in strip clubs in the United States. Katherine Frank, *G-Strings and Sympathy: Strip Club Regulars and Male Desire* (Durham, N.C.: Duke University Press, 2002), 191–94.

50. See also Hershatter, *Dangerous Pleasures.*

51. Yan Shi, *Tian Yi* (God's will) (Xinjiang: Xinjiang University Publishing House, 1998), 463.

52. Gilmore, *Manhood in the Marking,* 12–16.

53. Ibid., 16. See also Jankowiak, "Proper Men and Proper Women."

5. The Return of the Prodigal Daughter

1. During the early Qing, provincial governor Chen Hongmou (1696–1771) reminded his society of the Confucian principle that relationships within the empire were analogous to relationships within the family. Just as the father had complete control over his family, the emperor had complete control over his subjects. Subjects and family members were both bound to absolute obedience to those above them. All must be willing to sacrifice at the request of the father or the emperor. William T. Rowe, "Women and the Family in Mid-Ching Social

Thought: The Case of Chen Hung-mou," in *Jinshi Jiazu Yu Zhengzhi Bijiao Lishi Lunwen Ji* (Collection of articles on comparative history of contemporary lineage and politics), ed. Zhongyang Yanjiu Yuan Jindaishi Yanjiusuo (Institute of Contemporary History of Central China) (Taipei: Yongyu Publishing House, 1992), 505.

2. C. Cindy Fan, "Out to the City and Back to the Village: The Experiences and Contributions of Rural Women Migrating from Sichuan and Anhui," in *On the Move: Women in Rural-Urban Migration in Contemporary China,* ed. Arianne Gaetano and Tamara Jacka (New York: Columbia University, 2004). John W. Traphagan, "The Liminal Family: Return Migration and International Conflict in Japan," *Journal of Anthropological Research* 56 (2000): 365–85. James Ferguson, *Expectations of Modernity: Myths and Meanings of Urban Life on the Zambian Copperbelt* (Berkeley: University of California Press, 1999).

3. Bourdieu argues that within the institutions of sites of a struggle for domination, agents use their habitus to adapt to this struggle. In the process, they misrecognize the struggle as atemporal or natural truth inherent in the dominant structures. Because of misrecognition, agents' efforts of change end up preserving the very structures of domination that are threatened by those social changes. Pierre Bourdieu, *Outline of a Theory of Practice* (Cambridge: Cambridge University Press, 1977).

4. This is not very common among the hostesses, but I did encounter three such cases in one karaoke bar. Pimps from Japan often came to karaoke bars to recruit women. Each woman has to turn in 20,000 *yuan* and pass the interview in Japanese before being permitted to go through the visa process.

5. Louisa Schein, "The Consumption of Color and the Politics of White Skin in Post-Mao China," in *The Gender/Sexuality Reader: Culture, History, Political Economy,* ed. Micaela Di Leonardo and Roger N. Lancaster (New York: Routledge, 1999).

6. Hershatter, *Dangerous Pleasures.*

7. See Chan, *China's Workers under Assault.*

8. At home Dee was constantly pressured by her mother to get married. She felt that her elder sister's marriage could somehow save her from that pressure.

9. Fan, "Out to the City." In her study of southern Chinese migrant girls, Fan observes that expectations about the proper age for marriage and gender roles within marriage limit rural migrant women's opportunities for off-farm work and therefore limit the contributions they can make to their families. As Fan shows, these women face escalating pressure to marry in their early twenties, a pressure most women succumb to, returning from the city to the countryside. Married, they are confined to their homes, facing severe condemnation were they to leave

and seek migrant work. Thus, the strong cultural demands that they marry limit most of these women to lives of extreme poverty in the country.

10. Traphagen, "The Liminal Family." He argues that understanding reverse migration in Japan requires understanding the conflicting family ideologies between generations. According to Traphagen, the problem lies in the older generations' more rigid code of acceptable conduct that limits the freedom of the younger returnees, challenging habits newly acquired in the city. The older generation also emphasizes the parental obligation owed them. A compromise is reached in which this obligation by returnees is recognized but attenuated by taking up neo-local residence, preserving some independence of acquired freedom while tacitly recognizing their obligations. Traphagen argues that their "liminal" status is poised between "independence from and subjection to the family stem."

11. Ferguson, *Expectations of Modernity*. He argues that in the "back to the land push" in Africa, returning migrants have to adapt their lives to fit into what he calls "micro-political-economic" social relations that they cannot afford to ignore. Migrant workers have to be socially and culturally "compliant" with rural demands and expectations in order to enjoy a supportive and helpful network important for their economic survival in their hometown. Noncompliant migrant workers find themselves living in tension, insecurity, and fear, and are subject to their rural kin's outrage and sanctions (for example, accusations of witchcraft and sorcery).

12. Mary Beth Mills, *Thai Women in the Global Labor Force: Consuming Desires, Contested Selves* (New Brunswick, N.J.: Rutgers University Press, 2003). Nicole Constable, *Romance on a Global Stage: Pen Pals, Virtual Ethnography, and "Mail-Order" Marriages* (Berkeley: University of California Press, 1995). Sonia Ryang, "The North Korean Homeland of Koreans in Japan," in *Koreans in Japan: Critical Voices from the Margin*, ed. Sonia Ryang (London: Routledge, 2000), 32–54.

6. Clothes Make the Woman

1. Daniel Miller, "Consumption Studies as the Transformation of Anthropology," in *Acknowledging Consumption*, ed. Daniel Miller (London: Routledge, 1995).

2. Ibid., 264.

3. Jean Baudrillard, *Selected Writings* (Cambridge: Polity, 1988).

4. Sydney Mintz, *Sweetness and Power* (New York: Viking Penguin, 1985).

5. Jean Comaroff, "Goodly Beasts and Beastly Goods: Cattle and Commodities in a South African Context," *American Ethnologist* 17 (1990): 195–216.

6. Lila Abu-Lughod, "Bedouins, Cassettes and Technologies of Public Culture," *Middle East Report* (July–August 1989): 7–11. Arjun Appadurai, *Modernity at Large: Cultural Dimensions of Globalization* (Minneapolis: University of Minnesota Press, 1996). C. Waterman Barber, "Traversing the Global and the Local: Fuji Music and Praise Poetry in the Production of Contemporary Yoruba Popular Culture," in *Worlds Apart: Modernity through the Prism of the Local,* ed. Daniel Miller (New York: Routledge, 1995). Mark Liechty, "Media, Markets and Modernization: Youth Identities and the Experience of Modernity in Kathmandu, Nepal," in *Youth Cultures: A Cross-Cultural Perspective,* ed. Vered Amit and Helena Wulff (London: Routledge, 1995). Roland Robertson, "Glocalization: Time-Space and Homogeneity-Heterogeneity," in *Global Modernities,* ed. Mike Featherstone et al. (London: Sage, 1995). Lisa Rofel, *Other Modernities* (Berkeley: University of California Press, 1999). Yunxiang Yan, "McDonald's in Beijing: The Localization of Americana," in *Golden Arches East: McDonald's in East Asia,* ed. James Watson (Stanford, Calif.: Stanford University Press, 1997).

7. Marcel Mauss, *The Gift* (New York: Norton, 1967).

8. Benjamin Orlove and Henry J. Rutz, "Thinking about Consumption: A Social Economy Approach," in *The Social Economy of Consumption,* ed. H. J. Rutz and B. S. Orlove (Lanham, Md.: University Press of America, 1989), 211–52.

9. Pierre Bourdieu, *Distinction: A Social Critique of the Judgments of Taste* (Cambridge, Mass.: Harvard University Press, 1984).

10. Daniel Miller, *Material Culture and Mass Consumption* (Oxford: Blackwell, 1987).

11. Grant David McCracken, *Culture and Consumption: New Approaches to the Symbolic Character of Consumer Goods and Activities* (Bloomington: Indiana University Press, 1988).

12. See Lee, *Modern China.*

13. Jacka points out that rural migrant women in the city feel both "out of place" and "put in their place" as a result of the household registration system and accompanying regulations, discrimination, exploitation, and abuse. Tamara Jacka, *Rural Women in Urban China: Gender, Migration, and Social Change* (New York: Sharpe, 2006).

14. See Brownell, *Training the Body for China,* 235.

15. Eating is one kind of class-based consumption.

16. See Roy Ellen, "Fetishism," *Man* 23, no. 2 (1988): 213–35. Bourdieu, *Distinction.*

17. Xi Luo, "Shunu De Moyang" (The appearance of a fair lady), *Nu Zi Shi Jie* (Women's world) 3 (2001): 42–43.

18. Yue Wang, "Wenhua Paocai: Wuzuo Dacan de Shishang" (Cultural kimchee: Fashion of making the wrong dish), *Shenzhen Zhoukan* (Shenzhen weekly), 329 (2002): 41.

19. The meaning of *xiangqi,* the term used in the above quotation, is synonymous with *tuqi. Tuqi,* however, is more frequently used.

20. For instance, more than 70 percent of the Korean clothing consumed in Korea is made in Shandong Province. See Luan Luan, "Hanguo Fuzhuang Chaoguo Qicheng Shandong Zhizao" (Seventy percent of Korean clothing is made in Shandong), *Shijie Shangye Pinglun* (Comment on the World Commerce), December 1, 2004.

21. See Naishan Cheng, "Ni Jiang Pinwei Ma?" (Are you concerned about taste?), *Xin Zhou Kan* (New weekly) 7 (1999): 52–56. Min Li, "Shishang Zazhi Shidabing" (The ten ills of fashion magazines), *Xin Zhou Kan* (New weekly) 7 (1999): 43–45.

22. Sandra Niessen, *Re-Orienting Fashion* (Oxford: Berg, 2003), 7. Appadurai, *Modernity at Large,* 76.

23. For the fetish of Western women in Chinese advertising and popular culture, see Schein, "The Consumption of Color." Perry Johansson, "Consuming the Other: The Fetish of the Western Woman in Chinese Advertising and Popular Culture," *Postcolonial Studies* 2, no. 3 (1999), 377–88.

24. *Zhongguo Dierjie Dushi Nuhai Fushi Fengcai Dasai Dalian Sai Qu* (The Second City Girl Fashion Contest in Dalian) (Dalian: Committee for the City Girl Fashion Contest, 2001).

25. Fred Davis, *Fashion, Culture, and Identity* (Chicago: University of Chicago Press, 1992).

26. Ibid.

27. Ibid.

28. Wave clothing and other bodily ornamentation have made the most visible impact and hence have drawn a large proportion of attention from concerned parents and the media. As early as 2001, newspaper articles began to introduce the Wave as a startling new phenomenon to the general public. These accounts invariably provided a stock description of the young devotees of Japanese and Korean pop culture.

29. Jonathan Friedman, "Globalization and Localization," in *The Anthropology of Globalization,* ed. Jonathan Xavier Inda and Renato Rosaldo (Malden, Mass.: Blackwell, 2002), 233–47.

30. Ibid., 243.

31. Karen Tranberg Hansen, "Dealing with Used Clothing: Salaula and the Construction of Identity in Zambia's Third Republic," *Public Culture* 6 (1994): 503–23.

7. Performing Love

1. Wendy Chapkis, *Live Sex Acts: Women Performing Erotic Labor* (New York: Routledge, 1997).

2. Janet Theiss, "Femininity in Flux: Gendered Virtue and Social Conflict in the Mid-Qing Courtroom," in *Chinese Femininities, Chinese Masculinities.*

3. Ibid.

4. Anne Allison, *Nightwork* (Chicago: University of Chicago Press, 1994).

5. Pan Suiming, *Sheng Cun Yu Ti Yan.*

6. Liang, *Ningshi Jiuqi.*

7. Kate Millett, *Sexual Politics* (Garden City, N.Y.: Doubleday, 1970), 37.

8. Holland et al. also describe the way in which U.S. women are duped into subordination by the myth of romance. Dorothy Holland et al., *Educated in Romance: Women, Achievement, and College Culture* (Chicago: University of Chicago Press, 1992).

9. Catherine A. Lutz, "Engendered Emotion: Gender, Power, and the Rhetoric of Emotional Control in American Discourse," in *Language and the Politics of Emotion,* ed. Catherine Lutz and Lila Abu-Lughod (Cambridge: Cambridge University Press, 1990), 88.

Afterword

1. Xiaoyan Wang, "Dalian Xiaojie Quanluo Xianwu" (Dalian hostesses dance naked), *Dalian Bandao Chenbao* (Dalian peninsular morning post), April 18, 2003, 1.

2. Xuecheng Wen, "Riben KalaOK Huayang Fanxin" (Innovations of Japanese karaoke), *Zhongyang Tongxun She* (Central Communication Agency), March 16, 2004, 1.

3. In a few exceptional cases, hostesses have become government officials. See Donghui Zhao and Hongcan Liu, "Shanxi Yi 'Wu Nu' Dang Shang Fa Guan" (A hostess becomes a court judge in Shanxi)," *Bandao Chenbao* (Bandao morning post), October 16, 2001, 19. Huya Guan et al., "Jiekaisanpeinu 'Rongsheng' Xuanchuanbuzhang deheimu" (Unveiling the secret of a bar hostess promoted to general manager of Press and Propaganda Department), *Jia Ting* 12 (2001): 50–52.

Index

comfort women, 2. *See also*
    prostitution: in Dalian under
    Japanese and Russian
    colonialism
commodification: of bodies, 12, 184–
    85, 216, 218–19, 222; of intimacy
    and romance, 222–27, 231–32,
    240–41
commodity consumption: under
    Mao and during post-Mao era, 3,
    176–77, 194. *See also* hostesses
communes, 65, 119
competition: between Chinese and
    Japanese businessmen, 35; among
    clients, 134; between clients and
    hostesses, 140; among Dalian
    boys, 43; among hostesses, 94,
    99, 104, 187; of *jing*, 122; between
    jing and *liang*, 115; among
    karaoke bars, 89; among men
    under Mao, 118
condoms, 62
Confucian class, 6
Confucian culture, 19, 39, 41, 113,
    124
Confucian filiality and female
    virtues, 21, 43, 149
Confucian-socialist system, 106, 132
conspicuous consumption: of
    hostesses, 5, 162, 190, 194–95,
    206, 210; under Mao, 3; during
    post-Mao era, 10, 67, 112, 145
consumption: anthropology of, 175–
    77; and class, 137, 175–76; of
    clients, 77, 104, 145, 173; costs in
    hostesses, 208–10; discourse of
    rural-urban gap in, 165, 174–75,
    195–98; of hostesses, 73, 75, 173–
    75, 177, 189–91, 202–3, 241; in

karaoke bars, 54, 56, 66–67, 83,
    87, 100, 102; of *liang*, 55, 115, 119;
    public struggle in, 5, 174, 176–77,
    189–91, 208; sites of, 3, 10, 27,
    54–55, 102, 195; under socialism,
    56; of urban women, 196; of
    wives of clients, 12, 122. *See also*
    conspicuous consumption; sex
    consumption
cool: of bar culture, 102; of
    hostesses, 161, 200; masculinity
    of, 6, 106, 109, 231, 240; of
    medium, 267n15
cosmetics, 158, 188–91, 199, 210, 246
cosmopolitan images, 11, 21, 161, 173,
    180
country bumpkin, 5–6, 160, 174, 241
courtesan, 6, 37, 107, 245, 253, 262
crackdowns, 68, 69
criminal organizations, 87
criminals: in construction of
    hostesses, 24, 137; in construction
    of rural migrants, 52; during
    Japanese colonialism, 40; in
    karaoke bar industry, 32, 87,
    209
cuantai, 101
cultural capital, 241
culturalism, 6
Cultural Revolution, 14, 61, 118,
    148

Dalian: ambivalence toward
    Japanese, Maoist, and post-Mao
    state, 3, 46–47, 51–52, 59–62;
    dialect of, 62, 163; femininity
    in, 41–46; food under Japanese
    colonialism, 115; gender ratio
    under Japanese colonialism,

hometowns, 148–49, 151–52, 156–57; in hostesses vs. Western prostitutes, 213; and state, market economy, 20, 148–49, 157, 213

floating population, 4, 270. *See also* migrants

food: competition with *jing*, 115; hierarchy of under Japanese colonialism, 115; and *jing,* 115–16; rationing and state power, 11, 54–56, 113–17, 119; and state, 11, 106, 112–16, 119–20, 123

foreign fashion, 5, 199, 201–2, 207. *See also under* clothing

fortune telling, 80–81, 147, 227–29

foxes, 24, 259n53

freedom: of clients, 106, 119–21, 125, 128; of hostesses, 11, 159, 164, 171, 173, 208; of hostesses offstage, 214, 240; of Japanese women, 133; in karaoke bars, 77; of women under Japanese colonialism, 42

gangsters, 32, 87–88, 90, 142

gentry, 6, 254n11

gift economy, 135, 140, 175

globalization, 133

go offstage. *See* offstage

gossip: among hostesses, 82, 95, 97, 226; in rural hometowns, 149, 151, 154, 159, 161–63, 166, 169

grain tax. *See liang*

Great Leap Forward, 118

Guandong (Kwantung) Leased Territory, 35–36

guanxi, 3, 135, 273–74

guohua, 119

hairstyles, 161–62, 183, 188–89, 232

hanjian. See traitor

health: of clients, 117, 120; of hostesses, 186, 208; of socialist culture, 63, 65–68

Hershatter, Gail, 25

high-tier karaoke bar. *See* karaoke bars

home, 20–21, 27, 155–56, 169–71

hostesses: ambassador of modernity in rural hometown, 149, 151, 162–66; attitudes toward marriage, 103, 149, 151, 164, 170–71, 221; awareness of rural-urban dichotomy, 191–94; bodily alteration, 177, 186, 208; bodily modifications, 186; body practices/culture of, 182–210, 241; body refashioning, 185–86, 209; categorizations of, 3–4; and clients' feedbacks, 182–84; clothing of, 161–63, 173, 179, 183–84, 198–207, 246; commodification of bodies, 12, 218, 222; commodification of intimacy and romance, 222–27, 231–32, 240–41; comparison with Western sex workers, 158, 213; competition among, 94, 99, 104, 187; competition with clients, 140; complexity behind rational control, 227–32; conflicting feelings about home and city, 20–21, 27, 155–56, 169–71; conspicuous consumption of, 5, 162, 190, 194–95, 206, 210; consumption of, 73, 75, 173–77, 189–91, 202–3, 241; cosmopolitan image, 11, 21, 161, 173, 180; costs

the West, 133; women in, 133. *See also under* Dalian

Japanese businessmen: and Dalian hostesses, 62; Dalian men's competition with, 35, 58–59; Dalian men's emulation of, 10, 77, 134; with karaoke bars, 57–58, 77

Japanese fashion, 191, 199, 201, 204–5, 207

Japanese Military Flag Incident, 58

Japanese Street, 62

Japanese women, 43, 45, 133, 266n64

Jeffreys, Elaine, 69

Jiangsu National Painting Exhibition, 119

jiao gongliang, 112. *See also liang*

jing (semen): competition of, 122–23; conservation of, 105, 116–17, 123; economy of scarcity in and misappropriation of, 12, 106, 122–24; and *liang*, 115–16; and longevity, 116; and men's bodies, 116–17; relationships with state power, 11, 105–6; self-allocation of, 120–21

karaoke bars: and banquets and state power, 10, 54–55, 77; bar bouncers in, 9, 88, 217; barkeepers in, 89–91, 100; bar managers in, 9, 89–102, 104, 152; bribery in, 72, 76, 85; class in, 79–92; competition among, 89; complicity of state in, 65–67; in cultural milieu, 62–65; emergence of, 3, 53–55; erotic service in, 55, 66, 69–70, 72, 236; factions in, 85–86; hierarchy in industry of, 102;

in Japan, 244–45; madams in, 73–74, 82–87, 91–92, 98, 108, 214, 247; organization and management in, 80, 82, 86, 89; relationship with Japan, 4, 53–55, 57–59, 77; and status of clients, 102–4; target of state law, 9, 66–70. *See also* bar owners

kinship, 93

Korea: fashion, 191, 196, 199, 201, 204–6, 207; and karaoke bars, 54; prostitutes and comfort women under Japanese colonialism, 3, 44–45, 47, 262n6; relationships with hostesses, 158, 196

Korean fashion, 191, 196, 199, 201, 204–6, 207

land reform, 7

leisure, 3, 64, 253

liang (food): hierarchy of, under Japanese colonialism, 115; and *jing*, 115–16; rationing and state power, 11, 54–56, 113–17, 119; and state, 11, 106, 112–16, 119–20, 123

liange ting, 3

Liaoning, 2, 13, 35, 39, 48, 49–51

literati, 6, 253n6

Liu Dalin, 24–25

localist network, 92, 96

love: in clients, 109, 110, 131–32, 140–42, 153, 232; client's disillusions in, 130; discourses of, 240; in hostesses, 12, 92, 180, 228–31; in hostesses' boyfriends, 158; hostesses' performance of, 185, 211, 215–16, 219–26, 238; under Japanese colonialism, 43; of state, 63, 126

low-tier karaoke bar. *See* karaoke
    bars

madams, 73–74, 82–87, 91–92, 98,
    108, 214, 247
malnutrition, 54
Manchu Morality Organization, 41
Manchuria: accusations of, 42; in
    colonial era, 35–36; food
    hierarchy in, 115; under Mao, 49,
    51; prostitution in, 2–3, 36–46,
    51–52, 263n16; women in, 45–46
market economy: and gender, 21,
    127; and gift economy, 140, 175;
    and nature rhetoric, 126; and
    state, 8–9, 11, 66, 148, 157
marriage: clients' views of, 122,
    124, 131–32; under Japanese colo-
    nialism, 40; under nationalism,
    134; in peasant societies, 164–65;
    during post-Mao era, 127; and
    Western culture, 24. *See also*
    hostesses: marriage of
marriage law, 22
Marxism, 63, 105, 128
masculinity: cadre masculinity in
    post-Mao era, 134; elite masculin-
    ity under culturalism, 6, 107,
    245, 253; emasculation by wives,
    116, 121; emasculation in sex
    consumption, 131; emasculation
    under Mao, 4, 48, 77, 118–19,
    121, 145, 271; entrepreneurial
    masculinity and globalization,
    9–10, 13, 26, 126–28, 133–34, 145,
    173, 245; historical evolution of,
    245; under Japanese colonialism,
    3, 7, 42–43; and *jing,* 117, 120–
    24; on nationalism, 6–7; nature

rhetoric of, 124–26; performance
    of, 139–40; and power, sex work,
    13, 106, 131, 134, 139–41; quality
    of, 106, 139; rational control, 126,
    231; reclamation of, in karaoke
    bars, 55, 77, 105, 113, 118, 131; and
    rural girls, 235; and sex consump-
    tion, 144–45; and sports, 7, 43,
    88, 145; in state clientelism, 134–
    45. *See also* Japanese businessmen
masculinization of women, 118, 145
media: construction of hostesses,
    23–26, 136–37; construction of
    rural migrant women, 214, 236;
    construction of rural-urban body
    culture, 188, 195, 198; and host-
    esses, 182, 187, 189, 208; under
    Mao, 118; of pornography, 69;
    during post-Mao era, 127, 132
medium-tier karaoke bar. *See*
    karaoke bars
Meiji Restoration, 39
migrants: alliance of, 92–93, 96;
    discrimination and employment
    of, 4–5, 26, 178–79; migrant sex
    workers, 26–27, 34, 209; migrant
    workers, 165, 260n64; return of,
    148, 165, 170–71. *See also under*
    clients; Dalian
migrant women: employment of,
    4–5, 178–79; object of blame,
    23–26; sex workers in, 34, 150
migration: and sex work, 13, 26–27,
    209. *See also* rural
Miller, Daniel, 175–76
misappropriation, 12, 106, 123, 211.
    See also jing
misrecognition, 149, 275n3
mistresses, 22, 134, 140–41

TIANTIAN ZHENG is associate professor of anthropology at State University of New York, Cortland.

Made in United States
North Haven, CT
24 February 2024

49078595R00183